My God Always
Bless you & keep you
Safe N His Care
Pastor Steee

# OVERCOMING

Heb. 6:10

When the Lord called my husband, Paul, home, I stood at the crossroads of faith and utter despair as never before. Paul had been the undisputed head of our home, and when he died not only was I in deep mourning but I was also faced with myriad unfamiliar practical concerns. I was overwhelmed! Thanks be to God for the wonderful, godly counsel I received from Steve Mays. That the same powerful and practical counsel is now available in this book. At times of high emotion, deep hurt or the seeming "unfairness" of circumstances, it is necessary to have a spiritual compass to help guide us. *Overcoming* provides perfect direction!

DONNA P. ARLOW
Attorney at Law

American history is filled with overcomers—those who prevailed over racial injustice, broken families, physical danger or economic hardship. But why did they overcome? Were they lucky? Were they special objects of divine intervention? No. In each case, their ability to prevail was based on adopting a biblical way of thinking. Pastor Steve Mays, using his own personal experiences—both tragic and humorous—brings to light the simple but profound truths that produce an overcoming lifestyle.

DAVID BARTON
President, Wallbuilders

I can think of no better authority to speak on the subject of overcoming life's struggles than Pastor Steve Mays. The wisdom that he shares is not only grounded in God's Word but has also been tested and proven through his own experience. If you're someone who's questioning whether it's even possible to overcome your trials, you don't have to look any further than this author, and you won't have to read any further than this book.

PASTOR BOB COY
Senior Pastor, Calvary Chapel Fort Lauderdale, Florida

As an educator in the second largest school district in the nation for almost two decades, I have yet to come across a teenager who does not need to know what Dr. Mays clearly and courageously explains in *Overcoming*. How are our teenagers to face the challenges thrown at them in life with minimal resources and the lack of proper guidance? What a huge sigh of relief to know that between the covers of this book lie answers that all can use to overcome with flying colors; especially the most precious treasure that constrains us to be agents of change in our nation today—our children.

DIANA FAATAI, M.A.ED.
Los Angeles Unified School District


Steve Mays does a masterful job of mining the depths of Scripture, particularly from the life of Paul, to teach us how to be overcomers. This is no academic study. Steve has learned through many serious illnesses, setbacks and betrayals how to find God, peace and contentment in the midst of suffering and discouragement. Steve provides many word pictures and illustrations, along with practical strategies, to help us deepen our walk with God and receive His comfort when our world seems to be falling apart. Whichever of the "Big 13" problems you may be facing today (or tomorrow!), *Overcoming* can help guide you through and into the arms of Jesus, who gave everything so we might overcome the world!

TERRY FAHY
General Manager, KKLA Radio in Los Angeles, Salem Communications


Several years ago, I heard stories of Christians being persecuted in China. I received permission to go to China to meet with them. Before I left, a group of pastors who had been persecuted met with me to thank me for my efforts. I knew many of them had suffered much for their faith. I warned them of my concern that after I left China, there could be some retaliation for those who met with me there. One of the pastors grabbed my arm and said, "Congressman, please do not pray that we will not be sent to prison. We know how to suffer. If we are sent to prison, we will lead the prisoners to Christ. Today, many Christians feel overwhelmed with the circumstances of life. We feel like giving up if we cannot change those circumstances. Steve Mays, in his book *Overcoming*, describes how the power of the gospel of Christ does far more for us during those times than "strengthen" us and "sustain us." The power of the gospel of Christ is what enables us to overcome.

CONGRESSMAN J. RANDY FORBES
Fourth District of Virginia

Pastor Steve Mays is a *unique* human being. By unique, I mean someone the likes of whom one rarely comes across through the journey of life. Pastor, husband, father, counselor, mentor, friend, confidant, encourager. He is all of these things and much more to his family and the people of his congregation at Calvary Chapel who know him so well. I have had the privilege of knowing Steve in the role he plays outside of his church. His sole preoccupation is bringing lost souls into the kingdom of God and nurturing them in the faith, no matter who they are or where they come from. I know he has ministered to leaders of nations and major organizations and church and secular groups of many kinds, all with one objective in mind: bringing the message of the Word of God. But what makes him truly unique in my eyes is that he had the desire in his heart and found time to minister to me and my wife even though we live in Australia, on the opposite side of the world from him. During my time as World President of The Gideons International I valued his input, wise counsel and friendship. He was also a willing and helpful sounding board After I completed my term of office, he became pastor, confidant, counselor and friend to my wife and me during an extremely challenging period in our lives. What do you say about someone who calls you from the other side of the world every few days to check that you are okay and to pray with you and demonstrate a great love and compassion for you? I am honored to call him pastor and friend . . . and he is indeed *unique*.

KEVIN W. FULLER
Past World President, The Gideons International


Steve Mays has done something important in this book: He has succeeded in reminding us that regardless of the circumstances that life brings to our doorstep, the grace and mercy of Jesus Christ are the central realities. There is a joy and transcendence in this book that flows from the generous soul of its author.

TIM GOEGLEIN
Vice President of External Affairs, Focus on the Family
Former Deputy Chief, White House Office of Public Liaison for President George W. Bush


The biblical concepts shared by Pastor Steve Mays in *Overcoming* are powerful tools for the born-again believer's arsenal. This book is sure to spark an appetite for the Word of God. It is for anyone who aspires to rise above all circumstances and experience the level of freedom that God intended.

DR. RONALD C. HILL
Senior Pastor, Love and Unity Christian Fellowship

Steve Mays is an overcomer and role model for all ages. He is an example to all of us how to overcome obstacles that come our way. Learning this at a young age is important, and we are grateful for his use of the Bible and practical experience to teach us how we can be overcomers as well.

CLAYTON AND ELLEN KERSHAW
Los Angeles Dodgers Pitcher and 2011 National Cy Young Award Winner
Authors of *Arise*

Life is going to be hard—of that we can be sure. But as Christians we know that God is in control of our lives. Whatever He does or allows to happen in the lives of His children is motivated by His everlasting love for us. My friend Steve Mays has seen his share of troubles, hardships and setbacks, but like the phoenix rising from the ashes, Steve always comes back stronger. Now, in his new book *Overcoming*, he shares how he has been able to do that. I know this book will be an encouragement to you as you face the hardships of life. Chuck Swindoll wrote, "When God wants to do an impossible task, He takes an impossible individual and crushes him. Being crushed means being reshaped—to be a vital, compassionate, useful instrument in His hands." Steve is one of those instruments in the hands of God, and I trust this book will help you to become one as well.

GREG LAURIE
Pastor, Harvest Christian Fellowship

Steve Mays has been a dear and close friend for about 40 years, and we have been together through many experiences. As you read his book, you will see that he has been through many of the "surgeries" that can come in life. And when I say surgeries, I mean not just the physical surgeries, but all forms— physical, mental, spiritual, marriage, family, ministry, leadership and virtu- ally most of what can occur in life. As Steve has gone through these fires, he has not only survived but also thrived. He has grown, and he has much to teach others on the subject of overcoming the trials and circumstances of life. I used to tell Steve that most people wait until they die before donating their bodies to medicine, but Steve seems to have done it now. Yet it is through these times when the Lord does so much of His great work in us. "Blessed be the God and Father of our Lord Jesus Christ, the Father of mercies and God of all comfort, who comforts us in all our tribulation, that we may be able to comfort those who are in any trouble, with the comfort with which we our- selves are comforted by God" (2 Cor. 1:3-4). The apostle Paul knew the Lord had designed what he went through in life so that when he was comforted by the Lord, he would be able to comfort others. So too with Steve.

DON MCCLURE
Calvary Way Ministries

*Overcoming* is timely and encouraging. In an often defeated, overwhelmed culture, Mays's message resonates and challenges each of us to find the strength needed to achieve victory in Jesus Christ. We can overcome all that is holding us back. Pastor Mays shows us how.

KEVIN PALAU
President, Luis Palau Association

Steve Mays is one of our best Bible teachers, with one of the most popular teaching shows on our radio station. In *Overcoming*, he applies biblical wisdom to the real-world situations that certainly distract and many times overwhelm us, reminding all of us that we always have the choice to turn toward God.

FRANK PASTORE
Radio Host, The Frank Pastore Show
Salem Radio Network's KKLA, Los Angeles, California

How can you transform life's greatest challenges from barriers into stepping stones to lead to a meaningful and purposeful life? In *Overcoming*, my good friend Dr. Steve Mays provides time-proven biblical principles, combined with his personal experience and insight, which will enable you to overcome the barriers that are holding you back from experiencing and enjoying the purpose for which you were created.

TONY PERKINS
President, Family Research Council

Pastor Steve Mays is living proof that through all he has experienced in difficulty, crisis, suffering and life-long struggle, the grace of God is perfected in weakness. He has never wavered in faith or failed to trust the goodness of God. This book is a narrative that will bring hope and courage. God bless his story to every reader.

ROSS RHOADS
Chaplain, Billy Graham Evangelistic Association

I do not know anyone who is more qualified to deal with the subject of overcoming adversities than Pastor Steve Mays. He has spent more time on the operating table and had more operations than anyone I know. The thing that impresses me is his ability to bounce back from every trial with the joy of the Lord in his heart. I am certain that anyone who has faced problems and adversities in his or her life will find great help from the insights the Lord has given Steve, which he shares with us in this book.

PASTOR CHUCK SMITH
Founder, Calvary Chapel Movement

*Overcoming* is a must read. Steve Mays has authored a timely and relevant book full of hope. It may well be a life-changer for you.

JAY SEKULOW
Chief Counsel, American Center for Law and Justice

The life and ministry of Pastor Steve Mays is a commanding testimony to God's power and the perfect mirror for *Overcoming*. I believe this is the book God has been preparing Steve to write his whole life. Pastor Steve's outstanding teaching gift speaks through wisdom and discernment on overcoming failure, patterns of sin, poor choices and the daily grind of life that often leaves us spiritually empty and discouraged. Overcoming is possible, and Steve Mays provides the direction to get there!

JON WALLACE
President, Azusa Pacific University

FOREWORD BY JONI EARECKSON TADA

# STEVE MAYS

# OVERCOMING

DISCOVER HOW TO RISE ABOVE AND BEYOND

YOUR OVERWHELMING CIRCUMSTANCES IN LIFE!

**Regal**

For more information and for special offers from Regal,
email us at subscribe@regalbooks.com

Published by Regal
From Gospel Light
Ventura, California, U.S.A.
www.regalbooks.com
Printed in the U.S.A.

Library of Congress Cataloging-in-Publication Data
Mays, Steve.
Overcoming : discover how to rise above and beyond your overwhelming
circumstances in life / Steve Mays.
p. cm.
ISBN 978-0-8307-6200-2 (trade paper)
1. Emotions—Religious aspects—Christianity. 2. Self-actualization
(Psychology)—Religious aspects—Christianity. I. Title.
BV4597.3.M385 2012
248.4—dc23
2012000933

I wrote Overcoming *during some of the darkest days of my life.*
*I thought I would never catch my breath, but I did. God placed one of*
*His very special angels right in front of me—day in and day out—*
*to show me the way back to His goodness.*

*That angel was, and is, my lovely wife, Gail.*
*Some call her the pastor's wife, others call her Mrs. Gail,*
*but those who know her best call her "Mama"!*

*Therefore, with great humility and love,*
*I dedicate this book to my love, Gail. Her joy has always been*
*irresistible, her smile is the sweetest thing to look at, and her strength*
*has blessed not only me but also a multitude*
*of people around this country.*

*Gail, you are, and always will be,*
*"My little slice of heaven here on earth."*

# CONTENTS

# ACKNOWLEDGMENTS

Thanks to the many people who, after hearing my studies on overcoming the many issues in life, asked me to record my thoughts, my studies and my experiences into a book. Through the years, not only have I experienced and recorded many instances of overcoming my own hurdles, but as a pastor, I have also had the privilege of having others share their stories with me. Doing this has helped me to go even deeper in my study of God's Word and to bring this book to fruition.

Thanks to my co-writer and National Ministry Outreach Director, Melinda Kay Ronn, for her enthusiasm for this project, her tireless work in helping put this book together, and for bringing it to the attention of the publishing world.

Thanks to my good friend Don Modglin for his encouraging words and support over the years.

Thanks for the contributions of Kelly Click and Marian Guirguis, who helped with writing and editing; Tricia Bennett, my copyeditor; and Steve Chin, who also edited and helped manage the overall project. Thank you all for your labor of love and the many hours you spent helping to make this a reality.

I appreciate and benefited from conversations with friends and my staff at Calvary Chapel South Bay, who not only helped me with the critical critiques of the book but who also displayed confidence and shared encouraging thoughts that were desperately needed at times.

I appreciate the visionary insights and friendships of all those at Regal Books, including Steve Lawson and Bob Bever, who have made this journey so educational and inspiring.

Special thanks to my wife, Gail, to whom I have dedicated this book, for making all this possible through her prayers, love, counsel and generous support.

Last, but not least, my thanks to Jesus Christ, without whom this book would not have been possible. I thank Him for His strength, patience and enduring love that helped and empowered me to complete this project. To Him I give all the glory and praise.

# FOREWORD

# BEFORE YOU BEGIN . . .

It happens to every Christian—one minute you're spiritually skipping along, and the next, you've been ambushed. It could be a life-threatening illness or a sudden divorce, a painful injury that becomes chronic, or the death of a loved one. Fill in the blank with whatever overwhelms you right now. It comes with living in a fallen world.

Life can shrivel up when suffering becomes your dark and constant companion. You're able to keep your stride for a while, but in time, you find yourself spiraling into a whimpering slump. *Is this me? you ask yourself in the mirror. Does God know what He's doing? Will I never experience release?* Suffering can so sear the soul that you dread facing the day—and when night finally closes in, you pine for the morning.

My friend Pastor Steve Mays has been there. Yes, he leads a large Southern California church and preaches weekly; yes, he is a national radio broadcaster and author; but don't let the fame and titles fool you. Countless surgeries and injuries have forced him to go face to the floor. And when suffering overwhelms you like that, you search for someone, *anyone*, who might empathize. That's when Steve and I connected.

Long before we met, I had occasionally heard Steve's radio program on our local Christian station. His Bible teaching was honest and from the heart, and I appreciated his insights. It was only after we were introduced through a mutual friend that I began to realize how *honest* Steve's teaching really is. During a visit to my office, he shared his story with me—a journey through myriad surgeries on his back, neck and hips. Watching him smile through the pain, I thought, *Here's a man who understands affliction. Here's a brother who abides in the fellowship of my Savior's sufferings. Here is someone who can understand . . . me.* That's because I daily deal with pain, too.

That encounter began a string of notes, emails, phone calls and cards of encouragement—not to mention a few teaching CDs and books. At first I thought God had placed Steve Mays in my life so that I might lift *his* spirits—more than 40 years of quadriplegia and a decade of chronic pain somewhat qualified me to be an encourager. I soon realized it was only half the story.

God not only placed me in Steve's life to be a blessing, but also so that he could be a blessing to *me*. Around the time we met, I was struggling to free myself from my latest bout with pain. The jaws of nerve pain had clamped around my lower back and hips (how a quadriplegic like me can feel pain is still a mystery, but that's a different book :-). I was drawn to Steve's tenacious confidence in God . . . his joyful outlook . . . and his love and respect for God's Word. Here's a man who understood what I was going through and whose counsel I could trust.

And so, snippets of the psalms and slices of encouraging Scriptures flew between us. Each verse emailed from God's Word reminded us that God's purposes were perfect and that our Savior, intimately acquainted with grief and suffering, was pleading our case before heaven's throne. Occasionally, Steve Mays and I even prayed together on the phone. It was a pleasure when we were able to meet each other's spouses—I was touched by Steve's sincere concern for Ken, and I found his wife, Gail, to be delightful.

Years later, my pain is a little better. At times, it's *a lot* better. During the time since we met, Pastor Steve Mays has penned his insights about overcoming suffering in the book you now hold in your hands. Both of us still struggle with affliction, but we keep relying on the hope Jesus Christ offers every day. The Spirit of God puts it this way in Isaiah 45:3: "I will give you the treasures of darkness, riches stored in secret places, so that you may know that I am the LORD, the God of Israel, who summons you by name" (*NIV*). Whenever I occasionally feel the dark shadow of pain overwhelm me, I find heavenly treasures in such darkness: rock-solid, unshakable *hope*. And so do Steve and his wife, Gail.

That's why I'm honored to write these opening statements for this remarkable man. As I told him, pain is a strange and dark companion, but a companion nonetheless. Pain is an unwelcome visitor, but still a visitor. Pain is a bruising of a blessing; but it *is* a blessing from the hand of God. Who can tell the work of pain in our lives? I know that it drives me closer to that place of fellowship with Jesus that is nearer, dear and sweet. So, we take pain as though we were taking the left hand of God—better that than nothing.

And if, for you, that hand ever feels hard, be encouraged with this special paraphrase of Colossians 1:11-12 from *THE MESSAGE*: "We pray that you'll have the strength to stick it out over the long haul—not the grim strength of gritting your teeth but the glory-strength God gives. It is strength that endures the unendurable and spills over into joy, thanking the Father who makes us strong enough to take part in everything bright and beautiful that he has for us."

Friend, the fact that you are reading this book tells me that you, too, may be in the fellowship of sharing in your Savior's sufferings. Heartache and hardship surround you, and you may feel overwhelmed. I pray that the following pages of *Overcoming* will bring you "glory-strength" from God, as well as the happy confidence that the Lord of hope will supply every one of your needs.

Joni Eareckson Tada
Joni and Friends International Disability Center
Agoura Hills, California

1

# OVERCOMING DISCOURAGEMENT

*For we do not want you to be ignorant, brethren, of our trouble which
came to us in Asia: that we were burdened beyond measure, above
strength, so that we despaired even of life. Yes, we had the sentence of
death in ourselves, that we should not trust in ourselves but in God who
raises the dead, who delivered us from so great a death, and does deliver
us; in whom we trust that He will still deliver us.*

2 CORINTHIANS 1:8-10

*Discouragement is one of the deepest struggles I have had to overcome. I've had many surgeries through the years, but the last one on my back was probably the most difficult. One would think it would get better with each surgery, but actually it gets worse. I felt like a burden to my wife and to my church, and often I thought that I should just resign and let the church find a healthier pastor. My thoughts were not about copping out or quitting; rather, it was because I believed that the congregation deserves the very best. And being so sick all the time, I was not sure that I was the best. I had a discussion with the pastors and with the board after my last surgery, and they said they would take me as I am. I really had to wrestle with God over this because I questioned, "How do I serve God and the people with the strength needed when I don't feel good? I will probably have maybe four or five good days out of the year. I'm not moody or emotional; my body just hurts. The Lord has taught me over the years that if I could just have the strength to get out of bed, and then step into the shower, by the time I'm in my car driving to church, I would feel better. I am reminded that His strength is made perfect in my weakness. I really have to live one day at a time, but it weighs on me. It affects my outlook on life, and it is very discouraging. My friend Joni Eareckson Tada said that discouragement is like a handicap that no one can see. Joni is in a wheelchair. Everyone sees her in it, and therefore everyone has different expectations for her; but no one sees my struggles, and I don't think people are ever going to understand my condition. So I have settled it in my heart that my discouragements are really God's opportunities to shine and be glorified in my life. So I concentrate on my teaching, and I surround myself with great people to take care of the rest. When I do that, I feel that I have really done my job and am doing what the Lord has asked of me. So now I'm content with who I am.*

Have you ever been pressed beyond measure? I have, and I know that I am not alone. One of the most telling stories in the Bible about overcoming discouragement is of the apostle Paul's journey to share the gospel of Christ. Both historians and theologians credit Paul as being the most important person in the role of spreading Christianity throughout the world. But Paul had much to overcome. He spent 18 months at the church of Corinth, building up those believers in the knowledge of Christ and instructing them to live by faith and look for His coming. However, Paul was deeply troubled with some of the teaching, doctrine and practices that had developed in the church, which led to friction between him and some of the Corinthian believers. With his first letter to the Corinthian church, Paul spent a great deal of time correcting errors in the fellowship. Upon receiving his letter, some of those in the church began to turn on him. They spoke against him; they challenged his authority and became spiteful toward him.

How many of us have been in a work or personal situation in which we were the target of another's opposition, even when we were doing right? It is natural to feel discouraged. But Paul refused to live by feelings alone—he chose to live his life by faith and allow the Holy Spirit to empower every situation that came his way. He continued to love the church at Corinth, and his faith gave him the strength to press on. It's hard to envision the pressure and stress Paul was under. But the Holy Spirit bore witness to his situation, of which we read in 2 Corinthians 1:8-10: "We were burdened beyond measure, above strength, so that we despaired even of life. Yes, we had the sentence of death in ourselves, that we should not trust in ourselves but in God who raises the dead, who delivered us from so great a death, and does deliver us."

Paul had learned the importance of trusting in God. His circumstances were beyond his own ability to change, but they were not beyond God's, so he rested in God. We read that his strength was exhausted; he even said that he had a sentence of death within himself. In other words, there was a contract on his head. Consider this disheartening partial list of the things he faced: There were 40 men who took a vow that they would kill Paul before they would eat or drink anything; he was beaten at Lystra; he was chased out of Ephesus and almost killed because of a riot; he was rejected in almost every city he visited. Yet, in the midst of all these trials and more, Paul stood strong in his faith. Paul knew that God was able to raise the dead, so what could he ultimately fear from man? In each harrowing situation, Paul knew that God had been his help in the past and would be his help in the present and the future! Paul held firm to his understanding that God could change any seemingly impossible situation.

Today, maybe you find yourself at that very same place. You're exhausted. You have tried to do everything you can, but you have come to the end of yourself. The relationship is over. The love is gone; and though you desire to see God work, it seems impossible. I challenge you to remember that God is able to raise the dead. He is able to restore your heart; or as Ezekiel said, He is able to give you a new heart (see Ezek. 36:26). He is able to change the situation you are in if you look to Him.

Paul goes on to say, "Now thanks be to God who always leads us in triumph in Christ" (2 Cor. 2:14). Notice Paul's attitude in the midst of severe trials: "thanks be to God." How could Paul be thankful? How in the world could he ever rejoice in people turning against him? How can we be thankful and give God credit when things are beginning to go haywire in our life? How can we be thankful when people are speaking against us and our reputation is being questioned? How can we be calm and say, "Thanks be to God"? I believe the answer is found in the word "conscience," as seen in the following verse: "For our boasting is this: the testimony of our conscience that we conducted ourselves in the world in simplicity and godly sincerity, not with fleshly wisdom but by the grace of God, and more abundantly toward you" (2 Cor. 1:12).

## Clean the Window of Your Conscience

I agree with Paul. I believe that when we have a good conscience, we are able to stand like a rock before criticism and insults, and while facing the bleakest situations. The word "conscience" comes from two Latin words—one means "to be with," and the second means "to know." Therefore, the definition of a conscience is "the inward faculty that knows within our spirit what is right and wrong." Our conscience approves when we do right, but it accuses when we do wrong. It is inborn. The standards of our conscience are based on God's standards. Someone has said that our conscience is like a worm that never dies. It's a flame that will never be quenched. In other words, the conscience is not the law of God, but it bears witness to the law.

Another way to understand how the conscience works is to compare it to a window. A clear conscience, or window, allows God's light to shine through. What we turn our eyes to will dictate what the rest of our body sees. Jesus said, concerning the light that shines through, "The lamp of the body is the eye. If therefore your eye is good, your whole body will be full of light. But if your eye is bad, your whole body will be full of darkness. If therefore the light that is in you is darkness, how great is that darkness!" (Matt. 6:22-23). In other words, a person cannot seek both right and wrong any more than a window can simultaneously look upon the light and the dark. This illustration of a window has helped me to grow more than anything else in my Christian walk. It has given me the victory in so many different areas.

So when you think of your conscience, think of a window. Regularly ask yourself this important question: "Is my window clean? Is it clean because of God's Word, or is it dirty because of sinful habits?" God has given each of us a conscience. When that window remains crystal clear, it allows God's light to enter in, which helps us make God-honoring decisions. It warns us when we are going contrary to the Word of God. It convicts us when we begin to live in sin.

But when we become disobedient to God and choose to live in sin, Satan begins to tint that window of our soul, making it darker and darker, all because of our sinful behavior and unwillingness to surrender our conscience to the cleansing power of God's Word. Then one day, when we really need to say no, we'll look through the dirty, tinted window of our soul and not be able to make righteous decisions for our life. The only way out of this darkness and emptiness is to repent and have God once again make the window of the conscience crystal clear.

No wonder Paul kept his window so clean. He knew that he could not stand before kings and rulers in his own merit, but only with a pure heart and good conscience in Christ Jesus. I think this is what Paul was speaking about in Romans 1:9, when he wrote,

"For God is my witness, whom I serve with my spirit in the gospel of His Son." This one statement describes why we love this man Paul. Everything he was, and everything he did before his Lord and God was his witness. He stood and spoke with such authority that no man or king could resist his boldness. They trembled in fear, shook with insecurity and stumbled in unbelief, all because Paul stood before them with a pure heart. This is why he could resist and fight off any and all physical, spiritual and emotional attacks from those in the city of Corinth and elsewhere.

## Discouragement and Difficulty—Conquered

A clear conscience enables us to live in the light of eternity. Any believer whose hope is in Christ seeks the light, rejects the darkness and is empowered to stand in the midst of any difficulty. Let's look at four key truths enabled by a clear conscience:

### A Clear Conscience Enables You to Live in the Light

The apostle Paul lived his life with an incredibly strong desire to see Christ. He looked forward to the day of Christ's return, noting his rejoicing while waiting: "(As also you have understood us in part), that we are your boast as you also are ours, in the day of the Lord Jesus" (2 Cor. 1:14). The apostle John also wrote powerfully of seeking the light: "And everyone who has this hope in Him purifies himself, just as He is pure" (1 John 3:3). The men and women of the New Testament believed in the coming of Christ. Today, we also believe that Christ is coming; this truth gives us comfort and encouragement. The Bible teaches us that He will come at any moment. In fact, the Bible tells us that Christ will return when we are not expecting it. In a moment, in the twinkling of an eye, God will call His Church up to join Him.

Because we believe in the coming of Christ, and because our conscience is pure before God, we will not, we must not and we cannot be overwhelmed by our problems. Instead, we choose to believe that God is bigger than the problems we are experiencing. Even if you are going through a difficult time today, you know that tomorrow (or someday in the future), you will be standing in the very presence of Jesus Christ. If you look at stressful and painful situations with a clear conscience and the understanding that Christ is coming back, it will change the way you live, the things you choose to do and the way you treat other people.

There is no time for any of us to harbor bitterness or resentment. In other words, if God wants to heal us, we want to be healed. If God wants to use us, we want to be used. When we live in the light of Christ's return, all those burdens, trials and difficulties will be put in the right perspective, in the right light. Bitterness is not the will of God. Resentment is not the will of God. Harboring ill feelings is not the will of God. Being angry is not the will of God.

The Bible tells us, "Blessed is that servant whom his master, when he comes, will find so doing" (Matt. 24:46). The will of God is that we put our lives into the right perspective and do those things that please Him, all the way up to the day He returns. The book of Hebrews tells us that we are to trust God in all things and put our faith in Him. The writer of Hebrews 11:6 tells us, "But without faith it is impossible to please Him, for he who comes to God must believe that He is, and that He is a rewarder of those who diligently seek Him." If we believe that the Lord could return at any moment, we will be motivated to live a holy life—a life that pleases God.

With a pure conscience, we see God at work all over the place. The thought process is, *Yes, He's working in ways I don't understand. No, I don't understand why I'm going through this difficulty, and yes, I'm struggling in some areas. But because He's coming, my eyes are fixed upon the Lord, and I realize that many of my problems are petty. I realize that there is nothing too difficult for the Lord.*

Living in the light of eternity transforms us; it allows us to see our lives through a God-colored filter that is reflected in the way we think and act.

## A Clear Conscience Enables You to Do the Will of God

Very simply, Paul understood the importance of God's will in his life. He said to the Corinthians in 1 Corinthians 16:6-7 (paraphrasing),

"I'm going to be spending the winter with you, if God permits." His point was that "if God permits, and if it is possible, I will see you on my way out, and I'll catch you on my way in."

When certain parts of Paul's life fell apart—when those who hated his teaching and his stand for Christianity sought to destroy his light and his life—Paul was not shaken. Through challenges, uprisings and even riots, he simply chose to live in the victory that Christ both promised and provided, and he changed his plans to follow God's leading. We make plans, but sometimes God will change our plans. If we're not flexible, we're going to miss the will of God within our lives.

Paul was willing to live according to the will of God and answer to God, not to man. So consider, if you're seeking to please men, you're not going to be a servant of Christ. "For do I now persuade men, or God? Or do I seek to please men? For if I still pleased men, I would not be a bondservant of Christ" (Gal. 1:10). Ask yourself today: *To whom am I going to be faithful?*

Living out the will of God may require tough choices. It's not that you're going to be rude or mean, or break promises. But if God changes your direction, remember this little bit of wisdom: God never makes a mistake. Circumstances may change, or perhaps you need to admit that somewhere along the road, you chose the wrong path. *But if I am doing God's work,* you may be thinking, *why would He have to change my direction?* Yes, He knows all things and is sovereign, but He also has to contend with us; we don't always listen to His perfect will. So there may be a time when it is necessary for you to disappoint or even hurt someone by saying no.

Let me give you an example. Let's say that a young man is soon to marry. He thanks God every day for his future bride and is so excited that he cannot even sleep at night. He can't wait to marry her. Everything is ready. Everyone has been invited. The big day—the one he has dreamt about—is only a week away. Then the unthinkable happens. He finds out that she doesn't know Christ. (I'm not sure how this could happen, unless she was really beautiful and he was really dumb!) So the young man starts to pray. She says, "I'm not a Christian; I'm an atheist." Now they have to make a choice: (1) to go ahead with the wedding, or (2) to break it off.

Which choice should this couple make? Well, absolutely they should break it off! But many times (more than I would like to admit), people go through with the wedding. It's hard to believe, but they somehow convince themselves they are doing the right thing. The believer will justify his or her poor choice by thinking that he or she will win the other person to Christ after the wedding. Why? There are many reasons, but often it's about not wanting to offend parents or look bad before friends, so they keep a sinful commitment. Instead of saying, "You know, we need to stop this and reevaluate, because this is our whole life ahead of us," they go through with it instead, and they're definitely not in God's will.

Having a clear conscience before God means that each of us will seek the will of God above every other will in our lives. We will desire to do what God wants us to do, not what other people want us to do.

Though people hated Paul because of his message, he was not discouraged. He was willing and able to love those who wished him harm, because he knew he was acting according to God's perfect will.

God will change our plans, as He did in Paul's life. And if we're not flexible, we're going to be broken. Blessed are the flexible, for they shall not be broken. When plans change, it's important to be honest and not lie about it. One day we will stand before God, so better to stop lying and start living in purity and power with a clear conscience.

## A Clear Conscience Leads You to Glorify Jesus Christ

When we have a clear conscience, we will continually glorify and share Jesus Christ, wanting the preeminence of Christ to be the number-one priority in our lives. Malachi tells us, "Then those who feared the LORD spoke to one another, and the LORD listened and heard them; so a book of remembrance was written before Him for those who fear the LORD and who meditate on His name" (Mal. 3:16). When our conscience is dull or darkened because of sin, we do not see God. When our conscience has constantly rebelled and resisted the voice of the Holy Spirit, we do not consider or desire His will in our lives. When sin has dirtied the window of our conscience, the name of Christ is not on our lips. However, if we have a clear conscience before God, then we will confess Christ to a dying world and will shout with passion and love to all who can hear our voices, "Christ is coming; it's time to repent; it's time to get ready to meet your Lord in the clouds!"

**A Clear Conscience Puts You on Great Terms with the Holy Spirit**
What do I mean by "on great terms with the Holy Spirit"? The Holy Spirit is a person. He is part of the Godhead, and He now lives inside each believer to comfort, come alongside and help us know Christ better. He has the power to change our lives and use us for the glory of God. But when we constantly fight against Him and resist His ways, we put distance in our relationship. If we hear His voice and ignore it, we quench the Holy Spirit. If we choose to walk in sin and not in obedience, we grieve His heart. Grieving the Holy Spirit will bring such guilt and shame to our lives that we will no longer do what God wants us to do, and there will be a separation between the Holy Spirit and us. However, obedience produces intimacy:

> Now He who establishes us with you in Christ and has anointed us is God, who also has sealed us and given us the Spirit in our hearts as a guarantee (2 Cor. 1:21-22).

In this verse from Paul's second letter to the Corinthians, there are four important truths about the Holy Spirit that will help us overcome discouragement: The Holy Spirit *establishes us, anoints us, seals us* and *fills us.*

First, verse 21 tells us, "He who establishes us with you in Christ." The word "establish" basically means "to guarantee or to fulfill" a person's life. It's a business term that means He will honor the contract He has made in a believer's life. The day that a person accepts Christ, He comes into that person's life and stamps it with His seal— His guarantee.

I remember a commercial on television in which the owner asserted, "And I guarantee it." That little statement made him millions. Similarly, the Holy Spirit is saying to each of us, "I have guaranteed your life before God." What a great God we serve! He personally guarantees our lives. "He who establishes" means "He who guarantees." The Holy Spirit ensures that God is going to work out that which He has begun; He is able to do it and will complete His work. God is going to keep us for the Day of Christ. God is working through the Holy Spirit to establish our lives.

We also find in verse 21 that He will anoint us. Notice that Paul says, "Now He who establishes us with you in Christ and has anointed us is God" (2 Cor. 1:21). In the Old Testament, there were three groups who were anointed—the priests, the prophets and the kings. These groups were anointed for two reasons: They were anointed to be "set aside" and to be used "for" God's work. Sometimes we feel that God has brought us out of the world but we're not doing anything for the Kingdom. However, He brought us out of the world that He might bring us into Christ. God has established us and is now "setting us aside" and setting us apart "for" something else—to be an instrument in God's hands. Take heart, because God is pulling you out of the world and establishing your life; and He is beginning to use you in a very powerful way. God is doing that work because of your clear conscience.

Continuing in verse 22, we find another thing the Spirit is doing—He is sealing our life: "Who also has sealed us." The word "seal" means "to claim." It's an old word that was used to claim logs that had been cut down. A person would stamp the logs with his own personal seal. Then he would go back home and wait. When it was time to go get the logs, he would send somebody with the seal to retrieve the logs, and that person would claim and take those logs.

Similarly, Jesus Christ sent His Holy Spirit, and He has sealed each believer's life as a down payment. In other words, He's coming back. I like that song "Signed, Sealed, Delivered." The Spirit is going to get you there one way or another. God's Spirit is building you up; He is pulling you along by His side; and He has claimed you as His personal property. So no one had better mess with you! Because if they do, they're going to have to mess with the Lord!

God is with us and He will protect us. God will watch over us like He did Paul, who said in 2 Timothy 4:17 that the Lord had stood with him and strengthened him. Again, when Paul was on a ship that was going down, the Lord stood with him. And when Paul was in prison, Acts 23:11 continues to make it clear that God stood with him: "The following night the Lord stood by him and said, 'Be of good cheer, Paul; for as you have testified for Me in Jerusalem, so you must also bear witness at Rome.' " Just as God stood with Paul, He is willing and able to stand with us also.

Finally, I notice one more golden nugget in verse 22 (my paraphrase): "He will fill you." When God fills our hearts with His Holy Spirit, we have power—the ability to follow the Lord and do what we could not do in our own strength.

When we have a good conscience before God, when our lives are right in the very things of God, we can honestly look up and know that Christ is coming, and we can refuse to let the things we are going through bother us. His will is number one in our lives, and we want to be obedient to that will. We need to hear which way God wants us to go, how He wants us to live our lives, where He wants us to work and where He wants us to live. And when we have a clear conscience before God, we will be able to speak about the great things of our Lord. When we are right with God, the Holy Spirit will work in our lives to establish us, anoint us, seal us and fill us. God will, indeed, bless us in a wonderful way.

The apostle Paul was able to take the discouragement, the beatings and the rejection because he had a pure conscience before God. He knew he was on great terms with the Holy Spirit. What a wonderful way to live—no more double standards, no more secrets! We see this integrity and purity of heart in 1 Corinthians 15:10: "By the grace of God I am what I am." It's a very simple life.

## POINTS TO PONDER

- Do I have a clear conscience before God?
- Am I seeking the light and rejecting the darkness?
- How clean is the window of my life?
- Am I serious about doing the will of God?
- Am I on great terms with the Holy Spirit?

# 2

# OVERCOMING SUFFERING

*Blessed be the God and Father of our Lord Jesus Christ,
the Father of mercies and God of all comfort, who comforts us in all our
tribulation, that we may be able to comfort those who are in any trouble,
with the comfort with which we ourselves are comforted by God.*

2 CORINTHIANS 1:3-4

*There seem to be two types of suffering: (1) the suffering that comes of our own making, and (2) the suffering that comes when God prunes us. I have experienced both. The suffering of brokenness is never easy. The pain that I have experienced with surgeries has been pure agony. One day, I was reading in the book of Genesis the story about Joseph when he was in prison in Egypt. I read that the metal shackles around Joseph's ankles were iron, and they pierced his soul. God spoke to me that, just like Joseph, the suffering that He has taken me through has built character within my life and has made me strong—the very thing that God wants to accomplish in the midst of our suffering. Though suffering can be painful, devastating and deep, it can also be a privilege. I believe God chooses certain people to suffer, and when we understand that, the anointing of the Holy Spirit comes, and we can teach with passion and minister with grace. However, I have also learned to have compassion and empathy. Now when I see people suffer, my heart breaks for them. So my real suffering has not been physical or mental, but spiritual: a breaking of my soul. Now in those painful moments when I feel rejected, I know that He doesn't reject me. When I feel like no one understands, I know that my Lord does. Suffering has made me the man that I am today.*

Why talk about this subject of suffering? Can we please, please talk about something else, like buying another car, building a bigger house or maybe having a little bit more money? Why ruin a great day with the word "suffering"? Just thinking about the word or reading the book of Job is enough to frighten anyone. But what happens when God calls us to experience suffering firsthand? How can we bear it? It is a difficult pill to swallow, but we all suffer in one way or another. There are those who suffer physically; some suffer emotionally; others seem to suffer mentally; and, finally, many who constantly fight God's calling in their lives suffer spiritually. Why? We suffer because we refuse to surrender and yield everything to God's lordship. Suffering is a difficult truth, and without God in our lives, it's impossible to understand or see any good in it. But with God's help and His Spirit's empowerment, it can be the sweetest thing a believer ever experiences.

God's Spirit chooses certain people that He knows will accept the pain and sorrow of suffering. He knows they will trust Him fully and learn to love Him deeply. He will then take these vessels whom He has chosen to honor and will pour His glorious grace upon them with a touch of love and kindness directly from His own hands. He will make them an instrument so powerful, so special and so sweet that no one will be able to resist them. He's only asking us to do one thing for Him—simply put our trust completely in Him. It sounds like this: "Father, at this very moment, I place my pain, my sorrow and my sadness back into the hands of my Maker who has always loved me. Amen."

We often forget what God has already declared in His Word: God's ways are higher than ours (see Isa. 55:8-9). His wisdom and insight into who we are and what we need in our lives are perfect. And, much to our dismay, the Lord does not always reveal to us what He is doing in our lives!

When we get into the arena of suffering, often our faith begins to waver in disbelief, our hearts begin to question everything about God's love, and our minds begin to challenge God's authority. We take our eyes off of His love and begin to question God Himself. Satan then throws us into the pit of despair. We begin to spiral out of control. Faster and faster we fall until we finally end up in a horrible and sinful place, crying out, "It doesn't seem fair!" A question comes from our hearts: Why do the wicked prosper and the righteous have to suffer? Why, for example, does a young Christian woman, who is living her life for the Lord and with great virtuousness, get raped? Why, as in the case of Jim Elliot, was an evangelical Christian missionary to Ecuador murdered when he was trying to reach out with the love of the gospel? Why does a Christian couple have to experience the pain of a child suffering from cancer?

Even in my own life I have questioned why I have needed so many surgeries and am constantly plagued with physical afflictions. Quite frankly, I don't think any of us can truly answer these questions. If we didn't know God, we could likely brush it off as the way of human existence and go on. But because we know the goodness of God; because we know that He is filled with grace, mercy and compassion; and because we know that no experience—painful or otherwise—can touch us unless it goes through His hands, we struggle to make sense of the pain and suffering in life.

When we are struck with pain and suffering, we automatically think that we have done something wrong and that God is trying to teach us a lesson. This is not always the case. In fact, some of the most horrific suffering can take place when we are doing exactly what we should be doing! One thing is certain: Suffering produces character.

## Some Truths About Suffering

When we encounter trials, tribulations and sufferings, it's then that our Christian walk really meets the road. It is often during these times that the Scriptures truly become alive to us and the Holy Spirit does His greatest work in our lives.

### Suffering Helps Us Comfort Others

The Bible promises us that we will be comforted in our suffering. It does not promise that we will always understand our suffering, nor does it promise that God will deliver us from pain, suffering or even death; but it does promise He will always be with us. Perhaps the prophet Isaiah says it the very best: "When you pass through the waters, I will be with you; and through the rivers, they shall not overflow you. When you walk through the fire, you shall not be burned, nor shall the flame scorch you" (Isa. 43:2). We receive our comfort from God Himself, and He will use the very experience that is causing our suffering to help us comfort someone else! That is how the kingdom of God works.

Paul wrote, in his second letter to the Corinthians, "Blessed be the God and Father of our Lord Jesus Christ, the Father of mercies and God of all comfort, who comforts us in all our tribulation, that we may be able to comfort those who are in any trouble, with the comfort with which we ourselves are comforted by God. For as the sufferings of Christ abound in us, so our consolation also abounds through Christ. Now if we are afflicted, it is for your consolation and salvation, which is effective for enduring the same sufferings that we also suffer. Or if we are comforted, it is for your consolation and salvation" (2 Cor. 1:3-6).

At times God shakes up our lives. He brings us to a place in which we are uncomfortable in order to mold and correct us. As these verses state, sometimes we will suffer for no other reason but to make our hearts tender and to give us great compassion toward other people. When we experience difficulty in life, we are able to turn to the Lord for His comfort. The comfort of God is something that your spouse or your best friend cannot give to you. The Lord strengthens us by coming alongside us and walking with us through the storm.

## Suffering Turns Our Focus on God

The apostle Paul talks about the extent of his own suffering when he wrote, "For we do not want you to be ignorant, brethren, of our trouble which came to us in Asia: that we were burdened beyond measure, above strength, so that we despaired even of life. Yes, we had the sentence of death in ourselves, that we should not trust in ourselves but in God who raises the dead, who delivered us from so great a death, and does deliver us; in whom we trust that He will still deliver us, you also helping together in prayer for us, that thanks may be given by many persons on our behalf for the gift granted to us through many" (2 Cor. 1:8-11). What was the reason for Paul's suffering? He suffered so that he would not trust in himself, but in God, who raises the dead!

I believe that every bit of suffering God allows us to experience has at its core the purpose of bringing us to a place where we do not look to ourselves, but rather to God. The Lord wants to destroy that place of self-confidence in our lives and to bring us to a place in which we trust only Him. He wants us to understand and know His place of comfort and, in turn, be able to reach out and comfort others just as He has comforted and taken care of us.

## Suffering Helps Us Overcome Satan

Sometimes God uses suffering as a means to destroy the power of Satan in our lives. In the book of Job, we read the following:

Then the LORD said to Satan, "Have you considered My
servant Job, that there is none like him on the earth, a
blameless and upright man, one who fears God and shuns
evil?" So Satan answered the LORD and said, "Does Job fear
God for nothing? Have You not made a hedge around
him, around his household, and around all that he has on
every side? You have blessed the work of his hands, and his
possessions have increased in the land. But now, stretch
out Your hand and touch all that he has, and he will surely
curse You to Your face!" And the LORD said to Satan, "Behold, all that he has is in your power; only do not lay a
hand on his person." So Satan went out from the presence
of the LORD (Job 1:8-12).

In this exchange between God and Satan, God removed the
hedge of protection around Job, except to his person—meaning
that Satan could not take his life. Subsequently, in the course of
one day, 10 of Job's children were killed, his house was destroyed
and his wife told him to curse God and die. What was Job's response to his horrific suffering? The Bible tells us that Job tore his
robe, shaved his head, fell to the ground and worshiped the Lord,
saying, "Naked I came from my mother's womb, and naked shall
I return there. The LORD gave, and the LORD has taken away;
blessed be the name of the LORD" (Job 1:21). The Bible goes on to
clarify that in all this, Job did not sin nor charge God with wrong-
doing. Job maintained His faith in and love for the Lord in the
midst of his suffering!

God allowed His servant Job, a man whose eyes were always
looking to God, to suffer much pain and agony in order to allow
Job to demonstrate his love for God even in adversity. The Lord
allows suffering to glorify God in a way that destroys the power of
Satan's lies.

## Suffering Allows Us to Better Glorify God

In all ways, we want the Lord to be glorified in our lives. Sometimes
He gets greater glory in what may seem like nothing but suffering

on our end. Remember in the book of John when Martha and Mary were crying because their brother, Lazarus, had died? Martha told Jesus that if only He had been there, Lazarus would not have died. It's likely that the sisters had a hard time understanding why Jesus didn't drop everything to come and rescue His friend! And, understandably so, this furthered the suffering they were experiencing. But Jesus said to them, "This sickness is not unto death, but for the glory of God, that the Son of God may be glorified through it" (John 11:4). Jesus loved Mary and Martha. He allowed them to suffer temporarily because it was part of God's plan to do an even greater work than healing Lazarus, that is, to raise him from the dead. Not only would this greater miracle reveal Jesus' deity and give God glory, but it would also give Mary and Martha tremendous hope. God loves His children and uses suffering to bring about far greater glory than what we could ever imagine.

## Suffering Allows Us to Be More Christlike

Another reason why the Lord allows us to suffer is to make us more like Christ. There is nothing like a good dose of sorrow to make us cry out to the Lord. Depression, a broken relationship and overwhelming situations in our lives tend to drive us to God. It is in these difficult times that we learn to depend on God and not ourselves. Through the pain, God is helping us to grow, and He is teaching us about Himself. In the process, we are also learning about ourselves—that we are not self-sufficient and we are not able to handle everything on our own. We need the Lord in our lives. We need His guidance and help. In our horrible moments, God is able to comfort us, care for us and change our hearts because we are broken before Him. These are His appointed circumstances. It is in these broken moments of our lives that God is able to change us and make us more like Him.

## Suffering Allows Us to Be More Appreciative

I have witnessed time and again how suffering makes people more appreciative. When we struggle through difficult times, we find ourselves being thankful for the simple things, the blessings the

Lord has given us. Think of it this way: When we are sick, we become very appreciative of our health! When we are broke, we become very appreciative of basic provisions. When we experience a broken relationship, we become very appreciative of just having someone to eat meals with! So often we don't realize what we have until something is taken away. Too often we ignore God's daily provisions for our lives and the many blessings He has bestowed on us. Not taking things for granted is a key lesson of suffering. We need to appreciate what God has given us (including each breath we take) and live each day with a thankful heart. No one likes to suffer, but it's a necessary part of life. If our attitudes and hearts are right, we will thrive during the suffering and, on the other side, be better because of it.

## How to View Suffering and Cope with It

Ultimately, there are two ways to look at suffering. One way is like looking in a mirror. When trials come and difficulty hits, we immediately look in the mirror and all we see is *ourselves*. We see our hurts, our problems, our pain and what others have done to us, but we are oblivious both to God and to what is going on in *others'* lives. The more we look in the mirror, the further we slide into despair. If we deal with suffering when it comes by looking into a mirror, we will never overcome it. We will never enjoy and experience the fruit God wants to bring into our lives through our suffering.

However, God wants to take the mirror away and replace it with a window—a view on the rest of the world! If we look out the window, we will see other people who are also hurting. Although we may not see the purpose of our suffering at the time, we will see that God is moving, and He is placing people and circumstances in our life for a reason. When we are looking out the window, we have no time to look in the mirror.

### Time for a New View

What about you? Maybe you have been looking in the mirror for a long time. Maybe your attitude is that no one understands, no one has experienced what you are going through, and nobody cares. Every day you look into the mirror and find all the flaws of your life. Every day all you see is yourself; that is enough to destroy anybody. But the day you choose to throw out the mirror and, with God's help, look through a window, then you can look through the pain, the suffering and the agony of your own life and see another human being. This will produce in you an understanding that there are people around you who are putting up with you. They have been affected by your attitude and your life, and they are in need of your care and your ministry.

When we look in the mirror, we see ourselves. But when we look out the window during our suffering, we see God and others. Then, choosing to look out the window, we would not only receive God's comfort but also see other people going through difficult times as well. The Lord will lift us out of the sorrow, out of the situation, and use us as an instrument of righteousness within His Kingdom. He will give us His compassion to reach out to others who are suffering, to comfort them with the same comfort that we have received.

Suffering is common to all men and women. Every one of us goes through difficult times. Jesus, who did nothing wrong, suffered more than any other man or woman in history. Yet, He was able to say from the cross, "Father, forgive them, for they do not know what they are doing" (Luke 23:34). Throughout His life and His suffering, Jesus looked through a window instead of a mirror and was able to see others, not Himself.

## Help to Cope with Suffering

We need to get out from our looking position (the inward focus, the looking in the mirror) to a helping position—taking our eyes off our own situation and helping others through their suffering. But how do we do this? We do it by receiving God's comfort and strength. In the Bible, the word *paraclete* is given to describe the Holy Spirit. In the Greek, it means "one who comes as a pillar of fire by your side." God will be with us through the fire. He will be with us through the storm. He will be with us when the rivers begin to overflow. The Lord is able to comfort and help us in all situations of life. The apostle Paul, who had his own share of suffering, wrote, "And we know that all things work together for good to those who love God, to those who are the called according to His purpose" (Rom. 8:28).

Are you battling a painful time in your life? Are you trying to make sense of it all? It's important to stick with what you know the Bible promises to help dispel the horrible and nagging question of "Why?" So stick with these truths: You know that God loves you. You know that God is true. You know that He is righteous and holy. You know that God will not allow anything to come into your life that you cannot handle. You know that God will comfort you in the midst of your suffering. You know that God will use your suffering to help you minister to someone else. And you know that God will use your suffering for ultimate good.

We must look to the Lord and stand upon His promises. This is the only way to get through our personal suffering. We must remember what Jesus said: "These things I have spoken to you, that in Me you may have peace. In the world you will have tribulation; but be of good cheer, I have overcome the world" (John 16:33).

## POINTS TO PONDER

- Am I looking for ways to comfort others with the comfort I have received?
- Do I, like Job, maintain my faith and love for the Lord in the midst of my suffering?
- When I am suffering, where am I looking—in a mirror or out a window?
- What truths about God will help me get through my suffering?

3

# OVERCOMING DEPRESSION

*Therefore we do not lose heart. Even though our outward man is perishing, yet the inward man is being renewed day by day. For our light affliction, which is but for a moment, is working for us a far more exceeding and eternal weight of glory, while we do not look at the things which are seen, but at the things which are not seen. For the things which are seen are temporary, but the things which are not seen are eternal.*

2 CORINTHIANS 4:16-18

*I have been told that depression is repressed anger. There's no doubt that I have been through some things that have made me angry. A teacher molested me when I was in the eighth grade. I became violent, inflicting pain on others to dull the pain in my own heart. But the pain in my heart did not go away. My anger turned to depression. I was convinced that there was no real reason to live, and yes, I contemplated taking my own life. In that kind of depression, you can justify to yourself that no one loves you and that everyone else would be better off without you. But it's a lie from Satan, because ultimately I would have destroyed everyone who loved me if I had taken my own life. God began to speak to my heart about how selfish I was. Although it was the last thing I wanted to hear, it is exactly what got me into my depression—being consumed with self. I had to realize that God had a calling on my life and He had plans for me. Instead of serving myself, I needed to serve Christ and others.*

Who among us has not gone through difficult times within our own personal life? Who has not thought seriously about quitting or has not been tempted to give up or give in? Some of us have even had thoughts of suicide. Oftentimes, we go through these incredibly hard moments and don't really know how to deal with them or how we're to walk in the realm of the Spirit. So we look to other people; yet to our surprise, we often find that other people are in a worse condition than we are.

Paul gives us an answer in 2 Corinthians: *We are not to lose heart.* We must never give up or give in. It's time for us to start trusting God rather than staying overwhelmed at the things that are taking place around us and inside of us. People often ask me, "How can I do this, and why shouldn't I worry?" The apostle Paul gives us the answer to why we should trust God. He says that these difficult times are a "light affliction" working for us an eternal glory: "For our light affliction, which is but for a moment, is working for us a far more exceeding and eternal weight of glory" (2 Cor. 4:17). In this verse, Paul begins to share with us how to have victory over discouragement, how to overcome despondency, how not to allow despair or disappointment to overwhelm us. And he says these are light afflictions within our lives.

I don't know about you, but examples of things I call light affliction are that the coffee didn't come out right when I paid for it with my last two dollars, or that some store didn't have the stuff I needed, or that someone didn't say hi to me at church. That's about all it takes for some of us to get rocked into a terrible mood. But in the light of heaven, we need to change our perspective and start seeing the bigger picture. Christ died for our sins so that we might be a witness to all who are looking for hope.

Paul's definition of light affliction is far different from ours. He tells us, in 2 Corinthians 1:8, "For we do not want you to be ignorant, brethren, of our trouble which came to us in Asia: that we were burdened beyond measure, above strength, so that we despaired even of life." And in 2 Corinthians 2:4, he writes, "For out of much affliction and anguish of heart I wrote to you, with many tears, not that you should be grieved, but that you might know the love which I have so abundantly for you." Paul tells us that his anguish and affliction, and even the tears he weeps day and night, may be regarded as light affliction when compared to the eternal glory that comes with them. Paul continues to help put the discouragement of our lives into better perspective: "We are hard-pressed on every side, yet not crushed; we are perplexed, but not in despair; persecuted, but not forsaken; struck down, but not destroyed—always carrying about in the body the dying of the Lord Jesus, that the life of Jesus also may be manifested in our body" (2 Cor. 4:8-10).

What great lessons we can learn from Paul's teaching! We, too, can now say, "Lord, take my body and use it for the glory of God. We are troubled, but we are not distressed. We are pained, but not hopeless. We're victimized but not abandoned—cast down, but not undone." Paul understood what it meant to be afflicted. He had firsthand experience when it came to trouble, trials and mistreatment. Take a look at Paul's words in 2 Corinthians 11:24-27:

From the Jews five times I received forty stripes minus one. Three times I was beaten with rods; once I was stoned; three times I was shipwrecked; a night and a day I have been in the deep; in journeys often, in perils of waters, in perils of robbers, in perils of my own countrymen, in perils of the Gentiles, in perils in the city, in perils in the wilderness, in perils in the sea, in perils among false brethren; in weariness and toil, in sleeplessness often, in hunger and thirst, in fastings often, in cold and nakedness.

The truth is that any one of these difficulties would take us out! But when we look at Paul's life, we see that he's committed. Paul was a man who had a deep conviction concerning the "coming of Christ." He was a man who had tremendous courage when it came to the work of God. The fact that they could stone him in Lystra, yet he got back up and finished the message, proves his courage and steadfastness for the gospel! Paul knew that God had called him to do a work; because of that fact, he was committed and loyal and was never going to give up. His character was outstanding. This is the type of life I desire to live. How about you?

## Key Principles of Overcoming Depression

I'd like to state some key points or concepts that I believe explain how Paul dealt with despondency and depression. These truths will help us begin to face our own afflictions in a brand-new way and provide a glorious light in our darkest hours. God definitely desires to help us during the difficult times in our lives, even in the rejection that is happening or the barrenness we feel. God is willing to work in and through our lives, but we must let Him in and trust His ways.

### God Gives Us a New Start

God gave Paul a brand-new start in life on the Damascus Road. Paul later wrote to the church at Corinth about what God did for him that day and how this new start had changed his life. He noted in 2 Corinthians 4:1, "Therefore, since we have this ministry, as we have received mercy, we do not lose heart." I think the very reason why Paul was able to overcome countless difficulties was because he simply believed and trusted in what God had accomplished in his life.

We must never forget what Paul was before he came to Christ—a murderer of many Christians who confessed their faith and a persecutor of the Church and the followers of Christ. Despite Paul's wicked past, God had a marvelous plan for this man's life. God took Paul's failure and made him a trophy of grace. First Timothy 1:13 makes it clear that Paul received mercy and God forgave him for his heinous sins. The Scriptures also declare that Paul received "a ministry." So there is no doubt in my mind that Paul knew that God gave him this ministry—and that it was a gift of God's mercy. God simply gave him a second chance.

What is so exciting to me is that God has a marvelous plan for each of us as well. But there must be a Damascus Road experience in each of our lives. God must meet us and break our will; it's the place where God challenges us to go deeper into the life in His Spirit. It is that road where God speaks so clearly and so profoundly that nothing in this world will be able to call us away or distract us from the love of God. When we understand the nature of our God, we will come to understand and experience how often He graciously gives His people second chances. In fact, the Bible is filled with examples of those to whom God gave a second chance. I believe these second chances are the work of the Holy Spirit, who takes a broken life, sets it free and lights it on fire for Jesus.

Not only was this the apostle Paul's story, but it is your and my story too. God has given us a second, a third, a fourth chance. He meets us on our very own Damascus Road, fills us with His Holy Spirit and makes us a trophy of His grace, setting us on a broad path with a ministry of our own. This is all the work of His grace within us. Because of this incredible grace, I'm not going to quit. I'm not going to give up. I'm not going to be torn apart. I might be cast down, but I won't be destroyed. I might be persecuted, but I'm not going to give in. I might be totally perplexed, but I'm going to hang in there to the very end.

## God Gives Us a New Strength

We read in 2 Corinthians 4:16, "Therefore we do not lose heart. Even though our outward man is perishing, yet the inward man is being renewed day by day." Not only did God give Paul a new start, but He also gave Paul new strength for this new start. Paul received a fresh strength of the Spirit of God. The Bible says, in Deuteronomy 33:25, "As your days, so shall your strength be." In other words, no matter what we go through, God is willing to strengthen each day of our lives. But the key is being renewed day after day, not week by week or month by month.

God longs to give us His strength and His ability to overcome any discouragement in our lives right now. These difficulties can bring us closer to Christ. David, the great king of Israel, said it so well in Psalm 119:67-68: "Before I was afflicted I went astray, but now I keep Your word. You are good, and do good; teach me Your statutes." The great lesson from David is simple. These hated, difficult times in our lives have a unique way of enabling us to hear from God. These trials enable us to learn things about God we would never have known apart from this suffering in our lives. And these hardships enable us to see the glory and the power of the One who loves us and died for us. When we look at our afflictions, they are very "light" in comparison to what God is working out in us. Compared to our eternal glory, our earthly afflictions are only for a moment. Although they don't feel like it, they are like a vapor.

Paul declared that the afflictions work in us and for us so that we will be able to have a fresh start through the mercy of God and be strengthened by His Spirit. The Bible declares, "Not by might nor by power, but by My Spirit" (Zech. 4:6). God wants us to come to the end of ourselves. He desires to be glorified in our weaknesses. Paul says that we have this sentence of death in ourselves, "that we should not trust in ourselves" (2 Cor. 1:9). And that is the message that Paul himself came to understand. Because God was his strength, Paul didn't need any other resources. Nor did Paul need to figure anything out. When Paul went through it, God was there. When Paul was in prison, the angel came and ministered to his heart. When Paul was going down in the ship, God was there to encourage him. When Paul was discouraged, the angel of the Lord was there. God was a reality every day in Paul's life. When that truth becomes a part of our lives as well, we are able to look at life's struggles and deal with them in a whole different way.

The word *dunamis* is the Greek word meaning "power." It is where we get our English word "dynamite." In the book of Acts, God gives us our marching orders to win the world for Christ, but He must first give us His anointing, or His empowering Spirit. We find this word *dunamis* in Acts 1:8: "But you shall receive power [*dunamis*] when the Holy Spirit has come upon you; and you shall be witnesses to Me in Jerusalem, and in all Judea and Samaria, and to the end of the earth." The "*dunamis* power" of the Holy Spirit is His strength, His power, His knowledge of God Himself, and His fullness within our lives—it's like dynamite!

## God Gives Us a New Spirit

We learn from Paul's Damascus Road experience that God not only gives a new start and a new strength, but He also gives a new spirit. This makes sense, looking at it now. When God gives us a new start or beginning, He then must strengthen our lives and heart for the work He is calling us to do; and to top it off, He adds to our start and strength a brand-new spirit. Notice what Paul wrote in 2 Corinthians 5:5-6: "Now he that hath wrought us for the selfsame thing is God, who also hath given unto us the earnest of the Spirit. [The word "earnest" can be the same word as "comfort" of the Spirit.] Therefore we are always confident, knowing that, whilst we are at home in the body, we are absent from the Lord" (*KJV*).

No matter what happens, whether we live or die, we belong to God. That's why we are confident! He is our comfort. There's a great verse that says, "Nevertheless God . . . comforts the downcast" (2 Cor. 7:6). The word "comfort" is a Greek word that has two meanings: one is "to come alongside" and the second is "to be a pillar of strength." The reason why Paul was able to stand so strong was because he trusted the work of the Holy Spirit. He had a personal relationship with God Himself. He knew that when he was cast down, God was going to comfort him, and the Spirit of God would breathe into him new life. God Himself would quicken him and restore his life. So when we look at discouragement, when we see our life falling apart, when we see our marriage going haywire or our business failing, what are we going to do? Are we going to try to push through it, using our human wisdom and knowledge, or will we say to ourselves, *I need a new spirit, the Holy Spirit, and nothing else?*

God is going to get us through this struggle, first because He has called us His children and, as a result of His mercy, He is going to do a work in our lives. Not only that, but second, He's going to give us a new strength. We will not have to fight this thing in our own flesh. He has brought us to a point of weakness because of His strength, and He wants to be glorified in our weaknesses. God is going to do the work. God is going to bring His Spirit. He is going to comfort the loneliness. He is going to take away the sadness. He is going to come by our side and be a pillar of strength and comfort to our hearts. It is not necessary to fake this Christian walk. We don't have to say we're happy when inside we feel dead. No! We can say that He gave us life. He quickened us and gave us a purpose for living. Very simply, He came to bring His Spirit.

### God Gives Us a New Sight

Paul tells us, in 2 Corinthians 5:7-8, "For we walk by faith, not by sight. We are confident, yes, well pleased rather to be absent from the body and to be present with the Lord." Paul not only was given a new start, a new strength, and a new spirit, but on top of all that, he was also given a new sight. He saw things differently than he did before knowing Christ. He understood that the life he was living was being lived for the "glory of God." Paul lived in every way based on an eternal perspective. Yes, he saw the pain, the suffering, the bruises, the bleeding, but he also saw the glory of God. He saw the agony, the rejection and the shame, but he also saw the glory. He saw all that he experienced with heavenly eyes.

And we know that Paul suffered chronic pain. We know that he had a "thorn in the flesh" (2 Cor. 12:7). The word "thorn" in the Greek is a word that means a "tent post." What's referred to is not just a little thorn but something like a tent post being driven through his flesh. He agonized and was overwhelmed, but he chose to see heaven. When we choose to see heaven and the glory of God, we understand what life is all about—that whether we live or it actually costs us physical life, we belong to Christ.

This was the "philosophy" of my life, and it can be yours. Then, we can say to anybody: If you keep me alive, I'm going to talk about Jesus Christ; if you kill me, I'm going to be with Jesus Christ. This is what I believe, what governs my life, the principles that set my life apart from others. When we believe that God is going to start something brand new, that He is going to strengthen us and send His Spirit and open our eyes into a heavenly perspective, only then do we begin to realize that this depression is just for a moment. Better yet, this depression is really God's opportunity to do something big in our lives. When we see God in our lives, we have a different perspective and we understand that He will help us walk through painful circumstances.

### God Gives Us a New Season

Paul exhorted the Galatians, "And let us not grow weary while doing good, for in due season we shall reap if we do not lose heart" (Gal. 6:9). What a great word of hope: "for in due season." The key word for us is "season." God not only gave Paul a *new start*, a *new strength,* a *new spirit,* and a *new sight,* but He also gave Paul a *new season.* In the new season, we will reap. Right now, we are laboring and giving, and we do not see any reward. But when we get to heaven and stand before Christ, He is going to say, "Well done, good and faithful servant. . . . Enter into the joy of your Lord" (Matt. 25:21). Christ is going to reward us there at the Bema Seat of Christ. This term *Bema Seat* is not mentioned in the Bible, but the concept is found in 2 Corinthians 5:10: "For we must all appear before the judgment seat of Christ, that each one may receive the things done in the body, according to what he has done, whether good or bad." All things done in secret will be rewarded openly. So maybe in this life people don't recognize what you're doing, they don't give you credit where it is due, or they might steal your reputation. It doesn't make a difference, because we will all stand before God, and God knows the ultimate truth.

## Eyes Toward Heaven

Imagine Paul the apostle, the ugliest guy you had ever seen in your life, showing up at church. Remember, he was beaten five times with a whip around the face and around the body; three times with a stick; and he went down in a shipwreck on three separate occasions. His eyes, historians say, had malaria. He had drooping eyes that were constantly dripping. Bottom line, he was very difficult to look at. This is how I imagine it would go if someone came to my office and said, "This ugly guy wants to take you out for coffee." I would ask, "Well, who is it?" They'd answer back, "He says he's Paul the apostle." "You're kidding," I'd say! Then I would hustle out of my office and see this ugly, tiny guy, and we'd head out to the coffee shop.

Paul would probably say to me, "How have you been doing?"

"Well, you know, Paul, it's been hard. It's been tough. I'm thinking about quitting. I'm thinking about giving up."

And he would look at me with those beady eyes, with that cup of coffee in his hand—no doubt with a double shot of espresso—and I can almost hear him say, "Stephen, my boy, do you not know? Do you not have any concept of what God is doing in your life? Do you not know that He has given you a brand-new start? You were once on drugs and in desperate trouble, but God pulled you out of that pit. He put you in that pulpit, and He has turned your life around by His mercy. How dare you want to quit! After all that God has done, after all that God is doing, Stephen, you cannot quit."

As I looked at him, he would continue, "God has started a work in your life. Let Him finish that work. Don't be discouraged. Don't be despondent. Don't be overwhelmed. You hang in there and let God finish what He started."

By this time, I'd be feeling a bit ashamed of my attitude. But before I could reply, he would say, "Are you walking in strength?"

And I would answer, "Paul, I really want to, but I'm tired. I'm exhausted."

He would say, "You need to be strengthened every day with Jesus Christ. You need to hear the Word of God. You need to know which way to walk. You need to have the knowledge of God in your life. You need to be strengthened with the power from on high, because this is a supernatural work."

I imagine him finishing his double shot. Then, as he stared at the bottom of the cup without even looking up at me, he'd continue, "This is a supernatural work, and you cannot be a pastor or even a Christian in your own strength. Stephen, it's not by might, nor by power, but it's by God's Spirit [see Zech. 4:6] working through a broken instrument."

And then Paul would look at me and say, "You need a new spirit, Stephen. You're bitter and you have a nasty attitude. You're ready to quit. You're ready to throw in the towel." And he would look me right in my eyes that are filled with tears of discouragement and pain and say, "Do you not know that the Comforter is by your side? You're not looking to Him. You're not drawing strength from Him. You're not crying out to Him. You're not asking Him for help. You're not yielding to Him, and that's why you are facing this incredible storm in your own strength. Stephen, He wants to be your friend in both the good times and the bad. Remember He will never leave you nor forsake you, ever. He'll stick closer than a brother. You need to understand, Stephen, that there is someone to take away the loneliness, someone to take away the pain. And He is called the person and work of the Holy Spirit."

Paul would no doubt look at me with those dripping eyes and that beaten face and keep talking. "Have you seen heaven? Have you been in heaven lately? Have you been looking at the throne? Have you seen the streets of gold? Do you realize you're on your way? Have you had a sight of Jesus? What are you seeing? Are you seeing the church, the problems, the neighborhood, the house, the car, the finances, the kids and your job? What are you looking at?"

And I would say, so foolishly but honestly, "I'm looking at my problems, my house, my failures, my marriage." And he would respond, "Take your eyes off of all that and put your eyes on heaven. Gaze into heaven. Behold heaven. Understand that heaven is a whole different place, and it's almost here. It's almost over, and you can make it through."

I am sure that Paul would pat me on the shoulder, and say, "Listen, I want to tell you a secret. In my life, I was thrashed. In my life, things did not come out the way I thought, but I have received His glory, and a crown is waiting for me because I did this thing for God. In other words, very simply, I not only had a *new start*, a *new strength*, a *new spirit*, and a *new sight*, but I also had a *new season*. And, Stephen, there's going to be a new season when you will stand before Jesus Christ. I'll stand with you. God will say to you, 'Well done, good and faithful servant.' So, Stephen, it's time to stop your whining, complaining and murmuring. Do you not know that if you look to God, see God, hear God, know God and are heading toward God, that it will be enough to get you through the remaining years of your life?"

How do we overcome depression? We see Jesus. How do we overcome discouragement? We must let the Holy Spirit of God give us a *new start*, a *new strength*, a *new spirit*, and a *new sight* . . . with our eyes on a *new season*.

## POINTS TO PONDER

- Am I looking at my life with heavenly eyes?
- Will I allow God's Spirit to comfort me, and will I trust His work in my life?
- Am I standing in my own strength, or will I allow the Holy Spirit to lead me into victory?
- What is the "philosophy of my life"? What do I need to recognize to see with "heavenly eyes"?

4

# OVERCOMING FEAR

*So we are always confident, knowing that while we are at home in the body we are absent from the Lord. We are confident, yes, well pleased rather to be absent from the body and to be present with the Lord.*

2 CORINTHIANS 5:6,8

*God has really helped me overcome my fear of man. I was always questioning how I was doing—How's my ministry, my messages, my marriage? Do people respect me? Such fear and insecurity can bring paranoia. However, one day Christ showed me that He made me and bought me, and I became willing to fear only Him. That was the day that Satan lost and God won the victory in my life. I am convinced that Satan holds people prisoner to fear to hinder God's plan for their life. If I am afraid or insecure, then I am going to react and never fulfill God's purpose for my life. I had tried to be someone I wasn't. Finally, one day I knew that I had to face my fear head-on, and with the Lord's help, I did. I realized that God made me who I am and He has plans that only I can fulfill, so I started living and stopped being paralyzed by fear. All of a sudden, great things began to happen in my life. God has not given us the spirit of fear. Fear is Satan's foothold, where he can enter the mind and heart and keep us useless for the kingdom of God. Break the bondage. Be honest and be set free forever.*

It is so impressive to see a shepherd who really loves his flock, and we get personal glimpses of this when we read about the great compassion of the apostle Paul toward the Corinthian church. His heart's desire was for each of those in the church of Corinth to gain victory over this nagging fear about death. Just as Paul wasn't fearful of dying, neither should we be afraid, nor should we be afraid of giving our lives to Jesus Christ. Paul draws our attention to this in his second letter to the Corinthians: "Therefore we do not lose heart. Even though our outward man is perishing, yet the inward man is being renewed day by day. For our light affliction, which is but for a moment, is working for us a far more exceeding and eternal weight of glory" (2 Cor. 4:16-17).

Paul dealt with the issue of dying, which is a difficult topic for many people. In fact, he said he had the sentence of death within himself—that he should not come to trust in his own life. Paul had an eternal perspective. Ultimately, this is the key to a spiritual life. God's Spirit can open our eyes to the spirit world where He will show us incredible truths, like God's sovereignty, or one of my favorites—His providence. These truths of the Spirit can help us deal with our circumstances in a spiritual realm rather than a fleshly realm. We need to realize that heaven is the answer. Having his eyes on heaven is how Paul was willing to suffer all the things God said he would suffer and still have the testimony of the joy of Jesus Christ.

The other day, I was reading a very interesting article about a small congregation at an old Methodist church. As Pastor Henry M. Walters was addressing his congregation, he suddenly switched from his sermon and started to describe a vision of his own death. Everyone was horrified and wondered why in the world the pastor had switched his message off the sermon topic. "I see a light," he said. "The light is opening. I see the throne of God, and there are angels on both sides of the throne. I hear beautiful music. Jesus is coming down. I am dying." And then he fell down onto the platform. When his congregation had recovered from the shock, some of them thought this was just a sermon illustration. Yet, as they went up to the pulpit, they discovered that he was truly dead.

American evangelist Dwight L. Moody said it best:

Some day you will read in the papers that D. L. Moody of East Northfield is dead. Don't you believe a word of it! At that moment, I shall be more alive than I am now. I shall have gone up higher; that is all, out of this old clay pot tenement into a house that is immortal—a body that death cannot touch, that sin cannot taint, a body fashioned like unto His glorious body. I was born of the flesh in 1837. I was born of the Spirit in 1856. That which is born of the flesh may die. That which is born of the Spirit will live forever.[1]

Recently, while I was studying and preparing for my Sunday message, I received a phone call from a man who was dying. His friends called and said that he had to have an operation; otherwise he was going to die. It was going to be a quadruple bypass, and there was not a lot of hope for him. When I went down to the hospital and found him, he said, "I did not want to have the operation until I had talked to you." I looked into his eyes and saw a terror that I have never seen before. He said, "Pastor Steve, I am not right with God, and I know that. I have not been living for the Lord, though God has been after my life for a long time. I know exactly what He wants me to do, but I have been living in rebellion all these years, and now, as I am in bed ready to die, I am not prepared to meet the Master."

I looked at him and questioned, "You're not?" He said, "No, I have knowledge in my head, but I have absolutely no peace in my heart, and I believe that if I were to die now, I would not know where I would be." He trembled as I have never seen a man tremble before. His eyes were filled with fear and terror. "Do you think God will forgive me?" he said.

I replied, "As He forgave the criminal next to Him on the cross, He's willing to forgive you." Together we prayed the sinner's prayer. When we were done, there was an obvious peace and joy in this man's life that was just unbelievable. He proceeded into the operation, and the surgeons had great success. I expect God to do something very, very special within this man's life. The terror that I saw in his face, however, I will never forget.

The apostle Paul was living for Christ, serving Christ and longing to be with Christ in His kingdom. He knew he was going to die; he understood that. He was going through suffering and persecution. In fact, Paul didn't know if he was going to live through the day or be killed that evening. In Lystra, he almost died because they tried to stone him to death. He clearly knew that he had this sentence of death in himself. But he believed that his life was a vehicle for God—a place where God could manifest His glory and give evidence to the life of Christ. And so Paul faced death daily. He looked it right in the eye and understood it. And not being afraid of death, he was able to say with all confidence and boldness, "For to me, to live is Christ, and to die is gain" (Phil. 1:21). What a testimony of joy unspeakable and a life full of the glory of God! He sounds a little like his Lord, doesn't he?

# The Fear of Death

Many anxieties and fears tend to grip people's hearts, but the fear of dying is the most prominent. We are not really sure what to do with the subject of death, so we push it down and refuse to talk about it. Yet the Bible talks about death more than any other topic. Jesus talked prominently about death. It is certain that we will all die one day (or we will be raptured). Paul said, "We are confident, yes, well pleased rather to be absent from the body and to be present with the Lord" (2 Cor. 5:8). Paul's point, from the context of the previous verses, is that whether we live or whether we die, we belong to the Lord. God can take us at any moment, or He could take a loved one or a friend when we are not expecting it. So often we struggle with this fact. Paul faced death every day and did not have a problem with it because he knew that he was committed to God—first and foremost. He understood his home was in heaven with Christ. He had a clear window—he viewed his life in the light of eternity. He knew with certainty that to die was gain. Paul had complete assurance that he belonged to God and that he would live forever with Christ.

## Fear Conquered by Knowing

In 2 Corinthians 5:1, Paul begins, "For we know" (*KJV*). Here the word "know" in the Greek means "by experience." This certainty of "knowing" is based on an intimate experience. To understand the meaning of this word "know" in terms of its intimate certainty, we can turn to the book of Genesis: "Now Adam knew Eve his wife" (Gen. 4:1)—referring to their intimate relationship and thus conceiving of Cain. It was not just knowledge in the head, but also knowledge within the heart.

Paul notes, regarding the temporal body we live in, "For we know that if our earthly house of this tabernacle were dissolved, we have a building of God, a house not made with hands, eternal in the heavens" (2 Cor. 5:1, *KJV*). Not only does Paul not fear death, but he actually longs for it and the spiritual body that is promised; as he states in verse 2, "For in this we groan, earnestly desiring to be clothed upon with our house which is from heaven [our spiritual body]." That would be the righteousness of Christ. Paul takes comfort in his knowledge that it is God who has made the guarantee: "Now he that hath wrought us for the selfsame thing is God, who also hath given unto us the earnest of the Spirit. Therefore we are always confident, knowing that, whilst we are at home in the body, we are absent from the Lord" (2 Cor. 5:5-6, *KJV*). He urges that "we walk by faith, not by sight" (2 Cor. 5:7) and that "we are confident, I say, and willing rather to be absent from the body, and to be present with the Lord" (2 Cor. 5:8, *KJV*). The key words are "willing rather to be absent" (in other words, to depart), to have this body dissolve and to be present with the Lord. How do we conquer the fear of death? By knowing that we belong to God and by taking Christ at His Word that whosoever believes in Him shall never die but have eternal life.

### Fear Conquered by an Eternal Perspective

Looking at these verses, we begin to see the tremendous victory Paul experienced. Realistically, there are very few people who ever come to the point of victory that Paul displayed. He walked in complete confidence with the Lord. He knew exactly what God wanted in his life.

In the book of Acts, chapter 9, when God intervened with Paul that day on the Damascus Road, Paul's life was completely changed. God stopped Paul, and Paul responded, "Lord, what would You have me to do?" God told Paul, "I'm going to show you the things you're going to suffer." With the suffering, however, God opened to Paul a glimpse of heaven. He caught a glimpse of what the glory of God was within his life. Paul's whole life was governed around the principle of going to heaven. And because of this, he would not allow discouragement to be part of his life. He would not allow anxiety to consume him. And he would not walk through the door of fear, because he believed in and had confidence in the Lord.

Likewise, it's a wonderful day when God begins to intervene within our lives, for He now has the freedom to change our direction. Be thankful for those times when God has stopped you because of His grace.

Paul mastered the mindset that this world only offers temporal things. Paul said in 1 Corinthians 4:17 that these light afflictions, this moment that God was working in his life, was going to
be for far greater glory. Paul was focused upon the eternal things.

Therefore, I believe the key to surviving a life of suffering is to
get that eternal perspective. One day, believe it or not, it's all going
to be over. The pain is going to be gone. The disappointment, the
heartache, the broken relationships, the struggle within our flesh—
all the things we go through in our minds and hearts, all the areas
we would like to be different—these will all be over. And we are going to wake up in the presence of God. God is going to give us a
brand-new body . . . and we will see the Lord! There will be no more
tears, no sorrow, no pain, no agony; Christ will be the light and the
glory of heaven. We will absolutely enjoy every moment of it! So,
death should not be a fearful area within our lives. Remember what
Paul said: "For to me, to live is Christ, and to die is gain" (Phil. 1:21).

People whose only desire is to live in this temporal world think
Christians are crazy because we desire to merely maintain in this
temporal world—living for that greater house, that Kingdom that
is not made with hands, and that mansion that Jesus talked about
to His disciples when He said, "And if I go and prepare a place for
you, I will come again and receive you to Myself; that where I am,
there you may be also" (John 14:3). When we have an eternal perspective and anticipate heaven, God replaces our fear with joy.

Notice what Paul said: "So we are always confident, knowing
that while we are at home in the body we are absent from the Lord"
(2 Cor. 5:6). And he continued, "We are confident, yes, well pleased
rather to be absent from the body and to be present with the Lord"
(v. 8). Paul lived with three truths dominating his life: (1) He knew
that God could save him; (2) he knew that God could heal him;
and (3) he knew that God had a home for him in heaven.

## Three Eternal Perspectives

With that as background, I want to drive home the following
three facts that will help us overcome fear in our lives: (1) God

will hold us together; (2) God will work out all things on our behalf; and (3) God is going to take us to heaven.

## God Will Hold Us Together

In 2 Timothy 1:12, Paul wrote, "For this reason I also suffer these things; [and here's the key point] nevertheless I am not ashamed, for I know whom I have believed and am persuaded that He is able to keep what I have committed to Him until that Day." While writing these words, Paul was in prison in Rome (thanks to the emperor Nero), waiting for his beheading. Paul recognized that he was going to suffer for God, but he also knew that God would be there for him in the midst of his suffering.

The very first thing we must believe in and be confident of is that God is able to save us. He is able to forgive us and do a powerful work in and through our lives. Although this is a simple thing to say, I think we seldom really understand it. Too often we live in doubt and allow insecurity and fear to dominate our lives. Seeing that there are so many areas in our mind and heart that are not matching up to the life God wants us to live, we start questioning whether God has forgiven us. We allow Satan to condemn us. But the Bible very clearly states, "There is therefore now no condemnation to those who are in Christ Jesus" (Rom. 8:1). And Paul continues a few verses later, "Who shall separate us from the love of Christ?" (Rom. 8:35). We need to cling to these truths of God's Word and grasp the fact that God will hold us together.

Paul understood this saving grace of God from his own experience. He knew that God was able to deliver him—as He had done on that Damascus Road—and to forgive him of all the sins that he had committed. Paul had murdered many people. He had brought tremendous havoc upon the Church. He had brought tremendous pain into people's lives. But as I mentioned in chapter 3, on that day, God saved Paul. He intervened in Paul's life and made all things brand new. Paul knew without a shadow of a doubt that God was with him and was working on his behalf. Paul woke up every day knowing that God was able to save his life. He knew that God was doing a work in and through his life. Paul never gave up on God.

Sometimes we give up on God. Sometimes we do not see God because all we see is the troublesome situation and our problems. We are so concerned about the past, so worried about the present and so frightened about the future. Paul understood that the past, present and future are all held in God's powerful hands. Paul knew that God would hold him together. And I believe that God wants us to know today that He will hold us together, even though we feel like our lives are falling apart.

### God Will Work Out All Things

The second clear truth from Paul's eternal perspective is found in Romans 8:28: "And we know that all things work together for good to those who love God, to those who are the called according to His purpose." There are many people today who believe that God is able to save them, but they do not believe that God is able to work in their lives. They see a tough situation with their marriage, their children, their business or their finances, and they mistakenly believe they are left alone to deal with these aspects of life. Friends, God will always work things out for us for His glory. He will never withhold any good thing from us. We are the apple of His eye, and He loves us with an everlasting love! He will bear fruit in our lives if we let Him. Granted, things may not turn out the way we hope or expect them to. He may use our lives to be an example to others, to show the lost world His mercy and grace.

The Bible very clearly states that God's thoughts for us are not evil but good—to bring about an expected end. In other words, God is not seeking to hurt or punish us. But God does have a purpose and a plan, and He wants to work in and through our lives for good. The Bible says, "He who has begun a good work in you will complete it until the day of Jesus Christ" (Phil. 1:6). So that which He started (your salvation), He is able to carry through your life.

Paul was absolutely confident that everything that happened *to* him would be used by God to make things happen *in* him, so great things would begin to happen *through* him. That's why Paul could refer to those light afflictions working in him. The key is "working for us." All his trials, agony and pain were working in him to bring about God's glory. Paul was perplexed, distressed, beaten, whipped and shipwrecked—yet everything that happened to him was working out for the glory of God.

You might look at your marriage, at your single life, at your relationships or at all the things that are wrong in your life, but God is saying, "Listen, I am working in and through your life for My glory. That which I have started, I am going to complete." Ecclesiastes 3:11 tells us that "He has made everything beautiful in its time." Paul understood that God was able to order his day. He knew that God was going to guide him.

Remember the story I shared near the beginning of this chapter concerning the dying man with sheer terror in his eyes? I believe with all my heart that God had me answer the phone and go to the hospital to help this man from my church. God not only wanted to save him, but he also wanted me to see the terror in his eyes so that I could share with you the fact that there is no need to fear when we belong to God. That fear does not need to occur in your life, because when you know that God is able to save you, and when you understand that God is able to work in your life for His glory, your fears will be quelled.

**God Will Take Us to Heaven**
Finally, the promise of heaven kept Paul's fears at bay. He tells us, in 2 Corinthians 5:1, "For we know that if our earthly house, this tent, is destroyed, we have a building from God, a house not made with hands, eternal in the heavens." One day God is going to take each of us believers home. Paul said, "If you want to take my life, great! I know that God is in it. I know God is able. I know that God has prepared a place for me."

When we begin to believe these three simple truths, we can walk on this earth in a very powerful way—without fear. Nothing is going to stop us. We are not going to be afraid of one single thing because when we go through difficulties, we know God is going to work it out. When we have a difficult time, God is going to save us. When we die, we are going to heaven. As Christians, we are not to be afraid of dying. We are not to be frightened over the possibility of taking our very last breath. Remember that the Bible declares that our bodies are going to dissolve, but God will give us a body made without hands. We will stand before God absolutely pure. There will be no more tears, no more sorrow, no more pain and no more agony; heaven is going to be a wonderful place. We're going to see Christ face to face. We are going to have a brand-new body. And we're going to be able to rejoice that we are there, standing in the streets of gold. But most important, we are going to understand and see the glory of God.

## Embracing Our Light Afflictions

We look at all the anxiety of our lives and ask, "How do I get out of this mess? How do I overcome it?" We go to seminars, listen to CDs, consult doctors and read books about overcoming fear. In most cases, however, the answer is very simple: Do you believe that God can or has saved you in a wonderful way? Has God reached down, taken your heart, transformed you and given you a brand-new life in Jesus Christ? Do you really believe that? Are you a brand-new person in Christ Jesus, in whom God is going to do something very special in and through it? Knowing and believing these things is the secret seen in Paul's life, and we must embrace this secret too: God saves us, works it all out in the end and then takes us to heaven.

Someone may say, "Well, Steve, I am going through hardships." My answer is, "I know, but it's a light affliction." "No, Steve, I lost my wife." It is still a light affliction, because one day this husband is going to be with his wife. And one day there will be no more sorrow. But right now, God is working in and through our lives. And finally, we are going to go to heaven—so it's time to start rejoicing in Jesus now. As a result, we can wake up in the morning, have a terrible day and still say, "God, You are able to save me. And, God, You are able to work out this mess. If the whole thing falls apart and I die in an earthquake, I'm going to see You. So I am not going to live in fear. I'm not going to live discouraged. I'm not going to live in defeat. God, I'm going to look to You in a very powerful way." Like Paul, when we catch a glimpse of heaven, we will earnestly desire to go there and see Jesus Christ. What a wonderful way to live! There is no one who loves us more than God.

## POINTS TO PONDER

- Am I living with an eternal perspective?
- Do I really believe that God can and will work things out in my life for His glory?
- How do my current "light afflictions" compare to the glory of God and His promises for my future?

**Note**

1. Dwight L. Moody, cited in *Quotes and Notes: Echoes from Glory*, copyright 2011, www.WholesomeWords.org. http://www.wholesomewords.org/echoes/moody.html.

5

# OVERCOMING DISTRACTION: THE DIVIDED HEART

*Do not be unequally yoked together with unbelievers.*
*For what fellowship has righteousness with lawlessness?*
*And what communion has light with darkness?*

2 CORINTHIANS 6:14

*The greatest failures in my life occur when I am not focused. For example, when I am with my wife, I'm distracted with the things concerning the church. When I'm at church, I'm distracted with the things of my marriage. And when I'm alone, I'm distracted with the things of the world. Satan is a master at bringing distractions. This is when we need to look to Christ who is our example. He was never distracted from what was most important—the will of God. He had three years of ministry, and He always stayed focused on His mission. I look at my life and I'm often all over the place. Doctors have told me that I am a triple-A personality type and that I bounce all over. I used to put myself down because my brain was everywhere but still, but I have learned that God gave me this mind and it is my responsibility to bring it into focus. When everything seems equally important, then my priorities are always wrong. Distraction is anything that keeps us away from the will of God. We can't be master of everything, but we can place God first in our lives. If we can keep God first in our lives, then He will make sure that everything else is done well. So if I keep Him as my priority, stay in the middle of His will and keep my eyes on Him, I won't be distracted, but will see only Christ!*

---

Most of us have noticed how easy it is to get distracted whenever we have a close connection with someone who doesn't share our innermost values and beliefs. Paul calls it being "unequally yoked" (2 Cor. 6:14). When we align ourselves with unbelievers in dating, marriage or business, we put ourselves in a position to be drawn away from God. To be unequally yoked with a nonbeliever is contrary to the Word of God and is an act of disobedience.

This unequal yoking often occurs because we refuse to wait on God. We believe that God is being unfair or holding back on us, so we need to do it ourselves. But that line of thinking is simply wrong. God does not hold back any good thing from us. In the context of this verse, God's vision for us is held back due to our disobedience and ignorance. God weeps over the loss of those who have not surrendered their lives and for those who have walked away from His goodness.

This is nothing new. God's people have always wandered away from Him. We can read all through the Old Testament how God did so many things for Israel—provided for and protected them—but they began to walk away time and time again. He said He would give them houses that they had not built and vineyards they had not planted. When God finally brought them into the Promised Land, all He ever asked of His people was that they not become distracted but rather stay focused on His great love for them and trust Him. Unfortunately, left to themselves, they immediately turned from God, intermarried with idol worshipers and began to defile their lives.

## God Wants Our Loyalty

God is a jealous God (see Exod. 20:5-6). He does not want to share your love with any other lovers within your life. He does not want anyone or anything to take priority over Him. He seeks to be your Lord and will not share that position with anyone, not even with a wife or husband. So your relationship with God must be first.

When God is your priority, everything else will fall into its proper place. The Lord will give you a great marriage and great relationships. But without this foundation of giving God His rightful place in your life, you will find yourself pulling away from the heart of God and from the work of His Kingdom. Your first priority must be the Lord. When your first thought is to spend time with God in devotions, fellowship and prayer, then you can take that power and love to your wife, to your husband, to your children or to your dating relationship—all the while remaining safe and secure in the arms of Christ.

### The Goal Is to Be Separated Unto God

When you look at our culture and society, it's obvious that it's hard for men and women to commit to anything. Instead, people often go halfway, and as soon as things get rough, they walk away from their "half-hearted" commitment. God says that's not good enough. He desires a real and wholehearted commitment to Him. Why is it such a problem to be faithful to God and keep from being unequally yoked?

Let's look at a word most Christians despise and the world hates. That word is "separation," or "sanctification." Some of its synonyms are "consecration," "dedication," "commitment." The word "sanctification" is a powerful word, and it means "the process of making holy." God desires that we make a true separation (a split, a division or a disassociation) from the world.

The word "separation" gives us a better sense of its meaning as it relates to our relationship with God. In the Greek, "separated" is the word *choris*, or "without," which means "pure, or clean, or free from stain." In other words, we are not living so much *in* the world that the world has stained our lives. We're *in* the world, but not *of* the world. God wants us to walk through this world without being stained by it. But if we allow sin to come into our lives (if we continually ponder sin or do certain things that we know are not good), our consciences and our hearts become stained, and we are no longer pure before God.

Deuteronomy 4:37-38 tells us, "He brought you out . . . to bring you in." Often when God brings us out, we do not allow His Spirit to bring us all the way in. For example, we come out to church, but we end up not in the service but out having a cup of coffee in the café. We might have come out of our sinful habits, but we really don't get "into" what God is doing in our lives—through the community, through the church and through our family.

Webster's dictionary defines the word "sanctification" as "to set apart for a holy use." Often this "setting apart" is a reference to instruments that were used in the Old Testament concerning the Tabernacle, which were sanctified, set apart and consecrated; they were sprinkled with the blood, anointed and could only be used for this one purpose. So when we look closely at the word "separated," we begin to get a picture of what God is after. God desires that our lives be separate and stand out from the world.

A good example of this is when Jesus (in the synagogue) saw a man with a withered hand. He said to that man, "Stand up." The Pharisees thought that He was going to embarrass the man, but He said (my paraphrase), "Listen, would you like to be healed?" The man did what Jesus told him to do (see Luke 6:8), and God healed him instantly. There he was, standing separate, standing out for God. God wanted the people to know that He had blessed this man, ordained him and touched him. I'd like to be touched by God like that. But if I'd like to be touched, then I need to stand for the glory of God. So there are moments when I see that being separate can be embarrassing; but if God is going to do a work, I'm for it.

Another example is found in the book of Mark. In chapter 5, Mark tells the story of the woman who, in hopes of stopping her many years of bleeding, touched the hem of Jesus' garment. She had bled for 12 years. She was kicked out of the synagogue. She could not worship according to the law, because she was unclean. And finally, she had used all of her money on doctors, trying to find a cure for her condition. She knew that touching Christ was not what she should do according to the law, but she was willing to take a chance. Jesus stopped, turned around and asked, "Who touched Me?" And Peter, our beloved disciple with a big mouth, says, "How can we tell with so many people around us?" Jesus replied to Peter, "Someone touched Me—power went out from Me." And so the woman stood, trembling, and Jesus looked at her and said, "Daughter, your faith has made you well. Go in peace, and be healed of your affliction" (Mark 5:34).

Jesus' intent was not to embarrass her. Rather, it was to single her out to show her that she was special. She had been out of fellowship because of her condition, but when He put His hand upon her life, she was in fellowship once again with God. To be holy requires one to separate from the unholy. I wonder how many of us could say that our lives are really separate from the things of this world?

God not only wants to do an outward work in us, but He also desires to do an inward work. God now takes the instrument of difficult times and begins to work in our lives, allowing the Holy Spirit to broaden His territory within us. And so our eyes now become His eyes. Our body now becomes His body. We are now instruments in the hand of God, dedicated to doing His work. That great verse in 2 Timothy 2:21 comes to mind, in which Paul says, "Therefore if anyone cleanses himself from the latter, he will be a vessel for honor, sanctified and useful for the Master, prepared for every good work." So, here's the challenge. Each of us has the possibility of being touched by God. We have the possibility of being used by almighty God to do a work through His life and through ours. He desires to work in us and through us in a very powerful way.

**How God's Purposes Are Hindered in Us**
When we become unequally yoked, God's work and purposes are hindered in our lives. The blessings stop. God will not work through us when we are unequally yoked, because He's a jealous God. He is righteous, and His jealousy for us is righteous; therefore, He will not share His people with anyone. God's people have always had a problem staying by His side. God has chased us, ministered to us, healed us and worked in our lives. Yet we still have a tendency to not like the idea of being separated from the world and dedicated wholly to God. Even so, our freedom comes through a commitment to God.

> Do not be unequally yoked together with unbelievers. For what fellowship has righteousness with lawlessness? And what communion has light with darkness? And what accord has Christ with Belial [the devil]? Or what part has a believer with an unbeliever? And what agreement has the temple of God with idols? For you are the temple of the living God. As God has said: "I will dwell in them and walk among them. I will be their God, and they shall be My people." Therefore "come out from among them and be separate, says the Lord. Do not touch what is unclean, and I will receive you. I will be a Father to you, and you shall be My sons and daughters, says the Lord Almighty" (2 Cor. 6:14-18).

And then Paul exhorts us in 2 Corinthians 7:1: "Therefore, having these promises, beloved, let us cleanse ourselves from all filthiness of the flesh and spirit, perfecting holiness in the fear of God."

I have come to realize that God is after the goal of separation when it comes to those He calls His own. Let's examine this issue in three ways:

1. The need for separation (see 2 Cor. 6:14-16)
2. The call to separation (see 2 Cor. 6:17)
3. The benefit of separation (see 2 Cor. 6:18)

## The Need for Separation

Notice Paul's use of contrast. He says in 2 Corinthians 6:14-15, "Do not be unequally yoked together with unbelievers. For what fellowship has righteousness with lawlessness? And what communion has light with darkness? And what accord has Christ with Belial? Or what part has a believer with an unbeliever?" What I notice in this teaching is that there are no gray areas. Paul is saying that either we are for the light, or we are for the darkness; we are governed by Jesus Christ, or we are governed by the enemy; we are serving God, or we are not. Real Christianity puts a sword between my flesh and my spirit. The light speaks the truth, but the darkness lies. We are filled with God's righteousness, but the things that we are doing are unrighteous. We have been touched by the power of God, and therefore we should not be dating a non-believer. We have been filled by the power of God, and therefore we should not give ourselves to the things of the devil. The contrast is extremely important, because God once again is showing us the need for separation.

## The Call to Separation

In addition to the need for separation, we see a call to separation. Notice the "Therefore" that begins 2 Corinthians 6:17. The word "therefore" points backward to Paul's reasons for the call to be separate. He then continues, "Come out from among them and be separate, says the Lord. Do not touch what is unclean, and I will receive you." The Lord mentions three things in verse 17: (1) Come out from among them, (2) be separate from them, and (3) touch not the unclean thing.

Probably the best way to illustrate this is with an Old Testament story from the life of Samson in Judges 13–16. In my book *Crossing the Line*, I deal with this very subject of Samson's compromise and his being unequally yoked. Samson's incredibly heart-wrenching story describes a man who wasted God's efforts for his life. The story goes all the way back to Samson's mom and dad, before he was even born. The angel of God came to this couple not once, but twice, and told them that they were going to have a very unique child. God came to Samson's mom and said, "You need to sanctify your womb, and you need to sanctify your life." She obeyed the commandment of God, refusing to drink any wine or touch anything that would defile her, and she vowed to do what God told her to do. So when the time came for the child to be born and Samson came forth out of the womb, he was sanctified in the very heart of the belly of this woman.

Samson's parents took the ascetic Nazarene vow. *Nazir* means "consecrated" or "separate." Those who took this vow abstained from drinking any wine and from touching anything dead or visiting graves, and they let their hair grow long. Samson grew up to have tremendous power. God had a plan and a purpose for him. God was going to use this child to minister to the life of those written about in the book of Judges, because the Bible says, "Everyone did what was right in his own eyes" (Judg. 21:25).

In other words, they all did what they wanted, and the nation of Israel was falling apart, yet God wanted to save it. So He brought Samson into the world and ordained him for that purpose. Filled with the power of the Holy Spirit, Samson was tremendously strong. He was able to catch 300 foxes by himself, tying their tails together and lighting the cornfields of the Philistines on fire. He was able to take the jawbone of a donkey and smite a thousand men at one time and stack up their bodies. He was able to take the gates off the city, carry them 10 miles up a hill and stick them into the ground.

Yet, Samson had a problem. Though he was called by God and reared by godly parents, Samson loved Philistine women. There was a slow-burning lust within his heart. He couldn't stay away from the Philistine people, and so he would go and mingle with them. His parents said, "Don't do this. You have been called, consecrated, set apart and chosen—we've raised you our whole life. God wants you." But Samson basically said, "I don't care. I'm going." So he went down and married one of the women at Timnah. But the Philistines ended up killing his wife. For the next 20 years of his life, he was an angry madman wreaking tremendous havoc within the enemy's camp, destroying everything he could destroy, and not doing the will of God.

Finally, he falls in love with Delilah. I think a name like that ought to warn you a little bit. She flirted with him because she wanted to know the secret to his power. At first he wouldn't tell her his secret. But he was willing to flirt, to tease, and to get close; and finally, his flesh took over. He gave Delilah the secret—the vow of his commitment to God. She betrayed him and shaved his head. Then her cronies came in and plucked out his eyes and tied his hands. They made sport of him and made fun of Jehovah, and it broke Samson's heart. All of a sudden, Samson began to realize what he had done. He missed the call of God for 20 years. For 20 years, he had wasted his life—unwilling to heed the warning of God. Samson was unwilling to sanctify his life and set it apart, even though God wanted to use him.

What I see in this story is how necessary it is that we heed the call of sanctification (or separation). God sought to bring Samson out of the Philistine's camp, yet he wouldn't do it. God was warning him through his parents, yet he refused to submit. The prophets were coming to him, yet he wouldn't listen. His own people were begging him, yet he wouldn't listen. Samson was set in his own mind that he was going to do what he wanted to do. Even so, God had a plan, a calling, and He allowed this child to be born.

God has predestined us for a purpose; He gave each of us a name and called us from our mother's womb. God has filled us with the power of His Holy Spirit, and we are to fulfill the destiny that God wants. But we can hinder that work; we can have too many other things in our lives that are not pleasing to God. So here is another "therefore." Paul says, "Therefore, having these promises, beloved, let us cleanse ourselves from all filthiness of the flesh and spirit, perfecting holiness in the fear of God" (2 Cor. 7:1).

## The Benefit of Separation

On a very positive note, there's the benefit of separation. You might say, "Well, Steve, if I choose to live a dedicated life—let's say that I'm willing to really consecrate my life to God—what will happen in my life?" Let me explain what will happen. God promises, "I will dwell in them and walk among them. I will be their God, and they shall be My people" (2 Cor. 6:16). He says, toward the very end of this great promise, "I will receive you" (v. 17). Finally, He promises, "I will be a Father to you, and you shall be My sons and daughters" (v. 18).

When we choose to live a life separate unto God, we will receive the promises of God. God desires to live inside of us. He desires for us to know that He's around for us to take Him to work, to be with us in the daily things we do. The almighty God is saying, "I will dwell in you."

I hear so many people say, "Well, I am so lonely today." God says that He will never leave us nor forsake us. He says that each one of us is worth more than anything to Him, and what He has begun He's able to complete until the day of Christ. So, He's willing to dwell in us; but as 2 Corinthians 6:16 tells us, He's willing to walk among us. He is willing to walk with us through all the difficulties of life—the good, the bad and the ugly. He's willing to walk with us as we raise our children, as we go through the process of aging, as we recover from the devastation of being fired from a job and struggle through the learning curve of a new position that He has provided. God is willing, and He wants to walk with us through all the aspects of our life.

In the book of Luke, chapter 24, Jesus dropped in on two men who were walking down the road to a village called Emmaus. He asked them, "What are you guys doing?" They answered, "Man, haven't you heard? Jesus died." They, of course, didn't know He was Jesus. Then Jesus begins to speak the Word of God to them. When they got to their home, they invited Him in to stay and eat with them; when He broke the bread, their eyes were opened and they knew that it was Christ. God opened their eyes, and they saw the Lord.

Just as He was with these men, Jesus is with us. He's walking with us. He never leaves us, and He never forsakes us. To reiterate the Lord's words in 2 Corinthians 6:16, "I will be their God."

Think about this promise for a moment. What an incredible gift! God made the heavens and the earth, yet He wants to know us personally. He wants a close, intimate relationship with each of us. If we believe that God made the heavens and the earth, then God has the ability to change a heart and do absolutely anything in our lives!

We read in Numbers 16 that when Moses was hassled by Korah, a rebellious Levite who, with a number of other Israelite families, took exception to Moses' leadership in the wilderness and conspired to overthrow him and usurp his authority, God took care of the problem. God just opened the earth, and Korah fell in, and God basically said to Moses that his problem was taken care of. That's the guy to have around—God.

God says, in 2 Corinthians 6:17, "I will receive you." He is saying, "I'll take you just as you are. I'll accept you in all the situations you find yourself in, and I will always receive you." Yes, there are times when we are not received by other people because certain parts of our lives have not been pleasing to them; but God will always receive us. There is never a time, when we cry out to God in faith and ask for His forgiveness, that He is not there—because He'll never leave us nor forsake us.

The last thing the Lord says in this passage is a favorite of mine: "I will be a Father to you" (2 Cor. 6:18). God is saying that if we will surrender our lives, then He will be our Father. Certainly we are His sons and daughters, but because of our disobedience, we can hinder our Father's blessing. Let me illustrate this principle. I have a great relationship with my son. We go to hockey games, and we hang out together. What if, all of a sudden, he said to me, "I no longer want anything to do with you. I have found somebody else to hang out with, and I don't like you any longer—you're too strict." Would he cease to be my son? No, of course he would still be my son. Would I no longer be his father? No, of course I would still be his father. From his perspective, however, he doesn't want a father, and so he doesn't desire to have the relationship or blessings I can give him. However, if he would say to me, "Dad, I'm sorry; can we just restore what we had?" Like the father of the prodigal son, I would embrace him, give him a robe and a ring, and I would bless him with everything.

God makes clear in His Word that if we are equally yoked and we live our lives for the glory of God, He will do wonderful things through our lives. However, when we do not separate unto God, and we choose to become a part of the world, we close the door to His working within our lives. If we desire to see the goodness of God in our lives, then we will say, "Jesus, I understand that I need to have a life marked by separation." He'll respond, "Then I'll be your God; and not only that, I'll be your Father, and I'll show you how wonderful your life can be." The moment we surrender to God, He says, "Good, I have a bunch of promises I've wanted to give you. I'm going to dwell with you, walk with you, talk with you and do incredible things in your life."

## POINTS TO PONDER

- Are there any areas in my life in which I am unequally yoked?
- God calls me to separation—am I heeding that call?
- God rewards an undivided heart toward Him. How am I reaping the rewards of His presence? What, if anything, do I need to quit doing in order to have an undivided heart?

6

# OVERCOMING SELFISHNESS

*So let each one give as he purposes in his heart, not grudgingly or of necessity; for God loves a cheerful giver.*

2 CORINTHIANS 9:7

*When we are selfish, we give more honor to Satan than to God. The reason I say that is because I know from experience what happens inside and out when it's all about me; when it's all about what I think, how I feel, what I want and what I am going through. I magnify the trial and end up worshiping me. Every single sin springs up like a weed from the root of selfishness. It's the absolute opposite of contentment. That's when we have to ask ourselves, "Am I willing to bend, to be broken and let others have their way?" Thankfully, the grace of God has taken me out of myself and taught me how to give. When I started giving, really giving, with no strings attached, then God began to bless my life. I realized that Jesus lived His life giving to others. When we are selfish, we are not filled with the Holy Spirit. To get back to what God has called us to be, we need to submit to Christ and get focused on others' needs rather than on our own. It's called living the crucified life (death to self) and going the way of the cross.*

Selfishness is something that all of us can relate to and are guilty of almost every day of our lives. We see selfishness everywhere. If we turn on the television to any station and listen to the news for any length of time, we see just how selfish, corrupt and perverse this wicked world really is. As a nation, we have turned our backs on God. Our government, courts, politicians, corporations and, sadly, even some of our churches have left righteousness and chosen selfishness. The world is rejecting the cross of Christ, preferring to live in greed rather than repent and give God a chance to change their lives. No wonder God is going to judge this wicked world.

But where does the real blame lie? Is it not with the Church? We are losing our world, our culture, our Christianity all because of selfishness. The Christian life as we know it today is in serious trouble. If change does not occur, and occur *quickly*, we are going to lose our religious freedoms. Our only hope is for God to send a revival among us, which not only will change us, but will also change our communities. The key to any revival or the ability to live a victorious life is simply to die to oneself. The opposite of "self-centered" is "others-centered," and those who are "others-centered" are givers. That is the life that God desires in us—that we would first give ourselves to the Lord and then to others. That's not an easy thing to do.

But God declares that if we want to overcome a selfish life, we need to learn to give.

In the book of Job, it says that when Job prayed for others, then God delivered him from his captivity (see Job 42). Yet, we often stay in the same "stuck" place because we are unwilling to allow God to work in and through our lives. The Lord has the ability to love others through us; and He desires for us to learn to forgive others and be a blessing to them. But sometimes we impede what God wants to do because we have been hurt or devastated, and we then become extremely selfish in our thinking, feeling that we've been taken advantage of, either by God or by somebody else. And because of our own hurt, we hold back rather than understand that it's more blessed to give than to receive.

What should really spur our hearts in that regard is the commitment of our Lord Jesus Christ to us. God gave His very best when He gave us His own Son. And He gave Christ to us when we were alienated from God. Each of us was living in sin and on our way to hell when God reached out and gave us the gift of forgiveness of our sins and eternal life with Him. Christ came not to be ministered to, but to minister to.

Someone once said that there are three types of givers in life. One type is a flint, another is a sponge and the third is a honeycomb. To get anything out of the flint, it must be hammered; even then, all that results are chips and sparks. To get anything out of the sponge, it must be continually squeezed and put under pressure. Finally, there is the honeycomb, just overflowing with its own sweetness. We can apply this analogy to our hearts. Sometimes, like the flint, God needs to work in our hearts in a difficult way in order for us to receive His goodness and then give it out. Furthermore, like a sponge, there are some whom God needs to squeeze and put pressure on to bring forth any life out of their hearts. Finally, there are some, like the honeycomb, who have come to understand the goodness and grace of God; their love for other people overflows out of their full hearts.

Paul says, in 2 Corinthians 9:7, "So let each one give as he purposes in his heart, not grudgingly or of necessity; for God loves a cheerful [or, in the Greek, "hilarious"] giver." So let every one of us purpose in our own hearts to give, not with a selfish attitude or out of pressure, but rather with joy and cheerfulness, being "hilarious" in our giving. Solomon says it this way in Proverbs 3:9-10: "Honor the LORD with your possessions and with the firstfruits of all your increase; so your barns will be filled with plenty, and your vats will overflow with new wine." Solomon gives us a promise that our winepresses are going to burst, and God is going to bless our lives. Jesus said, in Luke 6:38, "Give, and it will be given to you: good measure, pressed down, shaken together, and running over will be put into your bosom. For with the same measure that you use, it will be measured back to you." That is a powerful verse. God is going to take what we give, and He is going to shake it. He is going to crush it. He is going to step on it. He is going to make more room, and He is going to add to it a hundred times.

I read this cute little story. A man called the church office. He wanted to speak to the "head hog of the trough." The secretary asked, "Who?" The man replied, "I want to speak to the head hog of the trough." Being sure now that she had heard him correctly, the secretary replied, "Sir, if you mean our pastor, you will have to treat him with more respect and ask for the reverend or the pastor. But certainly you cannot refer to him as the head hog of the trough." This time the man responded by saying, "Oh, I see. Well, I was going to give $10,000 to the building fund." The secretary hurriedly said, "Hold on, I think the big pig just walked in the door."

I hope my secretary doesn't do that! Too often, we think our life is our own, when it's not; we are dependent on God.

## Biblical Examples of the Danger of Selfishness

One of the great curses in the heart of man is selfishness. The Word of God repeatedly stresses that we are to live a Christlike life. In other words, we are to pattern our lives after Jesus Christ, who gave Himself for the sake of others, who was willing to walk that second mile, and who was willing to die so that we might live. Paul said, "I have been crucified with Christ; it is no longer I who live, but Christ lives in me; and the life which I now live in the flesh I live by faith in the Son of God, who loved me and gave Himself for me" (Gal. 2:20). So we are to die to who we are so that we can begin to live for the glory of God.

Why is selfishness such a dangerous issue? A selfish person looks on himself or herself as the ultimate answer and the ultimate point of concern. Yet the Bible says that we are not to look upon our own interests and needs; rather, we are to look upon the interests of others (see Phil 2:4). We're not to be concerned about our own lives; God will take care of all that (see Matt. 6:25-34). Instead, we are to be gracious. We are to be the givers, not takers. We are to be understanding and extend that gift of life to others.

In today's world, so many of our children have walked away from God, so many marriages have ended in divorce, so many businesses have been destroyed—all because of selfishness. God wants us to know about the dangers of living a life of selfishness. The Bible talks extensively on the subject.

## Lot's Story

In the Old Testament, we read the story of an exceedingly selfish man named Lot. He was the nephew of Abraham, who raised him and took him under his wing. As Lot grew, his sheep began to multiply. Abraham's possessions were growing in number as well, to the point at which there became a great contention between the herdsmen of Lot and the herdsman of Abraham. Abraham, being the gracious, faith-filled man that he was, came to Lot and said, "Why don't you choose the land that you want." So Lot, being very selfish, looked over and chose the plains of Sodom because it was well watered everywhere he could see.

We would think that he would say to Abraham, his uncle, "You have given me everything. I would like you to take first choice," but he didn't. And we would think that he would be overwhelmingly appreciative of what Abraham had done for him, but he wasn't. Lot was only concerned about his possessions and stockpiling even more than he was about the stability of his life. The Bible says that Lot turned his tent toward Sodom.

I've found that whenever I begin to turn my heart toward the world, things are bound to go wrong. When the angels came to warn Lot to get out of Sodom because of the sin that was all around him, the Bible declares that one angel had to grab Lot by the wrist because his soul was vexed. It was the angel of God who drew him out. Though Lot was a righteous man (see 2 Pet. 2:7), he was drawn to the sin around him. The angel had to pull him away from Sodom so he would not be destroyed. As it was, his wife, who was told not to look back at the destruction of Sodom, did look back and became a pillar of salt (see Gen. 19:26). Why? She looked back because she was consumed with the desire for material things and what she was leaving behind. Thus, Lot lost his wife, even though he himself had escaped. Furthermore, we find that his two daughters later raped him and bore Moab and Ben-Ammi—sons who would become the fathers of the Moabites and the Ammonites, enemies of Israel! Lot's life and family were a horrible mess because he pursued a life of selfishness and reaped the results.

## Achan's Fatal Mistake

Achan, whose story we read in Joshua 7, is another biblical example of selfish living. When the people of Israel came across the Jordan River, God told them not to touch anything of this area of Jericho. It all belonged to the Lord. It was the firstfruit of the land, and God wanted it for Himself. The Bible said that Achan spotted a Babylonian garment. His eyes looked upon it, his heart desired it and he took it, bringing it back to his tent and hiding it. Then God began to deal with the children of Israel. When Joshua fell to the earth on his face, God asked, "Why are you praying? There is sin in the camp." So Joshua got all the people together and went down through the tribes to find the problem. The very last tribe was Achan's tribe. Joshua started with the oldest man and went all the way down to Achan. By the way, the word "Achan" means "trouble." He was going to be an aching man pretty soon. Achan's selfishness cost him his life.

## King Saul

God gave King Saul such a great start, but because of his selfishness, Saul desired to make changes to what God wanted. As he was going after King Agag, as recorded in 1 Samuel 15, God spoke to Saul through the life of the prophet Samuel, instructing Saul to kill the king, kill all the animals and bring nothing back. But Saul, in his own selfish ambition, desired to make his own decisions; he therefore brought back King Agag as well as the animals. Now blind, Samuel asked Saul, "What do I hear in the background?" Saul replied, "You hear sheep." Samuel then asked, "Why did you bring the sheep back?" Saul said the people made him do it. Samuel continued, "Who is this man before you?" Saul replied, "This is King Agag." Samuel, shocked, asked further, "Didn't you listen to the Lord's voice?" Saul answered, "I thought it would be better for me to bring him back." And Samuel turned around and asked Saul, "Does God delight in sacrifice or obedience? Don't you know that rebellion is as the sin of witchcraft?" At that moment, Samuel took a sword and thrust it through Agag, killing him before God. Ultimately, we find that because of Saul's selfishness, because of his unwillingness to listen to and obey what God wanted, God took away his kingdom.

All throughout the Bible, we find countless examples of men and women who desired to make their own choices counter to God's expressed will. And that's the danger of selfishness—when we make decisions thinking that we know better than God or when we disagree with God and desire to live a certain lifestyle. God says that He is the Lord of all. He is always to have the preeminence over our lives. He made us; He bought us; we belong to Him. So it's vitally important to understand within our hearts the danger of a selfish life. Selfishness will breed contempt for others and for God's authority, destroy a marriage, chase the children out of the home, destroy a business and ultimately destroy a person's life. A truly better path is dying to self and living to Jesus Christ.

## Jesus' Words About Self-Centered Living

Jesus gives us a warning about living a selfish life. Luke 12:16-20 describes a parable He told:

The ground of a certain rich man yielded plentifully. And he thought within himself, saying, "What shall I do, since I have no room to store my crops?" So he said, "I will do this: I will pull down my barns and build greater, and there I will store all my crops and my goods. And I will say to my soul, 'Soul, you have many goods laid up for many years; take your ease; eat, drink, and be merry.' " But God said to him, "Fool! This night your soul will be required of you; then whose will those things be which you have provided?"

In this parable, Jesus tells us about a rich man who was becoming richer by the moment. He was an entrepreneur who wasn't afraid to expand his business to build barns and get his enterprise going in an even greater dimension. He made money honestly by farming. No doubt he worked hard, but he lived for himself. God was blessing the land, but instead of thinking about God's blessing and the needs of his neighbors, the rich man chose to "eat, drink, and be merry." God steps into the story and calls the man a fool. When Jesus Christ says this man was a fool, we should heed His words. There are very few times when Jesus makes such a statement. The rich man was gambling with his soul; he spent his whole life thinking about himself. God was not on his radar, and neither were other people. Let's examine this man's—and our—foolishness.

## Mistaken "Ownership"
If we were to look closely at these five verses in Luke 12, we would notice that six times the word "I" is used, and five times the word "my" is used. Herein lies the heart of the parable. This rich man thought that he was in charge of his life—that everything he had belonged to him. That was not the case. Truly we live, move, and have our being in God (see Acts 17:28). God made us in His image. The day that I asked Christ to come into my heart, He came into my heart in a very powerful way. My life is now to be given to the Lord, for the things of God. Our bodies are not our own; they belong to the Lord. We have a choice to yield our lives either to righteousness or to unrighteousness.

This parable in Luke describes a man who chose to live his life for himself, and we read that he was foolish in his ownership. His thoughts are revealing in verse 17: "What shall *I* do?" And then he thinks: "*I* have no room" and finally, "*my* crops." Verse 18 continues this selfish thinking: "*I* will do this: *I* will pull down" and "*I* will store." Then he says, "*my* crops and *my* goods." In verse 19, he says, "*I* will say to *my* soul . . . eat, drink, and be merry." His language reveals that there was no concept of God. It was all about him. A selfish man or woman does not bring God into the decisions of life. Sometimes we leave Him out of our marriage. Sometimes we leave Him out of our business decisions, or we leave him out of our daily personal lives and bring Him in only on Sunday morning. But God desires that we give Him preeminence in all of life. The Lord requires that we surrender our lives to His authority. So why don't we do that? It's because we're afraid of what we will have to give up.

Let me give you an example. If you are dating someone and you're thinking about marrying that person, then pray: "God, if this relationship is not Your will, then take him out of my life." If you're thinking, *No way am I going to pray that prayer!* It's probably because you're afraid He'll do it! Yet that's exactly the way you need to pray. God sees the destiny of a life. God understands the character of who a person is. God understands how long the endurance will last and who is going to end up at the very end. To leave God out of a decision as weighty as choosing the person you are going to spend your life with (and to think that you can make that decision with your own insight) is very foolish.

The truth is, we don't have the wisdom, the knowledge or the insight to make godly decisions. Too often we see life only from the outside. It's like the guy who married a gal, and on the night of their honeymoon, she took out her false teeth; he couldn't believe what he was seeing. Then she reached up and took off her wig, revealing her bald head, and he said, "Oh, no!" Then she reached down and undid her wooden leg (she had only one leg), and he was thrown for a loop because he was unprepared.

There is a prideful danger of "ownership," such as saying, "Well, I know how to run this business; after all, this is my background."

Yes, God gave you the mind, He gave you the vision and He wants you to succeed; but God also wants to be your partner—the One who co-labors with you in life. Too often, we are fearful that whatever we give to God, He will take away. But if it is taken away, that is ultimately good, because God knows it is dangerous to our hearts. The rich man in the parable wouldn't give up ownership of himself—and he paid the ultimate price.

### True Peace

The second thing I find interesting about this story is that the rich man was foolish in his own peace. He said, "And I will say to my soul, 'Soul, you have many goods laid up for many years' " (Luke 12:19). He is talking to his soul. In this man's reasoning, his peace came from his own life and what he had done—what he had accomplished. In reality, he had no peace whatsoever, because his peace was not in God, it was in things. The rich man was resting in his goods rather than resting in God. When you and I start resting in our possessions, we're going to have a difficult time.

### True Security

This rich man also said in Luke 12:19, "Take your ease; eat, drink, and be merry." In other words, he thought it was time to enjoy life. But notice God's response in verse 20: "Fool! This night your soul will be required of you; then whose will those things be which you have provided?" This man mistakenly believed that his whole life was ahead of him, just like we often do today. We think we're going to live forever and have a wonderful time in those years. But this man was on the edge of darkness. Living for himself, he had no knowledge that God was going to require his soul that very night. He spoke as though he were the master of his life. Jesus said this man was a fool because he left God out of the equation of his life.

Don't we do the same thing? We make decisions that we think are good, but we really don't seek the Lord or look into His Word. Sometimes we are very selfish in where we want to live, not even considering where our children need to go to school. We constantly think about what we need to make us feel better or more comfortable rather than what others might need. And we're not alone in that. We live in a very selfish world. People throw a marriage away when it doesn't go as they want. They throw babies away when they don't want to be a parent. All around us we constantly see people living for themselves.

Jesus came to stop that. He wants you and me to live for the glory of God; He wants us to learn what it means to die to self and put Jesus Christ first. We need to stop for a moment and pray, "What would Jesus do in this situation? How would God heal this marriage? How would God make this decision in business?" In other words, we must bring God into our daily lives.

The rich man was at the very brink of disaster, yet he had no concept what God was going to do in his life. Notice again the unmistakable words of verse 20: "But God said to him, 'Fool! This night your soul will be required of you; then whose will those things be which you have provided?' " In other words, he played with death and lost.

I recently read this illustrative and powerful poem:

He was unprepared, death knocked.
Who's there? Oh, wait awhile. I'm not ready yet.
No, tonight.
Wait until my crops are in.
No, tonight.
Wait until my new barn is done.
No, tonight.
Wait until I get right.
No, tonight, tonight in darkness you go.

We know in our hearts that God does not want us to be selfish people. We know that we need to learn how to give. That means giving beyond what feels natural. It means learning to love unconditionally. Even when my kids drove me crazy, I loved them; but regrettably, I realize now that there were times when I loved them conditionally. My son once said to me, "Dad, you love me because I love Christ, but you don't love me when I'm having a difficult time." Sadly, he was right. I had to learn to love my kids unconditionally. My conditional love was selfish, because I wanted them to do good so I wouldn't look bad.

Selfishness can be a very dangerous thing—just ask the rich man whose story is recorded in Luke 20. If you are going to follow Christ, you have to give up living a selfish life. Your life absolutely must be about Him first, and about others second. You come in last. The moment you start giving of yourself, God is going to do a wonderful work in your life. Maybe today you need to extend a little bit of forgiveness to someone. Maybe today you need to show a little bit of grace to someone. Maybe today you need to give a little bit of space to someone. As you learn to give, God will take your attempts to be a giving person and multiply them. If you don't learn to give, however, selfishness will destroy every relationship you embark upon and stop the hand of God in your life.

## POINTS TO PONDER

- What type of giver am I—a flint, a sponge or a honeycomb?
- Where is selfishness ruling in my life?
- Am I bringing God into both the daily decisions and the big decisions of life?

7

# OVERCOMING CRITICISM
# AND OPPOSITION

*Casting down arguments and every high thing that exalts itself
against the knowledge of God, bringing every thought into
captivity to the obedience of Christ.*

2 CORINTHIANS 10:5

*There is negative criticism and there is constructive criticism. With either type, we always need to be open to the Holy Spirit, because He may send something or someone our way to get us to stop and listen. We need to listen to how people feel, and we need to weigh it all before God. But if we're unwilling to listen, then we are going to get in trouble, because either we are going to fall upon the rock or the rock will fall upon us (see Ps. 18:2; Rev. 6:16). And that means that we are going to be broken. So how does God break us? How does God change us? Sometimes He will use our spouse; sometimes He will use other people. Either way, we need to always be ready to take the humble road and look into the mirror at ourselves. When we're not willing to look at ourselves, at our actions or at our teaching, we are in a dangerous place. I think a great leader is open to hear anything. But a great leader is also able to discern and therefore throw away things that are not from God and are discouraging for him. So the Word of God will separate between the bone and marrow. We need to give up our right to be right or we will begin to fall. If my children, my wife, and my pastors all tell me I'm wrong, then I am wrong! Better for me to listen, ponder and wait upon God before I make decisions. I have found over the years that criticism can be a great friend. It doesn't hurt so much when people don't like me or don't like what I've taught if I know it's from the Lord. Then I can accept the truth because He wants me to change things in my life.*

There are times when criticism is poison and creates division. Destructive criticism comes from the pit of hell. When people are bitter, or they have been hurt, they can become very critical. And even if they are not from God, we still need to respect them and respond with grace to let God do His work in their life. We can't let criticism eat us up. I think the character of a man is evident in how he deals with criticism. How does he discern what he hears? Does he wait on God? Both are dealt with at the cross of Jesus Christ.

The apostle Paul gives us great insight on overcoming criticism in 2 Corinthians, chapters 10–12. He faced a great deal of criticism in his ministry and was forced to defend himself and his ministry against some of the Jewish Christians who had begun to criticize him. In essence, they claimed that he was weighty in his letters, but weak in his presence. Paul responded to them, "Listen, unless you

repent, I'm going to come see you, and when I get there, we're going to see who is really weak." Paul stood strong on the foundation
of Christ, especially when being challenged by those in the church
of Corinth who believed it was necessary to keep all the Jewish fes-
tivals, feasts and traditions. What I find interesting is how Paul responded. Second Corinthians 10:3-5 records his words: "For though
we walk in the flesh, we do not war according to the flesh. For the
weapons of our warfare are not carnal but mighty in God for
pulling down strongholds, casting down arguments and every high
thing that exalts itself against the knowledge of God, bringing every
thought into captivity to the obedience of Christ."

The word "warfare" means "campaign." Paul did not see the criticism as a little misunderstanding between himself and a group of
men, but rather, he saw it as an attack of the enemy upon his life.
When people begin to say things about us, we can waste so much
time worrying that we allow our minds to go crazy. Paul refused to
go down that road. He understood that when people were seeking
to destroy his ministry, the true source was Satan. It was not a fleshly
battle, but a spiritual one. Paul had the ability to confront challenges. He had the confidence and belief that God worked through
his life. Because of this confidence, he saw the criticism for what it
really was—a campaign of Satan to hinder the work of God among
the Corinthians. Real Christianity is not a playground—it's a battle-
field that many times we do not take seriously.

Although prayer should be a Christian's strongest virtue, often
it is the weakest. What is the one great piece of equipment the Holy
Spirit has given us to find victory within our lives? Prayer. Prayer
is nothing less than warfare against the attacks of the enemy.
When we begin to pray for our spouse, when we pray about being
single, when we pray about being a single parent, or we pray for
our children or grandchildren, God begins to move in ways we
could never imagine. We can fret and worry all we want, but it
won't change our situation. Rather, it's the "weapons of our warfare" (2 Cor. 10:4) that bring down the strongholds in our lives.
God desires that we recognize the enemy. He wants us to understand the importance of resisting him—of refusing to cooperate

with the very ways the enemy wants to break down our lives. Criticism is one of his destructive weapons.

# Dealing with Criticism

Let's examine in depth four aspects in the battle to overcome criticism: (1) our walk, (2) our mind, (3) our weapons, and (4) our warfare—as well as several biblical examples.

## Our Walk

In 2 Corinthians 10:3, Paul declared, "Though we walk in the flesh, we do not war according to the flesh." Paul said this in a different way in Ephesians 6:11-12: "Put on the whole armor of God, that you may be able to stand against the wiles of the devil. For we do not wrestle against flesh and blood, but against principalities, against powers, against the rulers of the darkness of this age, against spiritual hosts of wickedness in the heavenly places."

Paul went for the very throat of the kingdom of Satan. He said there are powers, dominions, principalities and rulers of darkness that we go against in our lives. And then he said in verse 13, "Therefore take up the whole armor of God, that you may be able to withstand in the evil day, and having done all, to stand." His words make it clear that no matter how evil a day may be, we are going to be able to stand and not fall. We are to fight in the realm of the Spirit and know whom we are fighting against. The apostle Peter wrote of our adversary: "Be sober, be vigilant; because your adversary the devil walks about like a roaring lion, seeking whom he may devour" (1 Pet. 5:8). Notice that it's not everybody else's adversary. Rather, it's the adversary of each one of us. The enemy desires to take us away from the heart of God. He knows that he can't touch our salvation—believers belong to God. But he can touch our minds.

## Our Mind

In our Christian walk, the battle to follow Christ is fought in the mind. Too often, we allow imaginations and fantasies to grow in our minds and squeeze out the truth of God. Satan whispers in our ear, and we begin to question God and make decisions that are not pleasing to the Lord. Both the Holy Spirit and Satan are after our minds; whomever we yield to will affect what we believe, the way we live and the intimacy of our walk with God.

Though Satan cannot claim us, as born-again believers, he is seeking to make us sterile for the Kingdom—hoping that he can discourage us, bring us down and make us ineffective as a Christian. Our adversary knows we are going to heaven, but he's going to attempt everything he can to make our lives miserable here on earth. However, we don't need to allow that!

Two thousand years ago, Christ died for our sins and forever broke the penalty and the power of sin; so the battle over sin and death is won. But we need to walk in victory and believe that Satan has been destroyed. Scripture says, "He who is in you is greater than he who is in the world" (1 John 4:4). To live in that knowledge, we need to yield our minds to the authority of the Word of God. In the list of the armor of God, His Word is an offensive weapon against Satan; it's called the "sword of the Spirit" (Eph. 6:17), and with it we can vanquish Satan's attempts to control our minds.

There is an interesting story in the Bible that clearly illustrates this principle. It's found in the book of Nehemiah, chapter 6. Nehemiah had been sent to rebuild the walls of Jerusalem. Enter two interesting characters named Tobiah and Sanballat. These adversaries were extremely critical of Nehemiah's ministry. From the beginning they tried to stop the work of rebuilding Jerusalem's wall, but their every attempt to undermine Nehemiah failed. In chapter 6, though the wall was complete, the Bible says the gates had not yet been hung (see Neh. 6:1). Tobiah and Sanballat knew that their time was running out and they were losing the war against Nehemiah. Realizing that Nehemiah was about ready to hang the gates, Tobiah and Sanballat invited Nehemiah for a meeting at a place called Ono, preparing to ambush him. So, we see that the first way Satan comes against our lives is to draw us away from what we are doing, from the work of God within our lives. Nehemiah said, "I am doing a great work. . . . Why should the work cease while I leave it and go down to you?" (v. 3).

We should respond like Nehemiah if someone says to us, in essence, "come to Ono." Then our response should be, "Oh, no." Definitely, we should not go. But Tobiah and Sanballat kept coming against Nehemiah with the same message, seeking to draw him to Ono. In the same way, we need to understand that Satan is not going to let us off the hook easily. Finally, Nehemiah said, "Listen, I'm not going. I'm not going to allow you to draw me away from what God has called me to do."

Next, when Tobiah and Sanballat couldn't stop Nehemiah from doing the work of God, they wrote a condemning letter against him. They started a rumor, seeking to cause him pain. The letter indicated that Nehemiah was seeking to be king—charging that he was hiring prophets to prophesy that he would become the next king. The letter was circulated to his enemies in hopes of stirring them up. Furthermore, the letter invited Nehemiah to come and set the record straight. But Nehemiah was innocent, and such plans were not in his heart. He was humble before the Lord. Recognizing this as another attempt to get him to meet with Tobiah and Sanballat, Nehemiah simply denied the letter, sending a reply that they were making up these accusations. Tobiah and Sanballat were seeking to bring harm into Nehemiah's life, hoping his pride would cause him to react and take their bait. They hoped he would respond and defend his position—but he didn't. Instead, Nehemiah trusted in God.

Sometimes, when Satan cannot draw us out, he'll seek to lift us up—trying to make us prideful and get our anger at unjust charges to take over. Our heart cries, "How dare they! How can they do this? I need to stand up for myself. I need to fight for who I am." But when we do this, we are responding in the flesh rather than walking in the Spirit.

Then Satan tried one more attempt to bring Nehemiah down. Tobiah bribed Nehemiah's friend Shemaiah, who told Nehemiah that Tobiah and Sanballat were coming to kill him and that he should hide in the only safe place for him to go—the temple, a place forbidden to him. Nehemiah, who was suspicious, questioned his friend as to why he wanted him to take refuge inside the temple. Was he seeking to have him sin? And why should Nehemiah hide? Why should such a man as he flee into the temple and leave his work and the city unprotected? Nehemiah knew he had done nothing wrong, and so, wisely, he did not heed the advice of Shemaiah. With friends like that, who needs enemies?

Satan often seeks to pull us away from the work of God. He will try to lift us up in pride, tempt us to sin against God or just try to beat us down and drain us until we are exhausted with life. Nehemiah said no to all of Satan's attacks. And that should be our answer as well. To those who criticize us, and attempt to get us off our game, the answer is, "No, I'm doing a great work for God; leave me alone."

**Our Weapons**

Paul tells us, in 2 Corinthians 10:4, "For the weapons of our warfare are not carnal but mighty in God for pulling down strongholds." We must wage our spiritual battles with God's power. The first thing we need to realize about the "weapons of our warfare" is that we can count on God to fight the battles in our life. God uses supernatural means to destroy the very things that are against us. In the process, it's not uncommon for God to reduce us, to use the weaknesses of our flesh and our failures and turn them into tremendous building blocks for the kingdom of God.

# Ask God to Open Your Spiritual Eyes

Recognizing God and His power to help us in our battles is illustrated in the story of Elisha and his servant at Dothan (see 2 Kings 6:15-17). When Elisha's servant rose up in the morning, he looked out and realized that the Syrians had them totally surrounded. These were overwhelming odds—the men on his side—Elisha and himself—versus those of his opposition—2,000 in number. The servant went back and woke up his master, telling him they were surrounded. Elisha replied, "Do not fear, for those who are with us are more than those who are with them" (2 Kings 6:16). Then Elisha prayed, "LORD, I pray, open his eyes that he may see." The passage continues, "Then the LORD opened the eyes of the young man, and he saw. And behold, the mountain was full of horses and chariots of fire all around Elisha" (2 Kings 6:17). The servant had overlooked the supernatural power of God on their side. Yet God opened the young man's eyes. I imagine that Elisha never even got out of bed! He probably thought, *Oh, God, open this guy's eyes so I can go back to sleep.* The angels of the Lord surrounded them in chariots of fire. We need to remember in our own battles that the angels of the Lord encamp around the righteous.

Another example is found in 2 Chronicles 20. This passage says, concerning an incredible moment in a battle of the Israelites against the Moabites and the Ammonites, "For the battle is not yours, but God's" (2 Chron. 20:15). Verse 17 continues, "You will not need to fight in this battle. Position yourselves, stand still and see the salvation of the LORD, who is with you, O Judah and Jerusalem! Do not fear or be dismayed; tomorrow go out against them, for the LORD is with you." In verse 18 it tells us the Israelites were "worshiping the LORD." This great story concludes in verse 22: "Now when they began to sing and to praise, the LORD set ambushes against the people of Ammon . . . and they were defeated." Basically, all Hezekiah had to do was to worship the Lord; God destroyed the enemy.

Hezekiah encountered another supernatural incident described in 2 Chronicles 32:1-7. Sennacherib, king of Assyria, basically said, "I'm going to destroy you, Hezekiah." So Hezekiah brought the matter before the Lord. Second Chronicles 32:7-8 records that he said to his military captains, "Be strong and courageous; do not be afraid nor dismayed before the king of Assyria, nor before all the multitude that is with him; for there are more with us than with him. With him is an arm of flesh; but with us is the LORD our God, to help us and to fight our battles." In other words, Hezekiah is saying, the battle is not yours. The weapons to pull down this strong man are spiritual.

God desires to fight every one of our battles. He wants us not to fight from the flesh, but from the realm of the Spirit. Repeatedly, Scripture talks about strongholds—what we have allowed to build within our lives and take control. Often we allow imaginations and feelings to build up or we allow sin to go unchecked. We allow compromise in, subconsciously handing Satan seeds with which to plant in our minds. Those very seeds become thoughts and those thoughts become wishes. Soon those wishes become desires and the desires become the sin that destroys us. All of this happens because we have been listening to Satan instead of Jesus. Satan tries to build strongholds in us from which he mocks us and baffles us. Most likely we have tried to get rid of them, but can't. We've asked God to take them. We have fought with all our will. We have read, we have fasted, we have done everything, but they still stand in us and mock us, blocking our victory in Christ.

## The Mighty Weapon of Worship

Joshua was given the answer to bringing down strongholds in the story of the defeat of Jericho. In Joshua 6, the Lord told Joshua that He had given him the city. In essence, the Lord said, "I want you to walk around it. I want you to see it. I want you to be quiet, but on the seventh day, I want you to shout and worship." And when the children of Israel followed the Lord's instructions, that city was destroyed because of the presence of God within the life of the children of Israel.

If you are ever going to get rid of the strongholds in your life, it's going to be as you live in the presence of God and learn to worship Him. The real problem is not your husband or wife. It's not your children, so quit getting angry with them. It's not your boss, and it's not your friends. Rather, you are in a spiritual battle. Satan uses problems, a particular difficult person, for example, to get you to a point where you might walk away from God or say, "I quit." But when you understand that the battle is indeed bigger than a specific problem, you can begin to conquer the problem. Paul said, "For though we walk in the flesh, we do not war according to the flesh" (2 Cor. 10:3).

Let's look at a common example of fighting a spiritual battle: when we bring our children before God in prayer. When we use the spiritual weapon of our warfare, we ask God to fill them with the power of the Holy Spirit; we bind the works of Satan within their lives. We ask God to open their minds to see the goodness of God, and we begin to pray those kids into the Kingdom, asking God to set them free. This is undoubtedly a spiritual battle. We must pray for our spouses in the same way. Furthermore, if you are single, don't allow Satan to destroy you by magnifying feelings of loneliness. This is a season in your life when you have to draw closer to God. In all these instances, we must think on that which is good, that which is lovely, and that which is kind. When we realize that we are in a spiritual battle, we use spiritual weapons—prayer, God's Word, and worship—to tear down the strongholds in our lives.

## Casting Down Strongholds

Second Corinthians 10:5 says, "Casting down arguments and every high thing that exalts itself against the knowledge of God, bringing every thought into captivity to the obedience of Christ." There's an interesting picture in Ezekiel 8:3-10 whereby the Spirit of God yanks Ezekiel by a lock of his hair and takes him in a vision to Jerusalem. He takes Ezekiel through a doorway that leads underneath the city. Written on the walls were pornographic writings and every filthy thing. And God tells Ezekiel, "These are the thoughts of the people of God." The people of God are the ones who, up above, are telling others to worship God, yet in their hearts, they are corrupt. They've allowed these imaginations (pornography) to dwell in their minds. They've allowed these unholy things to dominate their lives, and this needs to be cast down.

You might say, "Well, Steve, I've allowed that to happen. How do I cast it down?" Well, you need to take your direction from God's Word. In the story of Gideon's calling (see Judges 6), there's a truth that happens prior to his victory. God said to Gideon, "Take your father's young bull, the second bull of seven years old, and tear down the altar of Baal that your father has, and cut down the wooden image that is beside it" (Judg. 6:25). So Gideon went with 10 men and they obeyed the Lord, tearing down this image (casting it down), using the young bull to do it. Then they took the animal and sacrificed it, using the wood of the image as fuel. The ox is the symbol of Christ. We need to realize that the only victory we have over our minds is the cross at Calvary. We need God to take the blood of Christ and cleanse our minds. We need Jesus Christ, through the power of our worship, to take us around the city of Jericho and destroy it.

Satan is going to seek to lift you up in pride—but don't go there. He's going to seek to drive you into some sin in your life—but you must resist him through the Word. He's going to seek to make you tired and exhausted and drain your life—but don't listen to him. Walk in the Spirit and you will not fulfill the lusts of the flesh (see Gal. 5:16).

## Fighting with Prayer and the Word of God

We've already established that Satan is going to seek to build a stronghold in your life—one brick at a time. He's going to take one thought and try to build on that. Proverbs 23:7 makes it clear that as a man thinks in his heart, so is he. How we think affects how we live. And that's why Satan puts deceptive thoughts in our mind. But when we know the truth of God's Word and stand firm on it, we can resist wrong thinking. The Bible makes it clear that we are chosen (see John 15:16) and special to God. Hence, we need to come back at Satan with the Word of God—with the weapon of the sword of the Spirit. Jesus said repeatedly to Satan when He was being tempted by him, "It is written" (Matt. 4:4,7,10). The Word of God is a powerful weapon. That's why it is critical for us to be in God's Word daily. The more we know what God says, the better we can resist the lies of the enemy.

God is seeking to cleanse our hearts and work in our lives, and He wants us to use our spiritual weapons effectively and precisely. Satan will never want us to pray. Often, the last thing we do is pray. Yet prayer is the most powerful weapon that God has given to us.

When we don't pray, it's because we are living in the flesh, fighting in the flesh, thinking about the flesh, loving the flesh. But God continually makes it clear that if we live and war after the flesh, we will not have victory. We need to fight the battle on our knees—for our children, for our businesses, for our marriages, for our relationships and for our witness in this world.

Prayer and the Word of God are mighty spiritual weapons to conquer the wiles of the devil. Tragically, these two areas are often lacking in the Church! Satan often has us whipped because of our ignorance of who our real enemy is and how to combat him. God wants us to know that Satan is after us (see 1 Pet. 5:8). And He wants us to be equipped to wipe him out in the authority of Jesus Christ. When a thought that is not pleasing to the Lord comes into your mind, arrest it by the power of the Holy Spirit. That thought is not of God. That imagination is not of God. Yet if you dwell upon that imagination, it will turn into a reality—and that reality is going to take you out.

Harboring a fantasy, taking a look where you shouldn't be looking—Satan will first plant a seed, then he'll plant a desire, and then he'll plant that hope. Finally, he'll fulfill it. When desire is conceived, it brings forth sin, and when sin is finished, it brings forth death (see Jas. 1:15). I challenge you: Don't go down that road—cast it down. If you are going to cast it down, it's going to be through the power of the cross. If you are going to pull it down, it's going to be by living a life of worship. Don't allow the enemy to rob you. Instead, get on your knees with your hands in the air, worshiping God, asking Him to give you victory over the habits in your life. You must take the Word of God and pray faithfully to stand against the wiles of the devil.

How do we handle opposition? First we must know where it's coming from. Criticism is not from God, it's from the devil. Fighting is not from God; it's from the devil. Pride does not come from God; it's from the devil. We must quit fighting in our own strength and get on our knees and pray. We must give our hearts to God and use His Word as the sword of the Spirit; then we will not be affected when opposition comes.

# POINTS TO PONDER

- Who is the source of my opposition? What is he using to oppose me?
- Who are the Tobiahs and Sanballats in my life?
- Am I effectively using the weapons of warfare God has provided for me? How is my prayer life? My daily time in the Word? My heart of worship?

# 8

# OVERCOMING JEALOUSY

*I am jealous for you with the jealousy of God himself. I promised you as a pure bride to one husband—Christ. But I fear that somehow your pure and undivided devotion to Christ will be corrupted, just as Eve was deceived by the cunning ways of the serpent.*

2 CORINTHIANS 11:2-3, *NLT*

*Jealousy is a destructive force. It will drive us to do crazy things. It can cause families to divide and people to lie in order to get ahead. There isn't much that is more damaging to the soul than jealousy, because it is void of God and void of the work of the Holy Spirit. Jealousy causes us to hate when someone else is being blessed. Instead of rejoicing, we look at the failure of our own heart and say, "Why don't I have that?" I remember one time when I was comparing myself to another pastor and to his successful ministry and large congregation. For a moment, I began to think that maybe I could do things better. Instantly, the Lord spoke to me that He gave that pastor his ministry, and He told me that I didn't have large numbers of people because I couldn't handle it. I had to really ask God why, because I didn't understand. And God spoke to me, saying that because I wanted it so badly, He wasn't going to give it to me. My motives were all wrong. You see, jealousy causes a person to feel like he has to have something, and that it has to be better. Satan was jealous of God. And it was God who had to punish him and throw him out of heaven. The only one who can really be jealous is God Himself. He says "I am jealous for you." And it's because of this jealousy that God will take away anything that keeps me away from Him.*

Years ago, I wanted my own church so badly that every weekend I drove from Twenty-nine Palms in the California desert to Costa Mesa near the coast to see Pastor Chuck Smith of Calvary Chapel. I sat on the steps of the church, waiting for him to come. Every Saturday, I would see Pastor Chuck and ask him, "Pastor, has the Lord spoken to you to hire me yet?" The answer was always the same: "No." Every Friday night, my wife would say, "You're not going to Costa Mesa tonight are you?" And I would say, defiantly, "Yes, I am, because this is the week." For 51 weekends, I made that trip; and 51 times, he said, "No." Jealousy drove me to do crazy things, and though my wife tried to stop me, I went anyway. Now I look back and wonder how I could have done that. My heart was jealous, and I wasn't content with what God had given me, when in reality, God knew exactly what I needed and when I needed it. After 51 weeks, I realized that he was never going to say yes, and I really had to let it go. I never asked again. Eventually, the call did come when I was busy with the things of God's kingdom and not my own.

steve mays · www.regalbooks.com

Dwight L. Moody told a story about a very jealous eagle that illustrates how far astray jealousy can take some people. The story goes like this: The eagle had envied another bird because it could fly higher than he could. Then one day, the bird saw a sportsman with a bow and arrow and said to him, "I wish you would bring that other eagle down." The man replied that he would if only he had some feathers for his arrow. So the jealous eagle pulled out a feather from his wing. The arrow was shot, but it didn't quite reach the rival bird because he was flying too high and too quickly. Then the jealous eagle pulled out another feather and then another, until he lost so many that he himself could no longer fly. The archer took advantage of the situation, turned around, drew his bow and killed the helpless bird! The moral of the story: The danger of jealousy is that a jealous person defends himself or herself to the point at which he or she becomes an open target for the enemy.

Jealousy appears as one of the seven major sins that Solomon talks about in the book of Proverbs. He says in Proverbs 6:16-19: "These six things the LORD hates, yes, seven are an abomination to Him: A proud look, a lying tongue, hands that shed innocent blood, a heart that devises wicked plans, feet that are swift in running to evil, a false witness who speaks lies, and one who sows discord among brethren." Jealousy existed even before the creation of man. The angel Lucifer became jealous of God. And it was because of that jealousy that he was transformed into Satan. The great evangelist Billy Graham said it well in his book *The Seven Deadly Sins*: "Jealousy can ruin a reputation, split a church, and cause murder. It can shrink our circle of friends, ruin our business, and dwarf our souls. Procrastination may be the thief of time, but jealousy is the murderer of the soul."[1]

Jealousy has gripped the hearts of so many people. It has broken more homes, destroyed more businesses, perverted more relationships, divided more churches, and crippled more personal lives than almost any other emotion. Solomon mentioned this sin in Proverbs 14:30: "A sound heart is life to the body, but envy is rottenness to the bones." Then he wrote in Proverbs 27:4, "Wrath is cruel and anger a torrent, but who is able to stand before jealousy?" The words "jealousy" and "envy" are similar yet there is a slight difference: Jealousy deals with what one has; envy hopes to be what another is. Paul, in 2 Corinthians 11, shows us how to deal with this horrible monster called jealousy and how we can overcome it. Harmful jealousy of others is destroyed with a righteous jealousy for God. If we are jealous *of* someone, we are looking out for ourselves; but if we are jealous *for* another, we are going to give of ourselves and minister to the heart of that person. When God is jealous *for* you, it is because you belong to Him.

## Righteous Jealousy

The apostle Paul's expression of jealousy for the Church was like the protective love of God for His people. Paul had brought the Corinthian church up in the ways of the Lord. He had spent 18 months teaching those believers how to live as those who are pleasing to God. After he was gone, he wrote two letters to them, which became the books of 1 and 2 Corinthians. Second Corinthians is actually a follow-up to the first letter. Paul was hoping that the Corinthian church would respond to the first letter in a humble and responsive way, but instead, they attacked his ministry and his integrity.

In 2 Corinthians, he lays out the importance of the calling of God and what God had done in his life. Paul makes the case that they must put God first. He does this by stating that he is jealous for them, just as God is jealous for them, meaning that he is protective of them. Here are Paul's words in 2 Corinthians 11:2: "For I am jealous for you with godly jealousy. For I have betrothed you to one husband, that I may present you as a chaste virgin to Christ." Notice that the Lord is jealous "for you" and not "of you." Paul holds out hope for the Corinthian believers that he can present them to Jesus Christ and that they would remain pure within their lives. Paul adds that he fears that Satan has beguiled many of them.

## The Antidote for Jealousy

Paul challenged the Corinthian church—and challenges us today—to love, labor and live for other people, if we're ever going to overcome this horrible monster of jealousy. We all struggle in this area, and

God wants to help us overcome by the power of His Spirit. In order to have real victory over jealousy, we must answer three important questions. The first question is often the hardest to answer: Am I willing to love other people? The second question has to do with the fruit of the first question: Am I willing to labor among other people? And the final question gets to the heart of the first two: Am I willing to live my life for others?

We can learn more about these three necessities by turning to Paul's second letter to the Corinthians, chapter 11, as he speaks to each one: Paul followed the example Jesus set for all of us in his life and ministry and was able to *love* the people of God (vv. 1-6); he was willing to *labor* for the people of God (vv. 7-12); and he was willing to *live* among the people of God (vv. 16-33).

## Love for People

Paul told the Corinthians in a letter, "I am jealous for you with the jealousy of God himself. I promised you as a pure bride to one husband—Christ. But I fear that somehow your pure and undivided devotion to Christ will be corrupted, just as Eve was deceived by the cunning ways of the serpent" (2 Cor. 11:2-3, *NLT*). What Paul mentions in verse 2, "I am jealous for you with godly jealousy," describes a healthy jealousy, *a love for people*, as previously noted. To better understand how Paul's jealousy is loving, we can look more closely at the word and its origin. The root word for "jealousy" is the same in the Hebrew as in the Greek: It means "warmth." It has to do with the passion, the fire and the emotions of someone's life, but it can be used as either a *positive* or a *negative* within that life.

Before Paul was converted, he had a passion to kill the Christians. The Bible says that he made havoc with the Church. And the Bible also describes that when Paul was saved, the whole Church rested. Like a madman, Paul was completely governed by a passion in his heart to destroy Christianity. He was committed to the dark side, a servant of Satan—ready to destroy the work of God. But it was God, on that Damascus Road, who took hold of Paul and changed his emotions, his mind and his will. God miraculously took the whole man and completely changed him.

We can take a lesson from that. Sometimes when God changes our lives, we will not allow Him to change our emotions; yet that's what needs to happen. God got hold of Paul's emotions on that Damascus Road. That's when Paul went from serving the devil to serving Christ. He went from being passionate about the kingdom of darkness to being passionate for the Lord Jesus Christ. Before his conversion, he was willing to kill Christians; afterward, he was willing to give his life for the sake of Christ. Nothing had changed except the direction of the passion in his heart. God turned Paul's life around and did something for him. Before the Damascus Road, Paul was jealous *of* people. He was jealous *of* the Christian walk; he was jealous *of* those around him. But after that day on the Damascus Road, Paul became jealous *for* the Church. He now lived his life by loving people.

God loves each of us. He has a jealousy for us. It's the same jealousy I have for my children. I want them to be blessed. I want God to use them. I want them to be secure. I really desire that they would have everything they need in their lives. Now, my kids would look at that love and say, "Dad, you are controlling." And I would reply, "No, I am jealous for you." Similarly, a person might say, "God, You are controlling my life. I can't go to R-rated movies. I can't go out with other women. I can't go out and get drunk. God, You are controlling my life." God would respond, "I am not controlling your life. I am jealous for you because those other things are going to take you to the kingdom of hell. Those other things are going to destroy every single relationship that is dear to you. Those other things are going to take you down the road of drugs or AIDS or homelessness. They're going to destroy your life."

God is not jealous *of* us, but rather, He is jealous *for* us, and it makes all the difference in the world. Satan came to Eve and said to her, "Listen, God is afraid you're going to be like Him." If she had understood that it is not the nature of God to be afraid or jealous of others, she would not have sinned against God. The Bible says in Habakkuk 1:13 that God's eyes are pure and cannot look upon evil. God is not jealous *of* anything; rather, He is jealous *for* us. Therefore, it's God's desire that we would walk in purity and in the power of the Holy Spirit so that He can bless us, use us and begin to prosper our lives.

When we become jealous of others—looking out for ourselves—everything seems to fall apart in our lives. For example, it's when we try to live a certain lifestyle that we go into debt. I believe with all my heart that the most wicked sin of all is jealousy, even more so than the love of money, because jealousy is behind most sins, especially because it originated in the heart of Lucifer. Paul conquered jealousy by truly loving people.

Do you really love people? Are you willing to show that love? Are you willing to manifest that love? You can, because Jesus Christ came to earth and died for us; and in so doing, He revealed and manifested His love for us. When we surrender our hearts to Him, His Holy Spirit gives us the ability to love others more than we love ourselves. It's not always easy, but the first way to overcome a jealous life is to let God form in you the ability to love others more than you love yourself.

God desires the mastery of our lives. He wants our passion. He desires our ambition. He will not share our lives with anyone because He wants the very best for us. And when we begin to bring in other loves, our lives begin to fall apart because no matter who or what these other loves are, they will never match up to the grace, power and anointing of God in our lives. Even my wife, as much as I love her, will never come close to loving me like God does. And so my commitment, my heart and my love need to be dedicated to God first. When that happens, I will love my wife—not because of who she is, but because of what Christ has done in her life and mine. I will not need anything from her. And that's the secret of living in contentment. Our love for others needs to be centered on a relationship with Jesus Christ. Then all other loves flow from that.

## Laboring for People

Paul emphasized the need to labor for people. Paul wrote in 2 Corinthians 11:9, "And when I was present with you, and in need, I was a burden to no one, for what I lacked the brethren who came from Macedonia supplied. And in everything I kept myself from being burdensome to you, and so I will keep myself." Here is the key. Paul was not willing to be a guy who would need to be ministered to. In other words, when we are void of jealousy, we are ready to minister to and labor among people. And if God blesses them, great; if God raises them up, great; if God uses them more than us, great. Yet, when we become jealous of others, the work of God is hindered. When we become jealous, a marriage can be destroyed. When we become jealous, children can be devastated. The opposite is true when we are willing to labor in our marriage, labor in our church, labor at work; then we are set free to do the task at hand.

In the book of Esther, we read an excellent illustration of jealousy in a story about two men: Haman and Mordecai. Haman was part of the government, and Mordecai was one of God's people. The Bible reveals Haman's heart, saying that he desired Mordecai to bow down to him (see Esther 3:5). Mordecai, however, wouldn't bow down. And this got underneath Haman's skin; it began to really bother him that he could not control Mordecai. He became extremely jealous of Mordecai, but Mordecai wasn't willing to yield his love to Haman. Mordecai was committed to God and in love with God. Haman, on the other hand, was in love with himself and was very jealous of Mordecai.

We see the fruit of Haman's jealousy when he builds gallows in his own backyard with a desire for Mordecai to hang. As the story unfolds, we also see the result and destruction of such jealousy. Who actually was hanged on those gallows before God? It wasn't Mordecai, but rather the one who built the gallows: Haman. Haman's jealousy led to his own death.

The Bible gives us other examples of destructive jealousy. We read in Genesis 16 that Leah had children, but Rachel didn't. Because of this, Rachel became extremely jealous of Leah and her family.

In 1 Samuel 18, King Saul was jealous of David. After David had killed Goliath, a song began to be sung throughout Israel, "So the women sang as they danced, and said: 'Saul has slain his thousands, and David his ten thousands' " (1 Sam. 18:7). The Scripture says that, from that moment on, Saul began to eye David; for the next 20-some years, Saul chased David throughout the land, wasting his life and losing his kingdom—all because of jealousy.

In Genesis 37, the 10 boys of the family of Jacob, except for Benjamin, conceived a plot to destroy their brother Joseph. Why? They were jealous because of Joseph's dream that his brothers would bow to him and also because Joseph was favored by their father, Jacob. Because of their jealousy, the brothers sold Joseph into slavery in Egypt.

There is a story of two people who owned businesses across from each other. Both of these men were entrepreneurs and were very competitive. One man began to see the other man prospering, and so the first man tried to one-up the second. When the other man started to prosper, then the first man tried to one-up him back. They both begin living a vicious cycle to outdo each other. One night an angel came and woke up the first man, and said, "Listen, you can have anything you want, but I'm going to give your rival across the street double whatever you get." So the guy says, "Well, you mean if I ask for a million . . . ?" "That's right; I'm going to give him $2 million." "You mean, if I ask for 10 buildings?" "Yes, I'm going to give him 20. Whatever you want, I'm going to give him double, understand?" "Yes." So the man thought about it, really thought about it, and said, "Okay, I've made my decision." The angel asked, "Are you sure?" The man confidently replied, "Oh, yes, I've made my decision." "Well, what's your choice?" the angel asked. The man responded, "I want you to blind one of my eyes."

Isn't that human nature? Some people would rather go around with one eye, as long as another guy is blind and can't get the edge! We humans seem to have this type of competitiveness about us in which we are willing to do just about anything to obliterate the competition, yet we are not willing to labor for the benefit of others and for God's purposes. Rachel was too busy being jealous of Leah. She was not willing to labor for her sister. Joseph's brothers were too busy being jealous of him, so they couldn't labor on behalf of Joseph.

In Numbers 12, concerning Miriam, Moses' sister, we read that although she worshiped God and had tremendous moments of faith, she became caught in a horrible moment of jealousy of her brother Moses. Moses married, but Miriam didn't like his choice. So when Miriam became jealous of Moses, she was smitten with leprosy. The very thing that festered inside turned outward and began to destroy the work of God and the whole nation of Israel. Jealousy will destroy the work a person is doing. We need to labor for the Body of Christ instead of for ourselves. Christ came to give His life. If we build His Kingdom, then He'll build our kingdom.

## Living for People

Paul's passion for the spiritual welfare of the Corinthian people is captured in the words of 2 Corinthians 11:24-29:

> From the Jews five times I received forty stripes minus one. Three times I was beaten with rods; once I was stoned; three times I was shipwrecked; a night and a day I have been in the deep; in journeys often, in perils of waters, in perils of robbers, in perils of my own countrymen, in perils of the Gentiles, in perils in the city, in perils in the wilderness, in perils in the sea, in perils among false brethren; in weariness and toil, in sleeplessness often, in hunger and thirst, in fastings often, in cold and nakedness—besides the other things, what comes upon me daily: my deep concern for all the churches. Who is weak, and I am not weak? Who is made to stumble, and I do not burn with indignation?

For this final challenge of Paul to the Corinthian church—and to us—let me put these verses in today's language: running the kids to their soccer game, going downstairs to get the clothes out of the washer, heading into the city and pulling permits, writing out checks and bills. We complain about all the chores we have to do and the fact that we don't have time for ourselves. "Woe is me!" Paul says. "Listen, I was beaten up; I was thrown down; I had to run away; I had to hide; I was let out the back of a window in a basket—but in all this, I have been faithfully living for people." He says in verse 27, "In weariness and toil, in sleeplessness often, in hunger and thirst, in fastings often, in cold and nakedness." So let me ask you: When was the last time you were hungry and not able to eat, thirsty and not able to satisfy your thirst? When were you sleepless, cold or naked because of persecution?

Paul carried the Church inside his heart. He was willing to live among the conflict, among the problems, among the discouragements in the midst of the turmoil in order to help others and fulfill God's purpose. What about us? So often when our kids have problems, we don't want to live with them. When our families begin to have problems, we want to run. When our church begins to have a problem, we want to leave. Often we're unwilling to live in difficult moments. Let me state it clearly—that's jealousy rearing its ugly head. The attitude is, "Listen, this is all about me. I'm in this thing for myself, and when life becomes tough, it's time for me to go."

Do you want to overcome jealousy? Then love people, labor for people and live for people.

## Step This Way

I want to close this chapter with four simple things you can do to overcome jealousy.

### Recognize
First, *recognize* whether you have jealousy. You might be jealous of your boss, a friend or someone else in your life. Recognizing the problem is the first step. Jealousy is an ugly monster seeking to destroy your life. Be willing to stop blaming others for your actions and recognize that you're jealous.

### Confess
Second, *confess* it: "God, I acknowledge that I have a problem with jealousy. I need Your help to overcome this area of my life. I renounce it and bring it once again to the blood of Christ."

### Accept
Third, I believe you need to *accept the grace of God*: Christ has come into your heart and taken the pain and sin of your life upon

Himself. It's Christ who is going to give you the strength and ability to overcome. You can't do it in your own strength, but in Christ you can do all things (see Phil. 4:13).

### Receive

Last, I believe that you need to *receive* the Holy Spirit. Because of the strength of jealousy, because it comes from the heart of Lucifer and its intent is to destroy the work of God, you need the power of the Holy Spirit to look jealousy in the eye and say to it, "I want to love. I want to labor for others. I want to live for others. I don't want to be jealous *of* others. Instead, I want to have a jealousy *for* others." If I could say that to my wife, "Honey, my jealousy is *for* you," then my whole life would be lived for her.

When you start to be jealous *for* people rather than *of* people, you will see a dramatic change in your life and in the lives of those around you.

## POINTS TO PONDER

- Do I really love people with a selfless love?
- Am I willing to labor for others, no strings attached?
- Am I jealous *of* people or *for* them?

### Note

1. Billy Graham, *The Seven Deadly Sins* (London: Marshall, Morgan & Scott, 1961).

# 9

# OVERCOMING WEAKNESS

*And lest I should be exalted above measure by the abundance of the revelations, a thorn in the flesh was given to me, a messenger of Satan to buffet me, lest I be exalted above measure.*

2 CORINTHIANS 12:7

*Having so many surgeries has really made me face the weakness of my own flesh. I find that I fight it so much because I desperately don't want to be weak. But weakness can be turned into a powerful force for God. Satan seems to point out our weaknesses and tries to use them against us. Some are weak in their minds and can't make decisions. Others are weak in the spirit and don't follow through with God. And some are weak in the flesh and give up too quickly. When we are weak spiritually, it's because we have been out of God's Word. The world tells us that everyone is so strong, but in reality we are all weak. I believe with all of my heart that God wants us to understand that it is our weakness that He wants. He wants to bring it into perfection; and when he has a weak vessel to work with, then He can strengthen us for His glory. He can heal and do miracles, but sometimes He chooses not to so He can manifest Himself and show the world how strong He is through our weakness. That's what God told Paul He was doing through Paul's physical weakness. In our lives, it's our weakness that drives us to despair, but as soon as we give it to God, His power is real. When we are empty, then He can fill us. I would rather choose weakness any day than to be full of myself and have no room for God's filling. So I choose today to be broken and weak, always looking for God—His touch and His power—in my life. Turn to God, He will fill you and strengthen the inner man, and people will be amazed that in your weakness His strength is made perfect.*

Sometimes we find ourselves fighting against God. We want to be strong. Often, guys want to be like John Wayne—take six shots and keep on walking. But the real world doesn't work that way. We do have failures; we do have insecurities; and we are, at times, rejected. Of course, women have these challenges as well. Often, we cover up or suppress our failures and weaknesses, hoping that we will never have to deal with them. But when God desires to do something far beyond what we could ever believe, often He will also bring us to a place of difficulty in which things do not make sense. And it's in that difficult time when God wants us to know that His "strength is made perfect in weakness" (2 Cor. 12:9). The very hardship you are fighting, the very trial you are trying to overcome is actually something He has sent or allowed. It is in that moment of discouragement that God often shows you the destiny of your life.

# How Do We Overcome Weakness?

Paul left us a pity-busting but encouraging truth in his words recorded in 2 Corinthians 12:7-10:

> And lest I should be exalted above measure by the abundance of the revelations, a thorn in the flesh was given to me, a messenger of Satan to buffet me, lest I be exalted above measure. Concerning this thing I pleaded with the Lord three times that it might depart from me. And He said to me, "My grace is sufficient for you, for My strength is made perfect in weakness." Therefore most gladly I will rather boast in my infirmities, that the power of Christ may rest upon me. Therefore I take pleasure in infirmities, in reproaches, in needs, in persecutions, in distresses, for Christ's sake. For when I am weak, then I am strong.

## Looking at Thorns

Paul gives us great insight, showing us four aspects of overcoming weakness. He tells us (1) the purpose of thorns, (2) the problem with thorns, (3) the provision of thorns, and (4) the power in thorns.

Before we explore these four aspects, let me focus your attention on the fact that the thorn was *given* to Paul: "A thorn in the flesh was given to me" (2 Cor. 12:7). He said in response, "Therefore most gladly I will rather boast in my infirmities, that the power of Christ may rest upon me" (v. 9). Paul said that these thorns come from God—therefore, in the midst of the pain, the loneliness, the agony or the failure, God is trying to speak to our hearts. Verse 10 continues the same theme: "Therefore I take pleasure in infirmities, in reproaches, in needs, in persecutions, in distresses, for Christ's sake. For when I am weak, then I am strong." Paul helps us realize the power of the thorn for doing God's will. The thorn is an instrument in the hand of God. Though Satan might have brought it, Jesus Christ is going to purify it. So no matter what happens to us, things are going to work out for our good. With all my heart, I believe that Paul came to understand that the secret of having victory in any situation is seeing Jesus Christ lifted high upon that cross.

Paul was now laying out to us the hand of God and how He works in our lives. Often people will spend a lifetime begging God to get rid of something, hoping that He will take "this thing" and remove it once and for all. Paul begged; we read in verse 8, "Concerning this thing I pleaded with the Lord three times that it might depart from me." People might say, "God, please take it out of my life." This "thing" might be a particular person: "God, get this person out of my life." But then we realize that the "thing" we have been trying to get rid of has now become the very instrument that God is using to bring us to the end of ourselves.

I find that when God desires to do a major work in my life, He will often cause me to lie down at His still waters, calling me to listen quietly to His voice rather than all the screaming voices of my pain and sufferings. The following great quote from Scottish preacher and theologian George Matheson (1842–1906) really encapsulates this point:

> To lie down in the time of grief, to be quiet under the stroke of adverse fortune, implies a great strength. But I know of something that implies a strength greater still. It is the power to work under stress, to continue under hardship, to have anguish in your spirit and still perform daily tasks. This is a Christ-like thing. The hardest thing is that most of us are called to exercise patience, not in the sick bed, but in the street.

Paul said, "We were burdened beyond measure. . . . We had the sentence of death in ourselves, that we should not trust in ourselves but in God" (2 Cor. 1:8-9). James said that we have need of this trial in our lives (see Jas. 1:2). Peter said that when we are tried, we will come forth as gold (see 1 Pet. 1:6-7). James further declared, "My brethren, count it all joy when you fall into various trials, knowing that the testing of your faith produces patience. But let patience have its perfect work, that you may be perfect and complete, lacking nothing" (Jas. 1:2-4).

With the understanding of the context of the origin of trials, let us examine the four aspects of overcoming weaknesses.

## The Purpose of Thorns

Paul said, "A thorn in the flesh was given to me, a messenger of Satan to buffet me, lest I be exalted above measure" (2 Cor. 12:7).

"Lest [we] be exalted above measure," we are given a thorn. This thorn that afflicted Paul was going to change his life. Fourteen years prior to this, God opened Paul's eyes—he was privileged to witness the majesty of heaven and God's throne. Because of that great moment (those great "revelations"), God understood that Paul was going to have a problem. To keep Paul in balance, to keep him from ruining the work God was doing in his life, there was sent a messenger of Satan to buffet his body.

We don't know exactly what the "thorn" was, but the word "thorn" in the Greek is a word that means "tent post." A tent post is about 18 inches long, and they were driven into the desert sand to hold the Bedouin tents in place. The thorn was something that Paul said was crippling—it became a handicap in his life—causing him so much pain that he began to cry out to God, "Get this thing out of my life; I cannot serve You with this in my way." The thorn became a major problem for Paul. He cried out, pleading three times for God to remove it from his life.

We saw a very similar thing with the prophet Habakkuk, whereby he trusted God, after initially questioning Him, even though God inflicted punishment upon his people. God told Habakkuk that the Chaldeans (an evil bunch) were going to rape his people's children, destroy their families and annihilate the southern kingdom of Judah (see Hab. 1). Habakkuk was devastated by this message, so the Bible says he climbed to the tower because he couldn't understand God (see Hab. 2:1). His whole basis of belief was shattered. He didn't understand why God would allow this to happen. After all, God is good and holy. But then God began to show him the sins of the people (see Hab. 2:2-20). And in that moment of Habakkuk's life, in the midst of the trial, he began to understand that these Chaldeans were now an instrument in the hands of

God, being used to purify the people of God and bring them to a point of turning back to the Lord (see Hab. 3). God works in our lives as well, allowing trials and hardships to happen to bring us closer to Christ.

We see still another example in the lives of Shadrach, Meshach and Abed-Nego, the three who were thrown into the fiery furnace for refusing to sinfully obey King Nebuchadnezzar's decree to fall down and worship a huge gold image of himself that the king had set up. To the king's amazement, the three survived the fire, and Nebuchadnezzar witnessed that the Son of God had joined them in the fire (see Dan. 3:19-27). Nebuchadnezzar had to ask the three men to come out of the trial because they were having more fun in this trial than outside. Because of their loyalty to God, these three followers of God were unharmed in the fire.

You may be saying, "Stephen, you are sick! Enjoy the pain?" But consider what Paul was saying: "I enjoy this pain; I thank God for this trial; I need this thorn in my life." God was doing a work through Paul that could not be perfected without the "thorn"; He was going to keep Paul humble.

God is not opposed to working in our lives to keep us humble or to allow circumstances to happen to bring us to a point of weakness so that He might be glorified. The greatest curse in our lives is our strength. When we are strong, we do not seek God. We tend to solve our own problems. But when life begins to fall apart, we are more apt to cry out to Him.

When the Israelites began to view the manna that God provided them for 40 years as a curse, they begged God to take the manna away (see Num. 11:4-35). When God finally took it away and gave them quail, the Bible declares that because of the leanness of their soul, they were seriously in trouble. The manna was not a curse at all—it was a blessing of God. But they murmured and complained so that God took it away, and the result was trouble.

Often we complain, murmur and gripe about things going on in our life. We refuse to see that anything good is happening. We don't like our boss. We don't like where we work. We don't like a certain family situation. We are having a difficult time in relationships. We are constantly fighting the system. Yet God is saying, "Time out. My life is committed to you, and this thorn is important for you."

Paul says in 1 Corinthians 1:27-29, "But God has chosen the foolish things of the world to put to shame the wise, and God has chosen the weak things of the world to put to shame the things which are mighty; and the base things of the world and the things which are despised God has chosen, and the things which are not, to bring to nothing the things that are, that no flesh should glory in His presence."

While Satan seeks to destroy you, God is seeking to vindicate your life. Going back to the situation in the book of Habakkuk, although the Chaldeans were going to destroy the southern kingdom of Judah, God was then going to destroy the Chaldeans and resurrect the nation of Israel. When God needs an instrument, He is willing to use whatever or whomever it will take. So the purpose of the thorn is to bring humility. We must try to understand that. The purpose of the trials and the difficulties is to bring brokenness and humility into our lives, to get us to rely on the Lord and not ourselves.

## The Problem with Thorns

Paul continues in 2 Corinthians 12:8, "Concerning this thing I pleaded with the Lord three times that it might depart from me." He was praying, "God, get rid of this thing. There is no way that I can handle this. God, surely You don't want me going through this difficult time." And Paul fervently sought the Lord three different times to ask Him to get rid of this horrible, painful experience. It is interesting that God said no. In the Garden of Gethsemane, Jesus pleaded, "O My Father, if it is possible, let this cup pass from Me" (Matt. 26:39), and the Sovereign Father said no. These pleas are mirrored in our lives: "God, please remove this obstacle, this trial, this pain," and God might be saying to us, "No." We might be asking, "For how long?" With Jesus, it was all the way to the cross. With Paul, God said, "Don't ever talk to Me about this again. This is needed in your life, and this is the only thing that will keep you broken and humble before Me."

God's greatest concern for us is the work He is doing in our hearts and our spirits. He wants to take us higher and bring us to a place of complete dependency on Him. We cry out, "But, God, the pain; Lord, the hospitals; God, the cancer. God, get rid of this thing, and I will then serve you with all my heart! God, give me somebody else in this relationship, and we could do so much better." Yet, we must consider that the very things we are going through today have been given to us by the hand of God—to keep us crying out for the mercy of God.

So maybe changing the other person is not the answer. Maybe it's not the boss, the spouse, the job; it's likely that the real issue is you and me. The very things that are happening in each of our lives—the hurt, the brokenness, the devastation, the physical pain—all likely come from the hand of God to keep us broken and humble before Him. Three times Christ prayed, asking the Father to let the cup pass from Him (see Matt. 26:39-44). And three times the Father said no. So Jesus responded with humility and acceptance: "Not as I will, but as You will" (v. 39). We are told in Hebrews 12:2, "For the joy that was set before Him endured the cross." With Jesus as our example, we know that it's not wrong to pray to get rid of a situation, but God's answer might be no, because walking through the situation might be the very stepping-stone He has orchestrated to make us into the man or woman He desires us to be.

## The Provision of Thorns

You can hear Paul's strength and contentment in 2 Corinthians 12:9: "And He said to me, 'My grace is sufficient for you, for My strength is made perfect in weakness.' Therefore most gladly I will rather boast in my infirmities, that the power of Christ may rest upon me." From these powerful words, we learn that in our weaknesses, God's strength is made perfect. If we will allow ourselves to be honest, if we are not afraid to humble ourselves and acknowledge the weaknesses of our life, then God will fill us with His power. This same power created the heavens and the earth. The reason why people are not seeing more of the hand of God within their lives is that they are so afraid of being weak. We live our whole life trying to be strong, but in reality, it's just the opposite in the kingdom of God. In this society, we show our strength by our military power. But in the kingdom of God, we show strength by weakness, by accepting, even embracing that weakness as God works in and through us for His glory.

On the flip side, when we become strong in ourselves, then we become weak with God and experience problems within our life. So God declares here in verse 9, "My grace is sufficient for you, for My strength is made perfect in weakness." And Paul responds, "Therefore most gladly I will rather boast in my infirmities, that the power of Christ may rest upon me." God wants to bring salvation in the midst of the sorrow. When I look around, as Habakkuk did (see Hab. 3:17-18), and I say, "There are no figs on the tree; there is nothing in the barns; and there is nothing in the pantry or refrigerator, yet God, You want me to rejoice?" God replies, "I'm bringing this situation into your life so that you would look to Me." God is sovereignly willing to bring us to an empty place so that He can sing His life into our hearts.

In the Old Testament, the words "rest upon" relate to "tabernacle." Christ will come and "tabernacle" among us. And what Paul is saying, in a very profound way, is that if we will allow our weaknesses to be seen by God, then God will come and tabernacle among us and we will become a "pillar of strength." But if we are not willing to humble ourselves and allow our weaknesses to be manifested, we will never see the power or the glory of God among us, because God cannot allow His glory to be part of the flesh.

If I said to you today, "I can guarantee that you will see heaven," would you be willing to have a difficult day in your life? Amen! Of course! You would respond, "For a glimpse of heaven, I'll go through hell. Just give me a glimpse of heaven." And that is what Paul did. He had a glimpse of heaven, so God said, "Paul, for the rest of your life I'm going to have to balance you out." Likewise, when God begins to work in our lives to balance us, to keep us broken, to keep us seeking Him, to keep us humble, we should view it as a wonderful day.

## The Power in Thorns

Paul tells us that the thorn becomes a place of power: "Therefore most gladly I will rather boast in my infirmities, that the power of Christ may rest upon me. Therefore I take pleasure in infirmities, in reproaches, in needs, in persecutions, in distresses, for Christ's sake" (2 Cor. 12:9-10). Paul really came to understand his thorny trial. When Christ humbled Himself and took upon Himself the form of a servant and went to the cross, God placed the sins of the world upon Him. From that cross, Jesus reached out and ministered, "Father, forgive them, for they do not know what they do" (Luke 23:34). So in the midst of His pain, in the midst of His agony, Jesus was able to minister and give life.

With that cross came a crown—the crown of thorns. Paul finally came to understand that if Jesus could die and go the way of the cross and humble Himself, then so could he. It was the cross of Christ that brought the crown, and it was the cross of Christ that brought sense to what was going on. A person might say, "Well, you're telling me that Paul was beaten five times?" Yes! Thirty-nine lashes each time! He was beaten with rods three different times by the Roman government. He was shipwrecked three different times. He went through hunger, pain and agony. He was stoned in Lystra. A typical response might be, "Well, now, time out! That is too much." Yet hold on a second; was he blessed? Yes! He saw heaven! How would God be able to balance him out? If you are thinking, "Oh, there's no way that I would want to live that life," well, then, you will live without a glimpse of heaven.

If we desire to grow, if we desire to have the best marriage or the best single life, if we desire to truly be a man or woman of God, then God is going to take the necessary steps to keep us humble, and that's a promise. When that thorn comes into your life and you begin to cry, complain and blame, it's vital to remember that God sent the thorn. You might say, "This thing is driving me crazy!" But what might the Lord say? "Let's not talk about this anymore because this thorn is from My hand." When your life is beginning to fall apart and you don't know what to do, you might even hear God say, "My grace is sufficient. I'm the answer—not finances, not the church, not government. I'm the answer for your life." When you finally look around and see the power, you realize it is all about Jesus.

With Paul's great revelation came a great buffeting. It was not Satan; it was God. Clearly we can blame others. We can blame Satan. We can blame our wife or husband. We can blame the church, or we can blame the government. But I just want to remind you—this thorn that you can't shake is a gift from your heavenly Father. God is saying to you, "Reach out your hand; I have a thorn for you." You respond, "Keep it! I don't want it!" God says, "Oh, by the way, it is not just a little finger prick. It is going to penetrate your heart; it is going to hurt." You say, "Oh, why would You do that, Lord?" God replies, "You see, my child, I have to keep you humble. I have to balance you, because I don't want to lose you."

"Is there any other way?"

"No, there is no other way."

Then you realize that there is one way: "God, give me victory over this thing." He responds, "Good. Finally!" But the best attitude yet would be to say, "God, give me victory in this thorn."

## POINTS TO PONDER

- Do I recognize God's power over the thorns in my life?
- Am I accepting all my circumstances as being sent from the hand of God?
- Am I seeking a way out of the trials or a way to draw closer to Christ in them?

# 10

# OVERCOMING DECEPTION

*Examine yourselves as to whether you are in the faith.*
*Test yourselves. Do you not know yourselves, that Jesus Christ is*
*in you?—unless indeed you are disqualified.*

2 CORINTHIANS 13:5

*One time when I went to lunch with a friend, the Lord spoke to my heart and asked me why I went. Although at times I can be quite discerning, sometimes I can even deceive my own heart. I told the Lord the same thing I reassured myself—that I wanted to help this person and do some things for him. But the Lord kept poking at my heart, asking me why I had lunch with this person. He was checking my motives, but I didn't realize it. I knew this man had a second home and I was hoping he would let Gail and me stay there for our upcoming vacation. My motives were not pure. I was getting together with this man to get something. Deception can be so subtle. Now, I am always willing to let God check my heart and motives in all things. Deception is dishonesty. I can fool people (or even myself), but I can never fool God.*

*Don't burn your conscience. You must keep it clean. Now when God brings people into my life my attitude is always for me to give something, not to get something. I would rather give my heart and life away to others and be a blessing than have impure motives. If God wants to do something for me down the road, that's up to Him, but God always checks my heart. This applies to my teaching as well. Some men teach on marriage while they are secretly in adultery! Sadly, our hearts can be that deceptively wicked. I don't ever want to deceive or be deceived. I see the same thing happening in regard to winds of doctrine or new methods and programs. I see other church fellowships growing, but if I try to bring that "new thing" into my fellowship, it flops. It's steeped in deception and twisted motives because it needs to be birthed within the heart of my own fellowship. I would be deceived in my thinking if I expected some new program to do the same spiritual work for my church as it did in another. Ultimately, all truth is found in the Word of God, and His Spirit separates the truth from lies.*

I read a funny little story about a man who went to the doctor for a checkup. After the doctor did a very thorough examination on him, the doctor asked the nurse to send in the man's wife so that he could talk to her. The wife said, "Well, doctor, how is he?" And he replied, "I'm afraid it's bad news. He might pass away, but I think there is a way we might be able to save him." She looked hopeful and said, "Well, what can we do?" The doctor said, "You need to fix him three meals a day for the next three months and take care of all his needs—whatever that may be." When the wife and her husband got in the car, her husband looked at her and said, "Well, what did the doctor say?" His wife looked at him with a straight face and said, "Honey, you're going to die."

Deception comes naturally to our sin nature. Though we are good at lying to others, we are even better at lying to ourselves. And so the apostle Paul exhorts us by saying it's good for us to examine our condition before God. We don't generally like to examine ourselves. In fact, we spend a great deal of time examining others—questioning their sincerity and their motives, and searching for "fruit" in their lives. But to examine ourselves is one of the great exhortations for us as Christians. We need to examine our walk with God. Often we can gauge our relationship with God by what we are doing in our everyday lives—the things we think, say and do.

"Examine" in the Greek means "to prove or to test under fire." We need to take a good, hard look at our faith when we are being attacked or find ourselves going through a difficult trial. We must never be afraid of asking the tough questions concerning our spiritual life. It's time to be honest with ourselves before our God. Are we really close to the Lord? Do we see spiritual growth in our lives? Are we battling habitual sins? Are we just giving up? Do we spend any time in God's Word, in prayer or in fellowship? First Corinthians 11:31 says, "For if we would judge ourselves, we would not be judged." Paul is saying that each of us needs to judge the condition of our own heart—are we truly in the faith? Are we saved, or are we deceiving ourselves? We need to examine everything by the fire of the Holy Spirit in order to prove it true.

Examining or proving your faith is not something you do in just a few moments. Rather, it's a true soul-searching, a concentrated effort that takes honesty, time and commitment. In other words, you can't go home and look in the mirror and think it's over and done with. Neither can you have an in-and-out conversation about how you're doing with the Lord. This type of soul-searching is really missing in today's Church. If this type of self-examination were happening, we would have less room to judge or criticize each other. There is so much sin and hypocrisy in our lives that we often seek to dig out the little splinter in someone else's eye while there is a huge two-by-four in our own eye (see Matt. 7:3-5). The things we gripe about the most in other people are often the very issues we are dealing with in our own lives.

## The Word of God Overcomes Deception

The Bible says that God discerns our thoughts. Hebrews 4:12 affirms that the Word of God is living and powerful, able to discern "the thoughts and intents of the heart." In other words, we don't even understand our own motives. Sometimes we do things we think are right, but down the road we begin to realize they're not. If we rely on the Word of God and read it every day, the Lord will begin to reveal areas in which we are deceived. He will guide us into the truth and show us the path that will transform our lives. Psalm 119:9,11 says, "How can a young man cleanse his way? By taking heed according to Your word. . . . Your word I have hidden in my heart, that I might not sin against You." And Psalm 139:23-24 says, "Search me, O God, and know my heart; try me, and know my anxieties; and see if there is any wicked way in me, and lead me in the way everlasting."

When we don't immerse ourselves in the Word of God, these verses make clear that we are going to believe a lie—we are going to be deceived and we are going to deceive others. When was the last time you took a good, hard look at yourself—your attitudes, thoughts and actions? Is it possible that you could be wrong about something? I know it's hard to believe, but is there a possibility that you're the ding-a-ling and not everybody else? When you say, "God, show me who I am," the Lord is more than willing to help you and to show you the areas in your life that are not right.

The problem comes when we don't want to hear what God has to say! So we go through life hurting people instead of ministering to them, because it's all about us. It's important to ponder and evaluate our lives because then we're going to have success. If we seek to cover our sin, we are not going to prosper. The Bible says,

"This Book of the Law shall not depart from your mouth, but you shall meditate in it day and night, that you may observe to do according to all that is written in it. For then you will make your way prosperous, and then you will have good success" (Josh. 1:8). So God is able to change the people who are paying attention to what the Word of God says. The reason why is because God, by the work of the Holy Spirit, uses His Word as His major tool for building or remodeling people's lives.

## Examine Yourself

The Bible tells us to put ourselves to the test—to judge ourselves. In 2 Corinthians 13:5-6, Paul says:

> Examine and test and evaluate your own selves to see whether you are holding to your faith and showing the proper fruits of it. Test and prove yourselves (not Christ). Do you not yourselves realize and know (thoroughly by an ever-increasing experience) that Jesus Christ is in you—unless you are (counterfeits) disapproved on trial and rejected? But I hope you will recognize and know that we are not disapproved on trial and rejected.

Paul's teaching is that when we look in the mirror, the evidence of the fruit of Christ should be seen in our character. We who love the Lord should meditate on Him and speak of Him often. Our commitment to Christ is reflected in our thought patterns, which in turn show forth in our conversations (see Mal. 3:16).

How do you examine yourself? Start with these questions: Are you committed to the lordship of Christ rather than to the things of the world? Are you joining God in the work He is doing in this world? Also, consider what you're putting in your mind: If you're reading magazines, you should not be reading worldly philosophies. You should not be listening to compromising music. You need to realize that you might be drifting. Hebrews 2:1 says, "Therefore we must give the more earnest heed to the things we have heard, lest we drift away." In other words, anchor yourself. And the word "drift" in this passage can be illustrated something like this: Your boat is tied off at the dock, but someone has untied it. You don't even know it because you are very peaceful, but then the boat begins to rock. As it begins to move out through the jetty, it heads toward the ocean. All of a sudden you feel the waves beginning to come and you realize you're in trouble. But it's too late!

As you dabble in the things of the world, you start to drift; before long you are walking away from the Lord and entangled in sin. You need to anchor yourself to Christ on a daily basis. And when you examine yourself, you can gauge whether you are anchored or drifting.

Paul exhorts the Church with these words: "Therefore, having these promises, beloved, let us cleanse ourselves from all filthiness of the flesh and spirit" (2 Cor. 7:1). The Scripture directs us to get rid of the work of the flesh and the filthiness of the spirit, which would include things such as deceit and malice—in other words, those things that destroy the spirit of a man. Paul is stressing the work of sanctification—reckoning the old nature dead by submitting ourselves to Christ's lordship. Basically, we have a responsibility, and that is to bring ourselves before God, saying to Him, "Lord, I need Your help. I see this problem in my life; I need You to strengthen me. Lord, I commit myself to You." When we ask this with humility, we allow the work of the Holy Spirit to really move in our lives.

What if this is your attitude? "Hey, I'm a cool Christian. I drink coffee at Starbucks. I have earrings and long hair, and I'm just cool." I suppose all that is okay, but what about the depth? What about the commitment? What about the lordship of Christ? If you respond, "Well, that's not really important to me," then you need to examine yourself and see if you are truly in the faith.

It is especially crucial that we examine ourselves in light of the times in which we live. The Bible tells us that in the last days, people are going to be living as if Christ doesn't exist (see 2 Tim. 3:1-9). So it is important to take a personal evaluation of ourselves before God. If we do that, man will not judge us, nor will we be judged by our Lord. But if we are too prideful to examine ourselves, then we will be judged by everyone, and we will judge everyone as well. Paul said, "I don't even judge myself because I have a pure conscience before God; I have laid this thing out consistently before the Lord" (1 Cor. 4:3, paraphrased).

We need to tell God, "You see my uptightness. You know I'm angry and want to drive that person off the road. Please, God, set me free and fill me with the power of the Holy Spirit." Or maybe your problem is with lust. "God, I'm struggling with lust. I can't keep my eyes off of the wrong things. Please put blinders on my eyes, through the Holy Spirit." Whatever your problem may be, you need to go to God and talk to Him. We are so good at telling everyone else our problems, but we need to go directly to the Lord, sharing our hearts and asking Him for help. Remember, He knows our hearts better than we do.

When I was molested as a junior high student, it wreaked a lot of damage in my life. As a result, relationships have been difficult for me because it's hard to trust people after being abused. Yet, I went to God and asked Him to give me the ability to trust and believe others once again. And He has done that miraculous work in my heart. In this life, we are going to get hurt; people are going to take advantage of us. But it's better to be gracious and gentle like Jesus than to be a snake like Lucifer. We must let God fight our battles.

## Truth Always Overcomes

In 2 Timothy 2:21, Paul says, "Therefore if anyone cleanses himself from the latter, he will be a vessel for honor, sanctified and useful for the Master, prepared for every good work."

How can we be the best example for Christ? How can we be a vessel of honor for God's use? We need to carefully evaluate our lives, asking the Lord to show us our sin, to show us the pride of our hearts and to show us the arrogance of our lives.

A person might say, "Well, I have a good heart!" No, actually, the Bible says "every man has a wicked heart" (Jer. 17:9, paraphrased). Only the work of the Holy Spirit gives us a good heart, but we can very simply and quickly go back to that wicked heart. So our hearts need to be submitted into the hands of Christ; by the grace of God, we can look to Him and be pure.

Paul consistently tells us that we need to be in Christ, in the faith, and in fellowship. It is not possible to "kind of" have Christ in your life. You need to be filled with Him. You need to be *in* Him—submitting to His lordship on a daily basis. That's where the strength of the Christian life resides—*in* Christ. When you dwell with Him, He permeates your life, your thoughts, your attitudes, your conversations and your behavior.

In 2 Corinthians 13:6-8, Paul tells us, "But I trust that you will know that we are not disqualified. Now I pray to God that you do no evil, not that we should appear approved, but that you should do what is honorable, though we may seem disqualified. For we can do nothing against the truth." Let's give attention to the fact that "we can do nothing against the truth," only *for* the truth. We cannot go against the truth or lie about it. We can never really attack the truth, but the truth can change us. There are atheists who have tried to come against the truth, but in the very end, God is going to destroy them. We need to quit fighting the truth, because the truth will set us free (see John 8:32).

Do you love God's Word? I want you to come to love the truth. His Word is the milk in our lives, the honey to our lips. The Word of God is the very thing that brings a lamp for our feet and a light to our path (see Ps. 119:105). The truth is God Himself. If we try to twist the truth or go against it, we are fighting God. Matthew 24:35 says, "Heaven and earth will pass away, but My words will by no means pass away." The strongest authority in the world is His truth. Heaven and earth are going to pass away; they're going to be rolled up as a scroll, but His Word (His truth) will endure forever.

How much time do you spend in the truth? How much time do you really give to understanding the knowledge of God? You can deceive yourself and say, "Hey, Lord, You know I'm cool, I'm together, and I'm a good Christian." But in Luke 12:3, we read Jesus' words that the truth is going to be shouted from the housetops. Ultimately, one day you are not going to be able to cover things; it's going to come out. Sin is like leprosy—the outside is going to show what's going on inside. If you love truth, it's going to show in your life.

We will see the effects of truth in our relationships. If we love the truth, we will listen to each other. That means that I will listen to my wife when she is speaking the truth to me, even though I may not initially like what I hear! Why don't we like to hear the truth spoken? It's because of our pride. We are so defensive. It is so hard to talk to each other. When others begin to share, we get defensive. We want to be heard, because we're a little bit prideful. However, when God breaks your heart, and you come to the end of yourself, then you really don't care. You say, "Lord, change my life; speak to me."

So break that alabaster box of perfume and let the fragrance go out. It's in the breaking that the fragrance begins to permeate. There is always beauty in the breaking. Listen, it's the truth that will break your heart, but it's also the truth that will heal it again. It's a wonderful thing when you come to realize that you can do nothing against the truth. So examine your heart. Are you in the faith?

## POINTS TO PONDER

- Am I willing to examine my heart to see if I'm truly in the faith?
- Do I love the truth of God's Word?
- Do I anchor myself in Christ every day, or am I drifting?

# 11

# OVERCOMING
# IRRESPONSIBILITY

*We are glad when we are weak and you are strong.*
*And this also we pray, that you may be made complete.*

2 CORINTHIANS 13:9

*There was a time in my life when I was very irresponsible; I put the ministry before my wife. We had one day off together a week, and for many years, even when we were together on our day of rest, my mind was still on the ministry and my responsibilities at the church. I was irresponsible in my marriage, and it really became a snare in our relationship. God gave me a wife whose one desire is me. Yet she is always willing to sacrifice time with me for the ministry. All she asks is for me to be totally devoted to her for one day.*

*Now, many years later, after having health issues and various sicknesses, successes and failures, and everything in between, I realize that there is only one person for me, totally devoted to me, and that is my wife. I look back over the years and realize that I needed to take the responsibility of being a husband and a friend seriously. Now I don't neglect our time together—body, mind and spirit are all for her. When I am with her, I don't think about the church, and our relationship has grown deeper and deeper.*

*It wasn't that I didn't love my wife. I just wasn't responsible to her. The Word of God says that the soul of the diligent is made fat (see Prov. 13:4, KJV). The truth in that proverb is manifested in the fact that now, after I made definite changes, our relationship is better than we could ever have imagined. Why should God entrust me with His ministry if I am irresponsible in my personal relationships? Well, He shouldn't. Oh, He blessed the pulpit messages, but it is because of the people, not because of me. The Lord taught me a valuable lesson, and now my wife and I get out our calendars and coordinate our time together. I am first responsible to her and to our marriage, then to the ministry.*

---

The Bible has a lot to say on the subject of responsibility, but here are Paul's words: "We are glad when we are weak and you are strong. And this also we pray, that you may be made complete" (2 Cor. 13:9). Let's examine this verse in different translations.

1. The *Amplified Version*: "For we are glad when we are weak (unapproved) and you are really strong. And this we also pray for: your all-round strengthening and perfecting of soul."

2. *New Living Translation*: "We are glad to seem weak if it helps show that you are actually strong. We pray that you will become mature."
3. *The Living Bible*: "We are glad to be weak and despised if you are really strong. Our greatest wish and prayer is that you will become mature Christians."

The point of this verse is that it's time for us to have perfection or completeness in our lives. It's time for restoration to start; maturity will then follow. It's time for us to be strengthened in our soul. It's time that others see a mature Christian standing before them. Sadly, very few of these qualities—perfection, completeness, restoration, maturity, strength—exist in the lives of people in our society today. In truth, the government, our families, our friends, and our churches show irresponsibility. Our culture wants more and more—yet people want to do less for it!

Paul's words show the heart of a loving Father: "For we are glad, when we are weak, and ye are strong: and this also we wish, even your perfection" (*KJV*). The word "perfection" means "to be complete, to strengthen, mature." Paul was willing to be weak as long as the Corinthian church was mature; he was willing to die that they might live. The apostle had a genuine love for people. He even said that he was willing to stay behind and miss the Rapture if that would help them come to know the goodness of God. He had the desire to depart and be with the Lord, but he realized that it would be better that he stay behind to encourage them in their walk. Paul was willing to delay going to be with the Lord in order to minister to those he loved.

## Facing the Problem: Letting Go of the Image

Imagine, for a moment, allowing your friends to be strong while you are humble. What type of relationship would begin to develop? It would be a very close and intimate relationship. Such humility would allow God to do a tremendous work. I believe the Church is often filled with pride and arrogance. In many ways it is too much like the world, especially when it comes to pride. It might even be worse than the world because of self-righteousness. We Christians seem to enjoy lording over others. We act and think too much like the Pharisees in the New Testament who thought they were perfect because they kept the law. In reality, Christ condemned them for their hypocrisy.

God said similar words to Habakkuk concerning the southern kingdom of Judah: "Look at the proud! They trust in themselves, and their lives are crooked. But the righteous will live by their faithfulness to God" (Hab. 2:4, *NLT*). The list of people's offenses in the book of Habakkuk included, among others, coveting, desiring, lusting, building, destroying and taking advantage of people—all of which are rooted in the sin of pride. Humility, on the other hand, cries, "I come from heaven; I pour out my life; I'm willing to die, to build up other people and be a blessing."

When I sit down with the Lord, take a walk on the beach or read my Bible, I hear God constantly saying to me, "Humble yourself. Sit before Me. Stephen, who do you think you are? Have you gone to the cross? Have you seen the way that I love people? Are you impatient?"

And I answer, "Yes, Lord, I am impatient."

Then He says, "Stephen, I want to change you."

"Well, Lord, how are You going to change me?"

"I'm going to bring people into your life that are going to drive you crazy."

"Oh, but, Lord, can I just go to sleep tonight and wake up tomorrow with the gift of patience?"

He chuckles and says no.

I have to admit that I'm not always a very patient man. While I was in Washington, DC, with my wife, she wanted to have tea. Now, I don't feel that comfortable having tea. I had my baseball hat on and was wearing my jeans. I used to ride a Harley-Davidson. I felt very uncomfortable with the idea of having tea. After all, my stubby hands are made for a mug and burritos, not tea and cake. My wife looked at me and said, "Are you kidding? We're in Washington, DC, and you won't have tea with me?"

Some of our friends who were with us heard this whole dialogue. My wife looked at one of our friends and said, "We cannot have tea." So, our other friend asked me, "Well, what are you going to do?" I said, "We're going to go to Starbucks like a man and sit down and have an espresso."

So we, of course, went and had tea.

Why didn't I want to have tea? It didn't fit the image I thought I should project. Image is 100 percent pride! After all that, I was willing to humble myself and do something for my wife, and guess what? I really enjoyed having tea!

Paul wishes for our perfection or maturity. The word "wish" in the Greek means "to equip," "to fit a ship, a sail, or make sure that it is ready for the storm" or "to climb a mountain." In other words, all the equipment is in our lives to sail the ship or climb the mountain; Paul is "wishing" that we would be "completely mature in Christ," ready to serve the Lord.

## Using Power Correctly: Build Up or Break Down

The power that comes with maturing in Christ allows us to build up others. In 2 Corinthians 13:10, Paul says, "Therefore I write these things being absent, lest being present I should use sharpness, according to the authority which the Lord has given me for edification and not for destruction." This verse reflects how Paul used his authority and power: for building up others. When we have authority, we have power. When God gives you a leadership position, power comes with it. The question is, how do you use the power? Do you use it for yourself, to destroy others, or do you use it to edify others? God gave you the power to build and to mend. Please note, God gives us power to minister, not to get our own way or to abuse situations. The more power we have, the more careful we need to be toward others.

In the book of Daniel, King Nebuchadnezzar had tremendous power, but it went to his head, and God turned it against him. Daniel warned the king to break off his sin of self-righteousness and humble himself before God humbled him, but Nebuchadnezzar refused to heed Daniel's counsel. The Mede-Persians came and destroyed Nebuchadnezzar, and he was driven out of his kingdom and was humbled for seven years.

There are other stories in the Bible regarding the abuse of power. Power corrupts—and absolute power corrupts absolutely. We must stay humble and look to the example of Jesus. Christ had power, yet He allowed the soldiers to tie His hands. Christ had the ability to do whatever He wanted, yet He let men nail Him to the cross. Power needs to be mingled with meekness and humility. There is nothing more damaging than a person with power but no humility; that person will hurt people every single day. We need to understand that power is a gift God has given to each of us. It is not a force; it is the person of the Holy Spirit. That is why the Bible says we can grieve, quench, resist and even tempt the Holy Spirit. We need to major on edification, not destruction.

# Grow Up!

I'd like to come back to the idea of perfection (maturity) by looking at 2 Corinthians 13:11: "Finally, brethren . . . become complete. Be of good comfort, be of one mind, live in peace; and the God of love and peace will be with you." In other words, grow up. It's time to be mature. It's time to get a job. It's time to take responsibility. It's time to quit running away from the things of God. In other words, it's time for us to be all that God wants us to be. The verse also says to "be of good comfort." We can allow the Holy Spirit to bring great comfort, peace and joy into our lives.

### Be of One Accord

Acts 1:14 tells us that we are to be of "one" mind. The Early Church prayed with "one accord," and the Bible tells us that the Spirit fell upon them. It also says in Nehemiah that "the people had a mind to work"; they were of one mind and one heart, and because of this, the walls were built in 52 days (see Neh. 4:6). If we're discordant, then we lose power. If there's confusion, then there's every work of the devil invited in. But when we come together, there is power.

A church body should be of one accord, both when the people worship and when they listen to the Word. God wants us to grow and be mature. Too often we feel sorry for ourselves. We might say, "I can't believe it, no one loves me." Well, of course people do. But the truth might be, you're hard to love; you're being a ding-a-ling; you're ornery, mean and nasty, and it's hard to get close to you. So if you want a friend, what do you have to do? Be friendly. It's time to take responsibility for our attitudes and actions. It's time we let God change our behaviors and moods.

Take me, for example. I could say, "I'm a mess because I was molested." But I had to work through it; I had to grow up and learn how to share my story. Just as Jesus told Thomas to reach out and touch His scars, I believe that when we allow others to reach out and touch our wounds, those wounds fade away into eternity. I believe God allowed this negative experience to happen to help me to minister to other people. I don't know why. It's just something that God allowed into my life, and I had to deal with it so I could move on. Through the cross, Jesus Christ forgives all. By His blood, He takes away the pain. Even being sick (as I've been sick most of my life), what are you going to do? Paul was sick, but he chose to go on.

**Behave Like Christ**

Either we whine and complain or we quit complaining because we have matured. It's important to see that responsibility and maturing are not negative things. The bottom line is that we need to grow up and be more and more conformed to the character of Christ! Our behavior should show our maturity. Are we peaceful? Are we kind? Are we approachable? In other words, chill out and just be nice. Yelling at people is not mature behavior. Neither is running over people in the market with your shopping cart! We are Christians, and it's time we behaved in a responsible way.

# Check Your Motives

One day, I went to the hospital to see a man who was dying. When I walked out of the emergency ward, I saw another person from our church in the emergency room, and so I went in to pray with him. Then, as I was leaving, I looked over and saw this woman drive by. She was a really pretty gal with blonde hair. I looked but kept on walking. The next thing I hear is, "Pastor Steve, Pastor Steve." And I breathed a prayer, "Oh, Lord, thank You that I just glanced and walked on!" God always checks our motives.

### Treat People Well

The way we act and the way we treat people are going to reflect on our walk with Christ. If I go to a restaurant and yell at a waiter because he gives me horrible service, and then he comes to my church service on Sunday morning, he'll remember how mean I was. So what does it prove to act like a jerk? Jesus Christ never acted like a jerk. He had Judas, He had Peter and He has you. And He's not treating you badly (even though He knows all about you)!

Jesus is full of grace toward us. He's patient with us even though we don't deserve it. And despite how much the Lord patiently and lovingly puts up with us, we still walk out of church, get in someone's face and say, "Pay me my money now!" We're like the servant in Matthew 18, who was forgiven a huge monetary debt but he wouldn't forgive another lesser debt owed to him (the parable of the unforgiving servant). It's remarkable that after being forgiven a debt to his master of 10,000 talents, he turns around and begins to choke someone who owed him far less! His master, hearing of that, threw him in jail to be tortured.

God wants us to be peaceful toward others. In 2 Corinthians 13:14—"The grace of the Lord Jesus Christ, and the love of God, and the communion of the Holy Spirit be with you all. Amen"—Paul is referring to (1) the love of God, (2) the grace of Jesus Christ, and (3) the communion of the Holy Spirit. I want to exhort you that God is for you, Jesus is praying for you and the Holy Spirit is working in you. If the Father, the Son and the Spirit are for you, then you cannot fail.

### Turn to the Holy Spirit

The Holy Spirit's work is to sanctify the believer's life. If you are a believer, you need to ask God to give you the courage to look in the mirror and not be afraid of what you see. Ask for His help to know who you are; for only through His grace can you know your weaknesses and accept and embrace your responsibilities. If you desire a dynamic, mature Christian walk, you need to come to a point at which you pray, "Holy Spirit, I am so sorry. I have grieved You, quenched You and stifled You. You are the One who builds me and raises me up and brings me close to Christ, yet I have stepped over You."

Have you been a great husband to your wife? Have you been a great wife to your husband? Have you been a great friend? Are you a great single person? Are you able to listen well to others? Are you able to show compassion? Are you growing and maturing? Are you willing to serve the Lord? Are you thinking about sinning? As you consider these questions, commune with God. He will change your heart, which will change your life.

## POINTS TO PONDER

- Am I humble before God and man?
- Am I willing to serve others first or only myself?
- What is God asking me to be responsible for today?

# 12

# OVERCOMING ANGER

*Be angry, and do not sin: do not let the sun go down
on your wrath, nor give place to the devil.*

Ephesians 4:26-27

*God has done many great things in and through my life, but by far, one of the most amazing works has been to soften my heart and deliver me from hostility and anger. God revealed my angry heart to me in different ways and allowed me to get a picture of what I was doing to my wife, Gail, and to others. One time, I actually frightened her with my hostility toward the dog because he messed everything up after I had worked hard in the yard. Gail locked herself in the bathroom because she feared I might hurt her. This happened a couple of times in the beginning of our marriage. Oh, I could make excuses—saying that I ran with gangs and that was all I knew, or that I had just come off of LSD, and my mind wasn't right—but ultimately, my anger was a spiritual issue.*

*The true revelation came one day through a specific incident. A cat ran in front of my car, and I honked at it. Another driver witnessed this and cursed at me from his car. I got so angry that I began to chase this man down the street in my car. Then the Lord said to me, "Steve, aren't you the pastor of Calvary Chapel South Bay?" I responded, "Yes, Lord." That was when my surrender began. I knew I was out of control. God knew the anger was there, and He allowed certain "buttons" to get pushed to reveal my heart. The Lord needed to work on my heart and teach me to respond with His love and patience toward others rather than react in my flesh.*

*I remember the day the Lord took the "button" away. I cried out to Him and confessed that I was out of control; the Lord said, "Then you are not filled with the Holy Spirit all the way." I had to humble myself and ask the Lord to take away the anger and to fill all those deep, dark areas of my heart with His Holy Spirit—and He did! He gave me both His peace and a righteous anger for the things of His Kingdom! I can never go down that road of out-of-control anger again, because I know it will disqualify me from the ministry. Praise be to God, He is faithful!*

Anger is a huge problem in our world. Whether it's domestic violence, road rage, terrorism or war, we are constantly reminded of the anger that is a part of the society in which we are living. People are ready to explode at the drop of a pin. Even in the Church we see uptightness among leaders, board members and churchgoers. People are just tense. They're angry about their relationships, their marriages, their walk with the Lord, their lack of faith, and with what is going on in this crazy world we live in.

Psalm 37:8 tells us, "Cease from anger, and forsake wrath; do not fret—it only causes harm." And Jesus taught in Matthew 5:22, "But I say to you that whoever is angry with his brother without a cause shall be in danger of the judgment. And whoever says to his brother, 'Raca!' shall be in danger of the council. But whoever says, 'You fool!' shall be in danger of hell fire."

There are three main ways that we deal with our anger. One way is to *repress it*—to not deal with it. But the problem with repressing anger is that it often turns into depression. When we seek to repress our anger, we find that it keeps popping up. Second, we sometimes try to *express it*. This can be problematic if we begin to explode and share our feelings in an ungodly way, pouring out our anger upon other people. Or lastly, we can learn to *confess it.*

## What Are You Going to Do with It?

I believe that we as a nation—as communities, churches and individuals—need to come to grips with the problem of anger. For example, a person watches the news and all of a sudden gets angry. What does he do with that anger? Or maybe a young lady is going out with someone, and he hurts her. What does she do when she feels rejected? Or what does a woman or man do when someone at church says something bad about her or him? What do we do with those moments of anger? If we do nothing, it is likely that we will become bitter, and this bitterness can absolutely destroy our lives.

The writer of the book of Hebrews gives wise words in Hebrews 12:15. I have paraphrased his intent: "If I do not deal with my hurts and allow God's grace to heal me and touch me completely, then my depression will grow, my thoughts will be filled with sorrow, and I will find myself turning away from everything that is good in my life. His grace will begin to disappear, and the seed of bitterness will begin to blossom into a plant of destruction that will finally destroy everything I love and everyone I love around me."

Bottom line, it's vital that we deal with anger.

# Feeding, Faking and Following

So how do we address anger in a healthy, constructive way? Is there anything we can do with our anger right now? There are three important actions we can take right now to achieve victory over hostility. First of all, we must *stop feeding it*. Second, we must *stop faking it*. And finally, we must *stop following it*.

### Stop Feeding It

Paul tells us in Ephesians 4:26, "Be angry, and do not sin: do not let the sun go down on your wrath." He does say here, "Be angry"; at first glance, these words cause a bit of confusion. Are we to be angry, or are we not to be angry? The truth is that God gave us this emotion. But it's definitely not to be used in a sinful way. There's an emotional place for feeling angry. Jesus turned over the money-changers' tables because they were defiling the temple of God. We ought to have anger toward the unrighteousness that is plaguing our nation. We ought to have a righteous anger toward ungodliness and the sinful behaviors of others. That is, we ought to have anger and be grieved in our spirit when we see our Lord mocked or watch people have no fear of Him. Yet, so often we have no feelings whatsoever. We can see someone get hurt and not even lift a finger. We're unwilling to get involved because we have no strength within our lives. God has made us human beings, and we absolutely should have convictions. We should be strong, not spineless. We should stand with conviction and not be cowards. To be angry and not sin means there is an end to our anger. And the way to experience that "ending" is to stop feeding it.

The verse continues, "Do not let the sun go down on your wrath." Very plainly, this means don't go to bed angry. Don't ponder it overnight. Don't allow the enemy to gain territory in your life. Ephesians 4:27 says, "Nor give place to the devil." How long can we think about it? When do we have to let the feelings go? Simple—we need to deal with it before we go to bed.

The prevailing attitude of talking about it in the morning is not biblical. We need to talk about it today. We must learn to deal with our differences with other people. We need to learn to listen to one another and be able to talk about what has happened. We cannot carry our anger to bed, where we are apt to think about it, ponder it and give Satan time to build a case against the other person within our heart. To keep feeding our anger is not healthy, according to the Word of God. And the reason why God has laid out this principle is because prolonged anger gets a foothold within our life and affects our emotions and our thinking.

If you are exploding and uptight, it is likely because you have repressed your anger and are unwilling to deal with it. So your emotions explode and you end up hurting or harming others. If your anger has gotten to this point, it's because you are unwilling to live according to the Word of God. For some of us, it's been many, many nights since things have happened to us, but we have held on to our anger and are now bitter and resentful toward other people.

Harboring resentment and bitterness stunts your spiritual growth. The beauty of walking closely with God disappears because you're feeding this anger. Instead of reconciling the anger, letting it go, growing up, dealing with it, putting it to bed and being mature in Christ, you are playing with it in your mind. Because you're feeding this anger, you're giving place to the enemy, and Satan will eventually destroy your life.

So many people hold on to offenses. They are mad about what someone said or did to them 25 years ago. And because they have not let it go, it has festered and grown. We have a responsibility to let things go, to give our actions or words to God, and deal with this heart issue. Guarding against bitterness is of utmost importance. Remember, anger, if ignored, turns into resentment, and resentment turns into bitterness, and bitterness turns into hostility.

## Stop Faking It

Not only do we need to stop feeding our anger, but we also need to stop faking it. "Pastor Steve, what are you talking about when you say to stop faking it?" The Bible says, "Bring your gift to the altar," which means you are going to give something more than a tithe. It might be a gift to missions, or it might be a commitment to do something for God. Whether it's time, talent or treasure, the gift needs to be genuine (real); and if you have not reconciled with those you have wronged, God won't accept the gift!

Matthew 5:23-24 teaches, "Therefore if you bring your gift to the altar, and there remember that your brother has something against you, leave your gift there before the altar, and go your way. First be reconciled to your brother, and then come and offer your gift." In other words, stop faking it. Stop going through the outward motions with an impure heart. When we are worshiping God, and our hands are lifted toward Him in praise and adoration, our hearts must be clean before Him. Or maybe we're studying God's Word or are just hanging out with the Lord, but no matter what we do, something is just not right. Our worship is weak, our devotions are dead, and our fellowship is fractured. Why? The Holy Spirit is telling you or me that something is not right.

What is it? I have found that it is rarely some*thing*, but rather some*one*. It's time to search your heart and then go and be reconciled with that person. Start listening to the voice of the Holy Spirit! He tells us not to go down a certain road. He tells us to back away from a relationship. He tells us to be careful about a situation. Yet, because we do not listen and obey, we make horrible mistakes. We get married to the wrong person. We make investments that are unequally yoked or we get devastated because we can't believe that something happened. Then we blame God, thinking He doesn't care. But God gave a warning. He prompted us to do the right thing, and we didn't listen.

We are responsible for having a heart that is pure before God, and when God begins to show us issues in our life that are not right, He is saying, "Put the gift down. I love the gift, and I want the gift. But if you listen to the Spirit, you will hear Him question how He can receive the gift if you won't even take care of what I've laid upon your heart." For example, if you feel that you've offended your children and all of a sudden in your heart you want to say you're sorry, you need to do that. Or if you've been cutting down your spouse and want to say right then and there, "I'm sorry," then definitely do it. It is critical to act on the conviction in your heart, because the Holy Spirit is revealing it to you.

It might not always be a case in which you have done something wrong. Rather, as you are praying, if you know that a person is struggling because of you, go to him. God wants us to be sensitive to other people. And when we become bitter or resentful, we are no longer sensitive. The Holy Spirit works to make us sensitive to our spouse, our family, our friends, children, boss, and so on. If your heart says, "I don't care," then why should God take your gifts to Him? God is looking for the sensitivity of a heart that is willing to build up the Body of Christ until we all come together in the unity of the faith. When God sees that the gift and the heart are the same, He'll receive the gift every time. But sometimes in our worship, we tell God we love Him, yet secretly, in the depths of our heart, we hate other people! God says, "Leave the gift. I appreciate it, but go take care of the situation, because this thing is destroying your life."

Listen, bitterness will stunt your spiritual growth, and anger will destroy your life. You need to say to the Holy Spirit, "God, I want to grow in Your knowledge and grace. I need help in this area—learning how to deal with my anger."

First, stop feeding the anger. Don't nourish the grudge. Second, stop faking it. Stop pretending that everything is right in your life, and be sensitive and obedient to the voice of the Holy Spirit.

## Stop Following It

Finally, we need to stop following our anger and choose instead to follow peace. Hebrews 12:14-15 exhorts us, "Pursue peace with all people, and holiness, without which no one will see the Lord: looking carefully lest anyone fall short of the grace of God; lest any root of bitterness springing up cause trouble, and by this many become defiled."

We need to follow peace and holiness, and we need to be diligent, looking to the grace of God. But if we are unwilling to both stop feeding our anger and stop faking it, we are not going to be looking for the grace of God. When this happens, anger is going to take root and spring up in bitterness, from which we will defile many.

The Word of God gives an illustration of this progression in the very next verse: "lest there be any fornicator or profane person like Esau, who for one morsel of food sold his birthright" (v. 16). In the book of Genesis, Esau, one of the sons of Isaac, despised his birthright. He did not see the value of it, and so he gave it up. And because he gave it up, Jacob, his younger brother, took it! But that bothered Esau. Bitterness took root, deceit began to sprout and, ultimately, Esau said that he was going to kill Jacob. Esau divided the family and went after Jacob, trying to kill him. The whole situation between Jacob and Esau and their parents was a real mess, but it was all built on this area of deception and anger.

Probably one of the saddest of all the stories in the Bible is found in 2 Samuel 15, about David's son Absalom. Absalom looked to his father, King David, to punish his half-brother Amnon for raping Tamar (Amnon's half-sister and Absalom's full sister). David's son raped his daughter, yet David did nothing about it. Absalom saw that this passivity wasn't right; so he took matters into his own hands and killed Amnon. Because of that murder, King David banished Absalom from the kingdom.

Finally, after many years, David invited Absalom back to his city. The people rejoiced because Absalom was coming home, but David said, "I do not want to see his face." That didn't go over well with the people. David was willing to forgive, but he was unwilling to reconcile. When the people saw David's reaction, their hearts turned away from him and turned toward Absalom. Absalom took advantage of the mood of the people and caused an insurrection to come against David. Thus, King David was driven out of his own kingdom. David was driven from his family, from his kingdom and from his popularity, because he was a bitter man.

That's what happens with anger. It drives you away from being what God wants you to be. It takes away what God wants you to have and it keeps you from all that God wants to do in your life. So what are you going to do about it? You get into a fight with your wife or your children and blow your stack—what are you going to do?

Number one: *You're not going to feed it.* You're not going to ponder or think about it. Instead, you're going to deal with it right off the bat because you know this thing is going to kill you if you don't. You're not going to give the anger an opportunity to grow in your life. You're not going to give Satan a foothold to build a wedge between you and someone else. Rather, you're going to take care of it before you go to bed.

Number two: *You're not going to fake it.* When you're worshiping and God is speaking to your heart about an issue (and you know there's an issue), you realize that you need to do something; you need to be obedient. You need to leave your gift of worship and take care of the situation, being sensitive to the person with whom there is an issue. Then you can come back and say to God, "Thank You, Father, for showing me my heart. I have made that phone call and dealt with this issue. Now, take my gift." And God will take the gift because your heart is in the right place.

Number three: *You need to stop following the anger* and *start following peace.* You need to seek to live peaceably with all men. Why? Otherwise, your bitterness is going to defile many. You need to completely forgive. Ephesians 4:31-32 says, "Let all bitterness, wrath, anger, clamor, and evil speaking be put away from you, with all malice. And be kind to one another, tenderhearted, forgiving one another, just as God in Christ forgave you."

Sin grieves the heart of the Holy Spirit. Why? Because the Holy Spirit comes to build us up. The Holy Spirit comes to mend us. The Holy Spirit comes to love us. And anger destroys all that.

## POINTS TO PONDER

- How do I resolve my anger (repress it, express it or confess it)?
- Do I have healthy anger toward that which is unrighteous?
- Am I feeding my anger, faking it or following the way of peace?
- Is there someone today with whom I need to reconcile?

# 13

# OVERCOMING WORRY

*We are hard-pressed on every side, yet not crushed;*
*we are perplexed, but not in despair; persecuted, but not forsaken;*
*struck down, but not destroyed.*

2 CORINTHIANS 4:8-9

*Worry is one of the monsters that have plagued my life. Early in my ministry, I worried about everything—my sermon messages, my staff, how the church building looked, and so on. Wanting to do things right the first time—worried and fearful of failing—I was insecure and did not trust God. I believe that worry and anxiety began to destroy my life; it definitely affected my health. Gail said to me one day, "Stephen, we have to leave the ministry because you're sick, you're not trusting God, you have no joy and this is not what God wants for our life. So either God has to give you shoulders to bear up under this ministry, or we have to leave it behind, because this cannot be the calling of God on your life." It was one of those moments when I knew she was right. Then and there, God miraculously and compassionately gave me the gift of faith to trust and rest in His peace.*

*Now, because of the gift of faith, when we have a building project or another big project, I don't worry about it. However, if God were to take that gift away, I would worry. As long as I know that God is in the project, I don't have to fret about anything. If I take my eyes off of God, however, then I want to do things myself, which will destroy me.*

*Some people think that God helps those who help themselves, but I think just the opposite is true. God says to me, "I have to stay up all night and take care of things; why don't you go to sleep and leave it to Me?" I know without a doubt that I can't change anything; the providence of God holds my life securely. I can't add a day to my life or an inch to my height by worrying, so I trust God. I don't worry because I can rest in knowing that I am doing what God wants me to do, and He will take care of everything else. I do my best and commit the rest. And even though my best isn't good enough, if I commit it to Him, then He will do it. He will take my water and turn it into wine.*

We live in a society that is filled with immense stress. Furthermore, we absolutely should confess that every one of us, at some time or another, has worried about something. Our personal lives and this crazy world we are living in today are filled with circumstances and situations that concern us. Yet the Bible tells us repeatedly not to worry. When we do worry, we are not trusting God. God really wants us to overcome this state of mind. In 1 Peter 5:7, the apostle Peter tells us what we are to do with all these worries, troubles and fears that often bring great stress and terror into our lives: We are to cast all our care upon Him, because He compassionately cares for us.

In chapter 12, I mentioned how David, in just one moment of folly, made a horrible mistake. He caused the children of Israel to go contrary to his own counsel. In the life of David, on his public side, he showed a pretty impressive ministry; but his personal life was largely a disaster. Sometimes, as we read through the psalms, especially Psalm 77, we see David crying out, "Oh, God, where are You? How long do I have to search for You?" David is often in this horrible state of insecurity and fear, and he's constantly worried about where he's at with the Lord. That's not where God wanted David to be, but because of David's sin, he found himself not right with God. David worried about his position because he had sinned against the Lord. Maybe today, in our hearts, we have to confess that we worry way too much, and we're not giving our anxieties to God.

When we're not in right relationship with God, when we do not trust Him, the natural result is worry. Even though we should be aware of and care about the world in which we live, and about the disastrous things that are occurring, if we know Christ and follow Him with all our heart, then the Bible says we are not to worry about anything (see Matt. 6). We are not to be anxious or terrified about anything.

Fear can destroy our lives. There's only one thing we can do to stop this fear and worry—draw close to Jesus Christ. Remember what He told His disciples, "Guys, we need to come apart for a time of prayer, before we fall apart by the pressures of this world."

For us, we need to give the economy to God. We need to give Him our jobs, or give Him our search for one. We need to give everything we do to God. He will guide, lead and direct us in the way that He wants us to go. Sometimes we have a ministry that looks tremendously strong on the outside when people look at us. But if those onlookers knew how much we worried—about the children, about what's going on, about finances, about the marriage (or being single or not being married or being widowed)—it would be a whole different picture. The Bible states, very simply, that we are not to worry. Instead, we're to trust the Lord with our lives. Jesus said in Matthew 6:25, "Therefore I say to you, do not worry about your life, what you will eat or what you will drink; nor about your body, what you will put on. Is not life more than food and the body more than clothing?" In other words, it's Jesus' responsibility to care for your life and mine.

When we worry or when we are filled with anxiety, we are pulling the responsibility away from God and assuming that responsibility over our own lives. God made a commitment to us the moment we came to know Him—that He would be our God and that we would be His people. He promised to be the Lord of our lives. We would have no need of anything. God would take care of us. We are promised that He knows when every sparrow hits the ground and He knows the number of every hair upon our heads. He knows exactly what's going on. So if we pull back and begin to worry about our day or about tomorrow or about yesterday, then we are basically taking things out of His hands and putting them into our own hands.

Jesus said, "Let not your heart be troubled" (John 14:1). In the Greek, it means, "Let not your heart be terrified." He was saying to the disciples, who were worried (actually, they were terrified) about what was going to happen, "Don't be troubled; don't be terrified; protect your heart and put your concerns back on the Lord." In this world, we're going to have persecution. But "He who is in you is greater than he who is in the world" (1 John 4:4). God is encouraging us, by this promise, to put our trust in Christ and never allow our hearts to become terrified. There are going to be moments of anxiety, and there are going to be fears that arise, but we need to give those things quickly to God.

Paul says, "Be anxious for nothing, but in everything by prayer and supplication, with thanksgiving, let your requests be made known to God" (Phil. 4:6). So, we're not to be anxious for anything in our lives. We're not to worry about ourselves, and we're not to worry about things that are going on. Here are the commands: Don't let your heart panic or become filled with anxiety. Don't be terrified. Don't be anxious for anything. God is holding things together until we figure it out. He knows that we don't understand all that is going on, and so He's going to help us. He's going to put things together. He's going to make sense of our lives. But we must see Jesus as the "Master plan of our heart."

First Peter 5:7 offers these assuring words, "Casting all your care upon Him, for He cares for you." "Casting" implies that we are not to hold on to anything in our lives. We have not been given the ability to hold on to things but to let them go. Great people who do great things for God are those who "let go." They delegate and they facilitate. The moment we begin to hang on, trying to become the "savior" of the world—worried about our children, worried about our marriage—we start to feel anxious and our strength gets zapped. Psalm 55:22 says, "Cast your burden on the LORD, and He shall sustain you; He shall never permit the righteous to be moved." In other words, He'll take care of the emptiness. He'll bring you to a point of security, and He will sustain your life.

So in a nutshell, God is saying that we're not to worry about our lives—that's His responsibility. Paul said, "He gave you His son; how much more will He give you all things freely" (Rom. 8:32, paraphrased). God desires that your heart and mind be at peace. And if your mind is stayed upon the Lord, you're going to have peace in your heart. According to Romans 8:28, "And we know that all things work together for good to those who love God, to those who are the called according to His purpose." Ecclesiastes 3:11 says, "He has made everything beautiful in its time." We have to give God time. He said to Ruth (through Naomi), "Sit still, my daughter, until you know how the matter will turn out" (Ruth 3:18). In other words, God will do the work. We remain silent, and God will speak. We stand, and God will move. God wants us to know that He's going to take care of it.

## Three Keys to Overcoming Worry

How do we overcome worry? There are three simple questions that will really help in this area. Number one: *What are we to do with our worries?* Number two: *How are we to do it?* And number three: *Why are we to do it?*

### What Are We to Do with Our Worries?

When worry or anxiety strikes, what are we to do? Notice how 1 Peter 5:7 answers this question: "Casting all your care upon Him, for

He cares for you." The apostle Peter gives us an illustration of what we're to do with our burdens or problems. The word he uses in the Greek, "to cast," is a unique word: It means "to pick up and throw at." Likely, we are tired of the burdens, tired of the pressures, and we want to get rid of them all, but we don't know who to give them to. Jesus is saying, "Give them to Me. Cast it—throw it to Me." So Peter is exhorting us to take this problem, this anxiety, these children, this husband, this job, this church and throw them all at the feet of Christ.

Ultimately, we are not capable of carrying these problems. We lose our joy. We lose our peace. The voice of God is no longer alive in our hearts because we have been hanging on to our burdens for dear life, but God doesn't want us to do that. We feel that we have to hang on to a problem. So we hang on to our kids and will not let them go, and because we hang on, we then lose our kids. When we are willing to let go of our kids, surrendering them to God, then it's more likely we are going to get them back. God is a better parent than we are. God can work inside of our kids' hearts. And God can get down to the very bottom of the issue. We see only the outside, but God knows the intent and motives of the heart. When we are willing to cast our kids before the Lord, or throw any other situation before God, He begins to work in a wonderful way.

Furthermore, we need to start casting the sin of our past before God as well. "Lord, I have been carrying this sin. I'm tired of it. Lord, You know what I've done. You have forgiven me. Here is my sin." The present, as well, should be cast to God. "Today, whatever happens in my life, God, I want to give it to You." Deuteronomy 33:25 says, "As your days, so shall your strength be."

Finally, concerning the future, we need to give that to God. Only He knows what the future will bring. Instead of worrying about it, we need to entrust our future to God. So, don't keep anything back; start throwing the past, the present and the future to Jesus Christ.

Both 1 Peter 5:7 and Psalm 55:22 tell us to cast not only our cares but also our burdens. In the Hebrew, the word "cast" means "to let go, to relax and to drop." Consider the visual of a weightlifter: When he picks up the weight, his legs begin to buckle, and his knees begin to come out of their joints. He knows that he's in trouble. What does he do? He lets go. And the weight just rolls out of his hands. Similarly, we must give our burdens to God, letting the weight of the burden roll off of us. Pray, "God—these kids, this marriage, this business, Lord, I can't bear it anymore." Then let go. And the moment we let go, God is able to pick up the burden. As it begins to roll off our hands and fingers, God is right there. He picks it up and puts it down. So the first key to overcoming worry is found in answering the question, "What do we do with our worries?" We have to cast our anxiety, our point of worry, to God, who will take it and turn it around in His time. We must give our burdens to God.

## How Are We to Do It?

How are we to cast our cares and burdens at the Lord's feet? Paul says, in Philippians 4:6, "Be anxious for nothing, but in everything by prayer and supplication, with thanksgiving, let your requests be made known to God." So the answer is to pray, asking earnestly and humbly, and with thanksgiving. What are the results? "The peace of God, which surpasses all understanding, will guard your hearts and minds through Christ Jesus" (Phil. 4:7). We need to start expressing to God how we feel and what's going on in our hearts. We should tell Him how upset we are about a situation. He already knows our hearts anyway. We're good at telling everybody else, but we need to tell God!

I believe that we need to come to a point at which we can come before God and say, "I am not happy with this whole situation." This honesty won't be a problem for God. In the book of John, chapter 11, Martha said, very simply, to Jesus, "Where were You? If You would have been here, my brother would not have died" (John 11:21, paraphrased). Jesus replied, "Martha, Martha. I'm the resurrection and the life. Roll away the stone from the tomb." She said, "But, Lord, he stinks."

Jesus: "Martha, I thought you believed."

Martha: "I do, but he still stinks."

Jesus: "Martha, roll that thing away. Lazarus, come forth."

And Lazarus came forth.

Sometimes we believe that the power of this story is in the resurrection of Lazarus. And it is. But it's easy to gloss over the fact that Jesus listened to Martha griping and complaining and making accusations against Him, yet He still had compassion on her! Just as Martha was talking to Jesus, God wants us to talk to Him, to pour out our hearts to Him. When we pray, "God, I don't understand. We've raised the kids the right way. We've been involved in their lives. What in the world is going on?"—God will speak back. He'll tell us exactly what we need to hear. By prayer and by supplication, we begin to overcome worry.

I remember a time early in my marriage when God said, "Pray for a car." I responded, "I can't pray for a car. I'm a pastor; I can't pray for carnal things." But we were in need and making only $25 per week. It was my first church as a pastor. And God said, "Pray for a car." Finally, I obeyed and prayed for a car. Within eight hours, a man knocked on the door and said, "You've been praying for a car?" I hesitatingly said, "Yeah." Handing me the keys to a brand-new car, he said, "Here are the keys. There's only one condition." In my mind, I thought, *Yeah, always a condition.* But I asked, "What is it?" He replied, "You need to drive me home. I have no way home."

Immediately I thought, *Oh, God, forgive me.* So what did I learn? I learned that God is in the car business. In fact, God is in any business that has to do with us—His children! We need to learn to talk to God. Too often we don't let God into our lives. Oh, we love God, we worship God, but we don't have time to talk to God. I want you to know that you need to cast your burdens; you need to share the burdens with Him and start talking to God in prayer. "Lord, here are my kids. God, here's my wife. God, here's my church. God, here's my finances." Talk to God about everything and watch what He does.

## Why Are We to Do It?

Why are we to cast our cares on God? Very simply, we are to cast our cares on God because He cares for us. First Peter 5:7 bears repeating: "Casting all your care upon Him, for He cares for you." Sometimes we don't like ourselves. Sometimes we don't like looking in the mirror. Sometimes we don't like the way we think or the way we're acting, and sometimes we're probably right about that. Our attitude probably really stinks. We might not really be friendly. We might have a tendency to be nasty and selfish. But in the midst of all that, God still cares. What He's saying is this: "Even if you don't care, I do care. So give Me the problem." Our response: "Well, Lord, no one wants this problem." He will always respond: "I do; give it to Me." God does care. And because He cares, we can cast our burdens on Him.

There are moments in my life when I get discouraged, depressed or become overwhelmed. I don't know what to do with my life. Is it time to move? Is it time to stay? What am I to do? I begin to say to myself, *Well, I just don't know what to do anymore. The pressure's too great.* And then I hear this voice, "Stephen, you don't care right now about anything except yourself. But I care about your future, about what you're doing here. You need to give Me the problem." When I give it to Him, I miraculously find peace. He's the One who really cares for my soul. Jesus Christ cares for us, and so we are able to give Him all our burdens.

A second reason why we're to cast our cares on God is because He sustains. Psalm 55:22 says, "Cast your burden on the LORD, and He shall sustain you." In other words, when you are empty and there's nothing left in your heart to give—there's no longer the ability to love your spouse, to go that second mile with your kids, or to get up and go back to work again—God wants you to know that He is your strength. He'll sustain you. He'll satisfy you. He'll put the longing in your heart. He'll satisfy the need deep within your life.

You might pray, "God, I can't go one more day." His response: "My child, I know that, but you know something? I care, and I'll be your strength. I'll sustain you. I'll fill your cup."

"Lord, I've been in sin."

"My child, I'll fill your cup, because I love you. And My love is so committed to you that I care for you, I'll sustain you and I'll fill you up."

Truthfully, God will get you through each day. And when you go to bed, you will think, *How did I get through this day?* It wasn't you, but God sustaining you. The third reason we are to cast our cares upon Him is because God keeps us. Philippians 4:7 says, "And the peace of God, which surpasses all understanding, will guard your hearts and minds through Christ Jesus." Sometimes we want nothing to do with the pressure, and we have been taught to walk away. We don't know how to face issues. We don't know how to deal with problems, so we run from them. Our hearts are often worried that everything is going to turn out bad in our lives.

But how in the world can we think this way if we have a God who cares, a God who sustains and a God who will keep us? In other words, what in the world can go wrong?

I read a statistic the other day that 85 percent of the things we worry about will never come to pass. Worry is Satan's way of robbing us of joy. So here's my challenge to you: I want you to make a commitment before God. Say, "Father, today I will learn to cast my cares and let go of my burdens at Your feet. So, God, take everything that is robbing my joy and killing my flesh and destroying my life. God, You take it, because I'm not capable. I'm losing heart. I want to start talking to You. I want to tell You what's going on in my heart. I need You to tell me it's okay." And then tell Him, "God, I know You care. You will sustain me and You will keep me in the midst of my problems. So no more worries. I'm going to trust You."

## POINTS TO PONDER

- What is keeping me from trusting God?
- What burden does God want me to cast upon Him today?
- Right now, can I trade my worry for His perfect peace— and rest in Him?

# CONCLUSION

What are you trying to overcome in your life today?

Have you been trying to change but feel like you keep slamming your head against a wall? Do you keep failing? Have you tried every 12-step program, self-help book and positive thinking exercise there is, only to come up short?

I want to encourage you to start with the right foundation—a personal relationship with Jesus Christ.

Only God, working in and through you, can give you the victory of overcoming.

Do you know Jesus Christ as your personal Savior? If not, pour your heart out to the Lord and say the following prayer:

*Dear Jesus, I admit that I am a sinner, and I ask You to forgive me of my sins. I ask You to come into my heart and fill me with the power of the Holy Spirit. Write my name in the Book of Life. Help me right now to surrender all to Your authority. Fill me with Your joy, and open my eyes to see Your love. In Jesus' name, amen.*

Welcome to the family of God!

In order to grow in your faith, I encourage you to find a good Bible-teaching church to attend and become a part of the fellowship. And I encourage you to start reading God's Word on a daily basis. Start in the Gospel of John, which is in the New Testament. If you need a Bible or other resources to help you in your walk with Christ, please contact my office at 310-352-3333.

If you are a believer, but you have become lukewarm in your walk with God, I encourage you to get back into God's Word and start praying on a daily basis. Get back into fellowship with other believers so that you have that encouragement and accountability.

The Lord wants you to live a victorious Christian walk and will supply you with the power and the ability to overcome some of life's most difficult problems. Walk closely with the Lord and you will be able to get above and beyond life's overwhelming circumstances.

# SCRIPTURE REFERENCE GUIDE

## CHAPTER 1:

## Overcoming Discouragement

**Joshua 1:9:** "Have I not commanded you? Be strong and of good courage; do not be afraid, nor be dismayed, for the LORD your God is with you wherever you go."

**Psalm 43:5:** "Why are you cast down, O my soul? And why are you disquieted within me? Hope in God; for I shall yet praise Him, the help of my countenance and my God."

**Isaiah 40:31:** "But those who wait on the LORD shall renew their strength; they shall mount up with wings like eagles, they shall run and not be weary, they shall walk and not faint."

**Isaiah 41:10:** "Fear not, for I am with you; be not dismayed, for I am your God. I will strengthen you, yes, I will help you, I will uphold you with My righteous right hand."

**Jeremiah 29:11:** "For I know the thoughts that I think toward you, says the LORD, thoughts of peace and not of evil, to give you a future and a hope."

**Matthew 6:25-34:** "Therefore I say to you, do not worry about your life, what you will eat or what you will drink; nor about your body, what you will put on. Is not life more than food and the body more than clothing? Look at the birds of the air, for they neither sow nor reap nor gather into barns; yet your heavenly Father feeds them. Are you not of more value than they? Which of you by worrying can add one cubit to his stature?

So why do you worry about clothing? Consider the lilies of the field, how they grow: they neither toil nor spin; and yet I say to you that even Solomon in all his glory was not arrayed like one of these. Now if God so clothes the grass of the field, which today is, and tomorrow is thrown into the oven, will He not much more clothe you, O you of little faith?

Therefore do not worry, saying, 'What shall we eat?' or 'What shall we drink?' or 'What shall we wear?' For after all these things the Gentiles seek. For your heavenly Father knows that you need all these things. But seek first the kingdom of God and His righteousness, and all these things shall be added to you. Therefore do not worry about tomorrow, for tomorrow will worry about its own things. Sufficient for the day is its own trouble."

**John 14:1:** "Let not your heart be troubled; you believe in God, believe also in Me."

**John 14:27:** "Peace I leave with you, My peace I give to you; not as the world gives do I give to you. Let not your heart be troubled, neither let it be afraid."

**Romans 5:3-5:** "And not only that, but we also glory in tribulations, knowing that tribulation produces perseverance; and perseverance, character; and character, hope. Now hope does not disappoint, because the love of God has been poured out in our hearts by the Holy Spirit who was given to us."

**1 Corinthians 10:13:** "No temptation has overtaken you except such as is common to man; but God is faithful, who will not allow you to be tempted beyond what you are able, but with the temptation will also make the way of escape, that you may be able to bear it."

**1 Corinthians 15:58:** "Therefore, my beloved brethren, be steadfast, immovable, always abounding in the work of the Lord, knowing that your labor is not in vain in the Lord."

**2 Corinthians 9:8:** "And God is able to make all grace abound toward you, that you, always having all sufficiency in all things, may have an abundance for every good work."

**Galatians 6:9:** "And let us not grow weary while doing good, for in due season we shall reap if we do not lose heart."

**Ephesians 6:10:** "Finally, my brethren, be strong in the Lord and in the power of His might."

**Philippians 4:13:** "I can do all things through Christ who strengthens me."

**Hebrews 6:10:** "For God is not unjust to forget your work and labor of love which you have shown toward His name, in that you have ministered to the saints, and do minister."

**Hebrews 12:2:** "Looking unto Jesus, the author and finisher of our faith, who for the joy that was set before Him endured the cross, despising the shame, and has sat down at the right hand of the throne of God."

**1 Peter 1:6-9:** "In this you greatly rejoice, though now for a little while, if need be, you have been grieved by various trials, that the genuineness of your faith, being much more precious than gold that perishes, though it is tested by fire, may be found to praise, honor, and glory at the revelation of Jesus Christ, whom having not seen you love. Though now you do not see Him, yet believing, you rejoice with joy inexpressible and full of glory, receiving the end of your faith—the salvation of your souls."

**James 1:2-4:** "My brethren, count it all joy when you fall into various trials, knowing that the testing of your faith produces patience. But let patience have its perfect work, that you may be perfect and complete, lacking nothing."

**James 1:12:** "Blessed is the man who endures temptation; for when he has been approved, he will receive the crown of life which the Lord has promised to those who love Him."

CHAPTER 2:

# Overcoming Suffering

**Psalm 23:4:** "Yea, though I walk through the valley of the shadow of death, I will fear no evil; for You are with me; Your rod and Your staff, they comfort me."

**Psalm 46:1-11:** "God is our refuge and strength, a very present help in trouble. Therefore we will not fear, even though the earth be removed, and though the mountains be carried into the midst of the sea; though its waters roar and be troubled, though the mountains shake with its swelling. *Selah*

There is a river whose streams shall make glad the city of God, the holy place of the tabernacle of the Most High. God is in the midst of her, she shall not be moved; God shall help her, just at the break of dawn. The nations raged, the kingdoms were moved; he uttered His voice, the earth melted. The Lord of hosts is with us; the God of Jacob is our refuge. *Selah*

Come, behold the works of the Lord, who has made desolations in the earth. He makes wars cease to the end of the earth; he breaks the bow and cuts the spear in two; he burns the chariot in the fire. Be still, and know that I am God; I will be exalted among the nations, I will be exalted in the earth! The Lord of hosts is with us; the God of Jacob is our refuge. *Selah*"

**Psalm 62:1-2:** "Truly my soul silently waits for God; from Him comes my salvation. He only is my rock and my salvation; he is my defense; I shall not be greatly moved."

**Psalm 73:26:** "My flesh and my heart fail; but God is the strength of my heart and my portion forever."

**Psalm 103:1-4:** "Bless the LORD, O my soul; and all that is within me, bless His holy name! Bless the LORD, O my soul, and forget not all His benefits: Who forgives all your iniquities, who heals all your diseases, who redeems your life from destruction, who crowns you with lovingkindness and tender mercies."

**Psalm 119:71-72:** "It is good for me that I have been afflicted, that I may learn Your statutes. The law of Your mouth is better to me than thousands of coins of gold and silver."

**Isaiah 63:7-9:** "I will mention the lovingkindnesss of the LORD and the praises of the LORD, according to all that the LORD has bestowed on us, and the great goodness toward the house of Israel, which He has bestowed on them according to His mercies, according to the multitude of His lovingkindness. For He said, 'Surely they are My people, children who will not lie.' So He became their Savior. In all their affliction He was afflicted, and the Angel of His Presence saved them; in His love and in His pity He redeemed them; and He bore them and carried them all the days of old."

**Lamentations 3:1-24:** "I am the man who has seen affliction by the rod of His wrath. He has led me and made me walk in darkness and not in light. Surely He has turned His hand against me time and time again throughout the day. He has aged my flesh and my skin, and broken my bones. He has besieged me and surrounded me with bitterness and woe. He has set me in dark places like the dead of long ago. He has hedged me in so that I cannot get out; he has made my chain heavy. Even when I cry and shout, he shuts out my prayer. He has blocked my ways with hewn stone; he has made my paths crooked. He has been to me a bear lying in wait, like a lion in ambush. He has turned aside my ways and torn me in pieces; he has made me desolate. He has bent His bow and set me up as a target for the arrow. He has caused the arrows of His quiver to pierce my loins. I have become the ridicule of all my people—their taunting song all the day. He has filled me with bitterness, he has made me drink wormwood. He has also broken my teeth with gravel, and covered me with ashes. You have moved my soul far from peace; I have forgotten prosperity. And I said, 'My strength and my hope have perished from the LORD.' Remember my affliction and roaming, the wormwood and the gall. My soul still remembers and sinks within me. This I recall to my mind, therefore I have hope. Through the LORD's mercies we are not consumed, because His compassions fail not. They are new every morning; great is Your faithfulness. 'The LORD is my portion,' says my soul, 'Therefore I hope in Him!' "

**Matthew 6:25-34:** "Therefore I say to you, do not worry about your life, what you will eat or what you will drink; nor about your body, what you will put on. Is not life more than food and the body more than clothing? Look at the birds of the air, for they neither sow nor reap nor gather into barns; yet your heavenly Father feeds them. Are you not of more value than they? Which of you by worrying can add one cubit to his stature?

So why do you worry about clothing? Consider the lilies of the field, how they grow: they neither toil nor spin; and yet I say to you that even Solomon in all his glory was not arrayed like one of these. Now if God so clothes the grass of the field, which today is, and tomorrow is thrown into the oven, will He not much more clothe you, O you of little faith?

Therefore do not worry, saying, 'What shall we eat?' or 'What shall we drink?' or 'What shall we wear?' For after all these things the Gentiles seek. For your heavenly Father knows that you need all these things. But seek first the kingdom of God and His righteousness, and all these things shall be added to you. Therefore do not worry about tomorrow, for tomorrow will worry about its own things. Sufficient for the day is its own trouble."

**John 14:1-3:** "Let not your heart be troubled; you believe in God, believe also in Me. In My Father's house are many mansions; if it were not so, I would have told you. I go to prepare a place for you. And if I go and prepare a place for you, I will come again and receive you to Myself; that where I am, there you may be also."

**Romans 5:3-5:** "And not only that, but we also glory in tribulations, knowing that tribulation produces perseverance; and perseverance, character; and character, hope. Now hope does not disappoint, because the love of God has been poured out in our hearts by the Holy Spirit who was given to us."

**Romans 8:18:** "For I consider that the sufferings of this present time are not worthy to be compared with the glory which shall be revealed in us."

**2 Corinthians 1:3-11:** "Blessed be the God and Father of our Lord Jesus Christ, the Father of mercies and God of all comfort, who comforts us in all our tribulation, that we may be able to comfort those who are in any trouble, with the comfort with which we ourselves are comforted by God. For as the sufferings of Christ abound in us, so our consolation also abounds through Christ. Now if we are afflicted, it is for your consolation and salvation, which is effective for enduring the same sufferings which we also suffer. Or if we are comforted, it is for your consolation and salvation.

And our hope for you is steadfast, because we know that as you are partakers of the sufferings, so also you will partake of the consolation. For we do not want you to be ignorant, brethren, of our trouble which came to us in Asia: that we were burdened beyond measure, above strength, so that we despaired even of life. Yes, we had the sentence of death in ourselves, that we should not trust in ourselves but in God who raises the dead, who delivered us from so great a death, and does deliver us; in whom we trust that He will still deliver us, you also helping together in prayer for us, that thanks may be given by many persons on our behalf for the gift granted to us through many."

**2 Corinthians 12:9-10:** "And He said to me, 'My grace is sufficient for you, for My strength is made perfect in weakness.' Therefore most gladly I will rather boast in my infirmities, that the power of Christ may rest upon me. Therefore I take pleasure in infirmities, in reproaches, in needs, in persecutions, in distresses, for Christ's sake. For when I am weak, then I am strong."

**Philippians 4:6-7:** "Be anxious for nothing, but in everything by prayer and supplication, with thanksgiving, let your requests be made known to God; and the peace of God, which surpasses all understanding, will guard your hearts and minds through Christ Jesus."

**2 Thessalonians 1:1-12:** "Paul, Silvanus, and Timothy, to the church of the Thessalonians in God our Father and the Lord Jesus Christ: Grace to you and peace from God our Father and the Lord Jesus Christ.

We are bound to thank God always for you, brethren, as it is fitting, because your faith grows exceedingly, and the love of every one of you all abounds toward each other, so that we ourselves boast of you among the churches of God for your patience and faith in all your persecutions and tribulations that you endure, which is manifest evidence of the righteous judgment of God, that you may be counted worthy of the kingdom of God, for which you also suffer; since it is a righteous thing with God to repay with tribulation those who trouble you, and to give you who are troubled rest with us when the Lord Jesus is revealed from heaven with His mighty angels, in flaming fire taking vengeance on those who do not know God, and on those who do not obey the gospel of our Lord Jesus Christ. These shall be punished with everlasting destruction from the presence of the Lord and from the glory of His power, when He comes, in that Day, to be glorified in His saints and to be admired among all those who believe, because our testimony among you was believed.

Therefore we also pray always for you that our God would count you worthy of this calling, and fulfill all the good pleasure of His goodness and the work of faith with power, that the name of our Lord Jesus Christ may be glorified in you, and you in Him, according to the grace of our God and the Lord Jesus Christ."

**James 1:2-4:** "My brethren, count it all joy when you fall into various trials, knowing that the testing of your faith produces patience. But let patience have its perfect work, that you may be perfect and complete, lacking nothing."

**James 1:12:** "Blessed is the man who endures temptation; for when he has been approved, he will receive the crown of life which the Lord has promised to those who love Him."

**1 Peter 1:6-7:** "In this you greatly rejoice, though now for a little while, if need be, you have been grieved by various trials, that the genuineness of your faith, being much more precious than gold that perishes, though it is tested by fire, may be found to praise, honor, and glory at the revelation of Jesus Christ."

**1 Peter 4:12-19:** "Beloved, do not think it strange concerning the fiery trial which is to try you, as though some strange thing happened to you; but rejoice to the extent that you partake of Christ's sufferings, that when His glory is revealed, you may also be glad with exceeding joy. If you are reproached for the name of Christ, blessed are you, for the Spirit of glory and of God rests upon you. On their part He is blasphemed, but on your part He is glorified. But let none of you suffer as a murderer, a thief, an evildoer, or as a busybody in other people's matters. Yet if anyone suffers as a Christian, let him not be ashamed, but let him glorify God in this matter.

For the time has come for judgment to begin at the house of God; and if it begins with us first, what will be the end of those who do not obey the gospel of God? Now 'If the righteous one is scarcely saved, where will the ungodly and the sinner appear?' Therefore let those who suffer according to the will of God commit their souls to Him in doing good, as to a faithful Creator."

**1 Peter 3:17:** "For it is better, if it is the will of God, to suffer for doing good than for doing evil."

**1 Peter 5:10:** "But may the God of all grace, who called us to His eternal glory by Christ Jesus, after you have suffered awhile, perfect, establish, strengthen, and settle you."

**1 John 4:4:** "You are of God, little children, and have overcome them, because He who is in you is greater than he who is in the world."

CHAPTER 3:

# Overcoming Depression

**Psalm 40:1-3:** "I waited patiently for the LORD; and He inclined to me, and heard my cry. He also brought me up out of a horrible pit, out of the miry clay, and set my feet upon a rock, and established my steps. He has put a new song in my mouth—praise to our God; many will see it and fear, and will trust in the LORD."

**Psalm 42:5-6:** "Why are you cast down, O my soul? And why are you disquieted within me? Hope in God, for I shall yet praise Him for the help of His countenance. O my God, my soul is cast down within me; therefore I will remember You from the land of the Jordan, and from the heights of Hermon, from the Hill Mizar."

**Psalm 55:22:** "Cast your burden on the LORD, and He shall sustain you; he shall never permit the righteous to be moved."

**Psalm 91:1-16:** "He who dwells in the secret place of the Most High shall abide under the shadow of the Almighty. I will say of the LORD, 'He is my refuge and my fortress; my God, in Him I will trust.'

Surely He shall deliver you from the snare of the fowler and from the perilous pestilence. He shall cover you with His feathers, and under His wings you shall take refuge; his truth shall be your shield and buckler. You shall not be afraid of the terror by night, nor of the arrow that flies by day, nor of the pestilence that walks in darkness, nor of the destruction that lays waste at noonday.

A thousand may fall at your side, and ten thousand at your right hand; but it shall not come near you. Only with your eyes shall you look, and see the reward of the wicked.

Because you have made the Lord, who is my refuge, even the Most High, your dwelling place, No evil shall befall you, nor shall any plague come near your dwelling; for He shall give His angels charge over you, to keep you in all your ways. In their hands they shall bear you up, lest you dash your foot against a stone. You shall tread upon the lion and the cobra, the young lion and the serpent you shall trample underfoot.

'Because he has set his love upon Me, therefore I will deliver him; I will set him on high, because he has known My name. He shall call upon Me, and I will answer him; I will be with him in trouble; I will deliver him and honor him. With long life I will satisfy him, and show him My salvation.' "

**Psalm 116:1-9:** "I love the LORD, because He has heard my voice and my supplications. Because He has inclined His ear to me, therefore I will call upon Him as long as I live. The pains of death surrounded me, and the pangs of Sheol laid hold of me; I found trouble and sorrow. Then I called upon the name of the LORD: 'O LORD, I implore You, deliver my soul!' Gracious is the LORD, and righteous; yes, our God is merciful. The LORD preserves the simple; I was brought low, and He saved me. Return to your rest, O my soul, for the LORD has dealt bountifully with you. For You have delivered my soul from death, my eyes from tears, and my feet from falling. I will walk before the LORD in the land of the living."

**Matthew 5:4:** "Blessed are those who mourn, for they shall be comforted."

**Matthew 6:25-34:** "Therefore I say to you, do not worry about your life, what you will eat or what you will drink; nor about your body, what you will put on. Is not life more than food and the body more than clothing? Look at the birds of the air, for they neither sow nor reap nor gather into barns; yet your heavenly Father feeds them. Are you not of more value than they? Which of you by worrying can add one cubit to his stature?

So why do you worry about clothing? Consider the lilies of the field, how they grow: they neither toil nor spin; and yet I say to you that even Solomon in all his glory was not arrayed like one of these. Now if God so clothes the grass of the field, which today is, and tomorrow is thrown into the oven, will He not much more clothe you, O you of little faith?

Therefore do not worry, saying, 'What shall we eat?' or 'What shall we drink?' or 'What shall we wear?' For after all these things the Gentiles seek. For your heavenly Father knows that you need all these things. But seek first the kingdom of God and His righteousness, and all these things shall be added to you. Therefore do not worry about tomorrow, for tomorrow will worry about its own things. Sufficient for the day is its own trouble."

**Matthew 10:30-31:** "But the very hairs of your head are all numbered. Do not fear therefore; you are of more value than many sparrows."

**Matthew 11:28-30:** "Come to Me, all you who labor and are heavy laden, and I will give you rest. Take My yoke upon you and learn from Me, for I am gentle and lowly in heart, and you will find rest for your souls. For My yoke is easy and My burden is light."

**Matthew 28:20:** "Teaching them to observe all things that I have commanded you; and lo, I am with you always, even to the end of the age."

**John 3:16:** "For God so loved the world that He gave His only begotten Son, that whoever believes in Him should not perish but have everlasting life."

**John 14:1:** "Let not your heart be troubled; you believe in God, believe also in Me."

**Romans 8:28:** "And we know that all things work together for good to those who love God, to those who are the called according to His purpose."

**Romans 8:38-39:** "For I am persuaded that neither death nor life, nor angels nor principalities nor powers, nor things present nor things to come, nor height nor depth, nor any other created thing, shall be able to separate us from the love of God which is in Christ Jesus our Lord."

**2 Corinthians 1:3-11:** "Blessed be the God and Father of our Lord Jesus Christ, the Father of mercies and God of all comfort, who comforts us in all our tribulation, that we may be able to comfort those who are in any trouble, with the comfort with which we ourselves are comforted by God. For as the sufferings of Christ abound in us, so our consolation also abounds through Christ. Now if we are afflicted, it is for your consolation and salvation, which is effective for enduring the same sufferings which we also suffer. Or if we are comforted, it is for your consolation and salvation. And our hope for you is steadfast, because we know that as you are partakers of the sufferings, so also you will partake of the consolation.

For we do not want you to be ignorant, brethren, of our trouble which came to us in Asia: that we were burdened beyond measure, above strength, so that we despaired even of life. Yes, we had the sentence of death in ourselves, that we should not trust in ourselves but in God who raises the dead, who delivered us from so great a death, and does deliver us; in whom we trust that He will still deliver us, you also helping together in prayer for us, that thanks may be given by many persons on our behalf for the gift granted to us through many."

**2 Corinthians 4:8-9:** "We are hard pressed on every side, yet not crushed; we are perplexed, but not in despair; persecuted, but not forsaken; struck down, but not destroyed."

**2 Corinthians 12:9:** "And He said to me, 'My grace is sufficient for you, for My strength is made perfect in weakness.' Therefore most gladly I will rather boast in my infirmities, that the power of Christ may rest upon me."

**Philippians 4:6-7:** "Be anxious for nothing, but in everything by prayer and supplication, with thanksgiving, let your requests be made

known to God; and the peace of God, which surpasses all understanding, will guard your hearts and minds through Christ Jesus."

**1 Peter 5:7:** "Casting all your care upon Him, for He cares for you."

**Revelation 21:4:** "And God will wipe away every tear from their
eyes; there shall be no more death, nor sorrow, nor crying. There
shall be no more pain, for the former things have passed away."

CHAPTER 4:

# Overcoming Fear

**Joshua 1:9:** "Have I not commanded you? Be strong and of good
courage; do not be afraid, nor be dismayed, for the LORD your God
is with you wherever you go."

**Psalm 23:4:** "Yea, though I walk through the valley of the shadow
of death, I will fear no evil; for You are with me; your rod and Your
staff, they comfort me."

**Psalm 27:1:** "The LORD is my light and my salvation; whom shall I
fear? The LORD is the strength of my life; of whom shall I be afraid?"

**Psalm 27:14:** "Wait on the LORD; be of good courage, and He shall
strengthen your heart; wait, I say, on the LORD!"

**Psalm 34:4:** "I sought the LORD, and He heard me, and delivered me
from all my fears."

**Psalm 56:11:** "In God I have put my trust; I will not be afraid. What
can man do to me?"

**Psalm 91:1-7:** "He who dwells in the secret place of the Most High shall
abide under the shadow of the Almighty. I will say of the LORD, 'He is
my refuge and my fortress; my God, in Him I will trust.' Surely He shall
deliver you from the snare of the fowler and from the perilous pestilence. He shall cover you with His feathers, and under His wings you

shall take refuge; his truth shall be your shield and buckler. You shall not be afraid of the terror by night, nor of the arrow that flies by day, nor of the pestilence that walks in darkness, nor of the destruction that lays waste at noonday. A thousand may fall at your side, and ten thousand at your right hand; but it shall not come near you."

**Psalm 91:10-11:** "No evil shall befall you, nor shall any plague come near your dwelling; for He shall give His angels charge over you, to keep you in all your ways."

**Proverbs 1:33:** "But whoever listens to me will dwell safely, and will be secure, without fear of evil."

**Proverbs 3:25-26:** "Do not be afraid of sudden terror, nor of trouble from the wicked when it comes; for the LORD will be your confidence, and will keep your foot from being caught."

**Proverbs 29:25:** "The fear of man brings a snare, but whoever trusts in the LORD shall be safe."

**2 Chronicles 20:15:** "And he said, 'Listen, all you of Judah and you inhabitants of Jerusalem, and you, King Jehoshaphat! Thus says the LORD to you: Do not be afraid nor dismayed because of this great multitude, for the battle is not yours, but God's.' "

**Isaiah 35:4:** "Say to those who are fearful-hearted, 'Be strong, do not fear! Behold, your God will come with vengeance, with the recompense of God; he will come and save you.' "

**Isaiah 41:10:** "Fear not, for I am with you; be not dismayed, for I am your God. I will strengthen you, yes, I will help you, I will uphold you with My righteous right hand."

**John 14:27:** "Peace I leave with you, My peace I give to you; not as the world gives do I give to you. Let not your heart be troubled, neither let it be afraid."

**Romans 8:15:** "For you did not receive the spirit of bondage again to fear, but you received the Spirit of adoption by whom we cry out, 'Abba, Father.' "

**Hebrews 13:6:** "So we may boldly say: 'The Lord is my helper; I will not fear. What can man do to me?' "

**2 Timothy 1:7:** "For God has not given us a spirit of fear, but of power and of love and of a sound mind."

**1 John 4:18:** "There is no fear in love; but perfect love casts out fear, because fear involves torment. But he who fears has not been made perfect in love."

CHAPTER 5:

# Overcoming Distraction: The Divided Heart

**Genesis 4:7:** "If you do well, will you not be accepted? And if you do not do well, sin lies at the door. And its desire is for you, but you should rule over it."

**Joshua 1:8:** "This Book of the Law shall not depart from your mouth, but you shall meditate in it day and night, that you may observe to do according to all that is written in it. For then you will make your way prosperous, and then you will have good success."

**2 Chronicles 20:15-17:** "And he said, 'Listen, all you of Judah and you inhabitants of Jerusalem, and you, King Jehoshaphat! Thus says the LORD to you: Do not be afraid nor dismayed because of this great multitude, for the battle is not yours, but God's. Tomorrow go down against them. They will surely come up by the Ascent of Ziz, and you will find them at the end of the brook before the Wilderness of Jeruel. You will not need to fight in this battle. Position yourselves, stand still and see the salvation of the LORD, who is with you, O Judah and Jerusalem! Do not fear or be dismayed; tomorrow go out against them, for the LORD is with you."

**Psalm 119:15-16:** "I will meditate on Your precepts, and contemplate Your ways. I will delight myself in Your statutes; I will not forget Your word."

**Proverbs 3:5-6:** "Trust in the LORD with all your heart, and lean not on your own understanding; In all your ways acknowledge Him, and He shall direct your paths."

**Isaiah 26:3:** "You will keep him in perfect peace, whose mind is stayed on You, because he trusts in You."

**Isaiah 54:17:** " 'No weapon formed against you shall prosper, and every tongue which rises against you in judgment you shall condemn. This is the heritage of the servants of the LORD, and their righteousness is from Me,' says the LORD."

**Matthew 6:34:** "Therefore do not worry about tomorrow, for tomorrow will worry about its own things. Sufficient for the day is its own trouble."

**Luke 10:38-42:** "Now it happened as they went that He entered a certain village; and a certain woman named Martha welcomed Him into her house. And she had a sister called Mary, who also sat at Jesus' feet and heard His word. But Martha was distracted with much serving, and she approached Him and said, 'Lord, do You not care that my sister has left me to serve alone? Therefore tell her to help me.' And Jesus answered and said to her, 'Martha, Martha, you are worried and troubled about many things. But one thing is needed, and Mary has chosen that good part, which will not be taken away from her.' "

**Philippians 4:8:** "Finally, brethren, whatever things are true, whatever things are noble, whatever things are just, whatever things are pure, whatever things are lovely, whatever things are of good report, if there is any virtue and if there is anything praiseworthy—meditate on these things."

**Philippians 4:13:** "I can do all things through Christ who strengthens me."

**Romans 8:28:** "And we know that all things work together for good to those who love God, to those who are the called according to His purpose."

**Romans 12:1-2:** "I beseech you therefore, brethren, by the mercies of God, that you present your bodies a living sacrifice, holy, acceptable to God, which is your reasonable service. And do not be conformed to this world, but be transformed by the renewing of your mind, that you may prove what is that good and acceptable and perfect will of God."

**1 Corinthians 7:35:** "And this I say for your own profit, not that I may put a leash on you, but for what is proper, and that you may serve the Lord without distraction."

**1 Corinthians 10:13:** "No temptation has overtaken you except such as is common to man; but God is faithful, who will not allow you to be tempted beyond what you are able, but with the temptation will also make the way of escape, that you may be able to bear it."

**Hebrews 12:1-2:** "Therefore we also, since we are surrounded by so great a cloud of witnesses, let us lay aside every weight, and the sin which so easily ensnares us, and let us run with endurance the race that is set before us, looking unto Jesus, the author and finisher of our faith, who for the joy that was set before Him endured the cross, despising the shame, and has sat down at the right hand of the throne of God."

**2 Timothy 2:15:** "Be diligent to present yourself approved to God, a worker who does not need to be ashamed, rightly dividing the word of truth."

**1 John 2:15-17:** "Do not love the world or the things in the world. If anyone loves the world, the love of the Father is not in him. For all that is in the world—the lust of the flesh, the lust of the eyes, and the pride of life—is not of the Father but is of the world. And the world is passing away, and the lust of it; but he who does the will of God abides forever."

## CHAPTER 6:
# Overcoming Selfishness

**Proverbs 11:26:** "The people will curse him who withholds grain, but blessing will be on the head of him who sells it."

**Proverbs 28:27:** "He who gives to the poor will not lack, but he who hides his eyes will have many curses."

**Isaiah 56:11:** "Yes, they are greedy dogs which never have enough. And they are shepherds who cannot understand; they all look to their own way, every one for his own gain, from his own territory."

**Matthew 19:21-22:** "Jesus said to him, 'If you want to be perfect, go, sell what you have and give to the poor, and you will have treasure in heaven; and come, follow Me.' But when the young man heard that saying, he went away sorrowful, for he had great possessions."

**Luke 6:32-34:** "But if you love those who love you, what credit is that to you? For even sinners love those who love them. And if you do good to those who do good to you, what credit is that to you? For even sinners do the same. And if you lend to those from whom you hope to receive back, what credit is that to you? For even sinners lend to sinners to receive as much back."

**1 Corinthians 10:24:** "Let no one seek his own, but each one the other's well-being."

**1 Corinthians 10:33:** "Just as I also please all men in all things, not seeking my own profit, but the profit of many, that they may be saved."

**2 Corinthians 8:9:** "For you know the grace of our Lord Jesus Christ, that though He was rich, yet for your sakes He became poor, that you through His poverty might become rich."

**Romans 15:1-2:** "We then who are strong ought to bear with the scruples of the weak, and not to please ourselves. Let each of us please his neighbor for his good, leading to edification."

**Galatians 6:2:** "Bear one another's burdens, and so fulfill the law of Christ."

**Philippians 2:4:** "Let each of you look out not only for his own interests, but also for the interests of others."

**Philippians 2:3:** "Let nothing be done through selfish ambition or conceit, but in lowliness of mind let each esteem others better than himself."

**James 2:15-16:** "If a brother or sister is naked and destitute of daily food, and one of you says to them, 'Depart in peace, be warmed and filled,' but you do not give them the things which are needed for the body, what does it profit?"

**James 3:14-16:** "But if you have bitter envy and self-seeking in your hearts, do not boast and lie against the truth. This wisdom does not descend from above, but is earthly, sensual, and demonic. For where envy and self-seeking exist, confusion and every evil thing are there."

**1 John 3:17:** "But whoever has this world's goods, and sees his brother in need, and shuts up his heart from him, how does the love of God abide in him?"

## CHAPTER 7:
# Overcoming Criticism and Opposition

**Proverbs 19:3:** "The foolishness of a man twists his way, and his heart frets against the LORD."

**Matthew 5:11-12:** "Blessed are you when they revile and persecute you, and say all kinds of evil against you falsely for My sake. Rejoice and be exceedingly glad, for great is your reward in heaven, for so they persecuted the prophets who were before you."

**Matthew 7:1-5:** "Judge not, that you be not judged. For with what judgment you judge, you will be judged; and with the measure you use, it will be measured back to you. And why do you look at the speck in your brother's eye, but do not consider the plank in your own eye? Or how can you say to your brother, 'Let me remove the speck from your eye'; and look, a plank is in your own eye? Hypocrite! First remove the plank from your own eye, and then you will see clearly to remove the speck out of your brother's eye."

**Matthew 18:6:** "But whoever causes one of these little ones who believe in Me to sin, it would be better for him if a millstone were hung around his neck, and he were drowned in the depth of the sea."

**Romans 1:29-32:** "Being filled with all unrighteousness, sexual immorality, wickedness, covetousness, maliciousness; full of envy, murder, strife, deceit, evil-mindedness; they are whisperers, backbiters, haters of God, violent, proud, boasters, inventors of evil things, disobedient to parents, undiscerning, untrustworthy, unloving, unforgiving, unmerciful; who, knowing the righteous judgment of God, that those who practice such things are worthy of death, not only do the same but also approve of those who practice them."

**Romans 2:1-2:** "Therefore you are inexcusable, O man, whoever you are who judge, for in whatever you judge another you condemn yourself; for you who judge practice the same things. But we know that the judgment of God is according to truth against those who practice such things."

**Romans 14:10:** "But why do you judge your brother? Or why do you show contempt for your brother? For we shall all stand before the judgment seat of Christ."

**1 Corinthians 2:14:** "But the natural man does not receive the things of the Spirit of God, for they are foolishness to him; nor can he know them, because they are spiritually discerned."

**Ephesians 4:29:** "Let no corrupt word proceed out of your mouth, but what is good for necessary edification, that it may impart grace to the hearers."

**Ephesians 6:12:** "For we do not wrestle against flesh and blood, but against principalities, against powers, against the rulers of the darkness of this age, against spiritual hosts of wickedness in the heavenly places."

**Ephesians 6:14:** "Stand therefore, having girded your waist with truth, having put on the breastplate of righteousness."

**2 Timothy 3:16:** "All Scripture is given by inspiration of God, and is profitable for doctrine, for reproof, for correction, for instruction in righteousness."

**Hebrews 11:6:** "But without faith it is impossible to please Him, for he who comes to God must believe that He is, and that He is a rewarder of those who diligently seek Him."

**Hebrews 12:14-15:** "Pursue peace with all people, and holiness, without which no one will see the Lord: looking diligently lest anyone fall short of the grace of God; lest any root of bitterness springing up cause trouble, and by this many become defiled."

**James 1:19-20:** "So then, my beloved brethren, let every man be swift to hear, slow to speak, slow to wrath; for the wrath of man does not produce the righteousness of God."

**James 1:26-27:** "If anyone among you thinks he is religious, and does not bridle his tongue but deceives his own heart, this one's religion is useless. Pure and undefiled religion before God and the Father is this: to visit orphans and widows in their trouble, and to keep oneself unspotted from the world."

**2 Peter 3:3-4:** "That scoffers will come in the last days, walking according to their own lusts, and saying, 'Where is the promise of His coming? For since the fathers fell asleep, all things continue as they were from the beginning of creation.' "

**2 Peter 3:9:** "The Lord is not slack concerning His promise, as some count slackness, but is longsuffering toward us, not willing that any should perish but that all should come to repentance."

CHAPTER 8:
# Overcoming Jealousy

**Song of Solomon 8:6:** "Set me as a seal upon your heart, as a seal upon your arm; for love is as strong as death, jealousy as cruel as the grave; its flames are flames of fire, a most vehement flame."

**Psalm 37:1:** "Do not fret because of evildoers, nor be envious of the workers of iniquity."

**Proverbs 3:31:** "Do not envy the oppressor, and choose none of his ways."

**Proverbs 27:4:** "Wrath is cruel and anger a torrent, but who is able to stand before jealousy?"

**Titus 3:3:** "For we ourselves were also once foolish, disobedient, deceived, serving various lusts and pleasures, living in malice and envy, hateful and hating one another."

**James 3:16:** "For where envy and self-seeking exist, confusion and every evil thing are there."

**Romans 13:13-14:** "Let us walk properly, as in the day, not in revelry and drunkenness, not in lewdness and lust, not in strife and envy, but put on the Lord Jesus Christ, and make no provision for the flesh, to fulfill its lusts."

**1 Timothy 6:4:** "He is proud, knowing nothing, but is obsessed with disputes and arguments over words, from which come envy, strife, reviling, evil suspicions."

**Galatians 5:16-18:** "Walk in the Spirit, and you shall not fulfill the lust of the flesh. For the flesh lusts against the Spirit, and the Spirit against the flesh; and these are contrary to one another, so that you do not do the things that you wish. But if you are led by the Spirit, you are not under the law."

**Galatians 5:19-20:** "Now the works of the flesh are evident, which are: adultery, fornication, uncleanness, lewdness, idolatry, sorcery, hatred, contentions, jealousies, outbursts of wrath, selfish ambitions, dissensions, heresies."

**Titus 3:3-6:** "For we ourselves were also once foolish, disobedient, deceived, serving various lusts and pleasures, living in malice and envy, hateful and hating one another. But when the kindness and the love of God our Savior toward man appeared, not by works of righteousness which we have done, but according to His mercy He saved us, through the washing of regeneration and renewing of the Holy Spirit, whom He poured out on us abundantly through Jesus Christ our Savior."

**1 Peter 2:1-2:** "Therefore, laying aside all malice, all guile, hypocrisy, envy, and all evil speaking, as newborn babes, desire the pure milk of the word, that you may grow thereby."

CHAPTER 9:

# Overcoming Weakness

**Psalm 31:24:** "Be of good courage, and He shall strengthen your heart, all you who hope in the LORD."

**Psalm 34:17-20:** "The righteous cry out, and the LORD hears, and delivers them out of all their troubles. The LORD is near to those who have a broken heart, and saves such as have a contrite spirit. Many are the afflictions of the righteous, but the LORD delivers him out of them all. He guards all his bones; not one of them is broken."

**Psalm 145:14:** "The LORD upholds all who fall, and raises up all who are bowed down."

**Isaiah 35:3-4:** "Strengthen the weak hands, and make firm the feeble knees. Say to those who are fearful-hearted, 'Be strong, do not fear! Behold, your God will come with vengeance, with the recompense of God; he will come and save you.'"

**Jeremiah 17:9:** "The heart is deceitful above all things, and desperately wicked; who can know it?"

**Jeremiah 17:10:** "I, the LORD, search the heart, I test the mind, even to give every man according to his ways, according to the fruit of his doings."

**Matthew 7:1-2:** "Judge not, that you be not judged. For with what judgment you judge, you will be judged; and with the measure you use, it will be measured back to you."

**Matthew 26:41:** "Watch and pray, lest you enter into temptation. The spirit indeed is willing, but the flesh is weak."

**Luke 18:1:** "Then He spoke a parable to them, that men always ought to pray and not lose heart."

**Romans 8:26:** "Likewise the Spirit also helps in our weaknesses. For we do not know what we should pray for as we ought, but the Spirit Himself makes intercession for us with groanings which cannot be uttered."

**Romans 12:19:** "Beloved, do not avenge yourselves, but rather give place to wrath; for it is written, 'Vengeance is Mine, I will repay,' says the Lord."

**1 Corinthians 1:26-29:** "For you see your calling, brethren, that not many wise according to the flesh, not many mighty, not many noble, are called. But God has chosen the foolish things of the world to put to shame the wise, and God has chosen the weak things of the world to put to shame the things which are mighty; and the base things of the world and the things which are despised God has chosen, and the things which are not, to bring to nothing the things that are, that no flesh should glory in His presence."

**2 Corinthians 12:9-10:** "And He said to me, 'My grace is sufficient for you, for My strength is made perfect in weakness.' Therefore most gladly I will rather boast in my infirmities, that the power of Christ may rest upon me. Therefore I take pleasure in infirmities, in reproaches, in needs, in persecutions, in distresses, for Christ's sake. For when I am weak, then I am strong."

**2 Corinthians 13:4:** "For though He was crucified in weakness, yet He lives by the power of God. For we also are weak in Him, but we shall live with Him by the power of God toward you."

**Philippians 4:19:** "And my God shall supply all your need according to His riches in glory by Christ Jesus."

**1 John 4:17-18:** "Love has been perfected among us in this: that we may have boldness in the day of judgment; because as He is, so are we in this world. There is no fear in love; but perfect love casts out fear, because fear involves torment. But he who fears has not been made perfect in love."

## CHAPTER 10:
# Overcoming Deception

**Proverbs 12:5:** "The thoughts of the righteous are right, but the counsels of the wicked are deceitful."

**Matthew 24:4-5:** "And Jesus answered and said to them: 'Take heed that no one deceives you. For many will come in My name, saying, "I am the Christ," and will deceive many.' "

**Romans 16:18:** "For those who are such do not serve our Lord Jesus Christ, but their own belly, and by smooth words and flattering speech deceive the hearts of the simple."

**1 Corinthians 3:18:** "Let no one deceive himself. If anyone among you seems to be wise in this age, let him become a fool that he may become wise."

**1 Corinthians 6:9-10:** "Do you not know that the unrighteous will not inherit the kingdom of God? Do not be deceived. Neither fornicators, nor idolaters, nor adulterers, nor homosexuals, nor sodomites, nor thieves, nor covetous, nor drunkards, nor revilers, nor extortioners will inherit the kingdom of God."

**1 Corinthians 15:33:** "Do not be deceived: 'Evil company corrupts good habits.' "

**Galatians 6:3-4:** "For if anyone thinks himself to be something, when he is nothing, he deceives himself. But let each one examine his own work, and then he will have rejoicing in himself alone, and not in another."

**Galatians 6:7:** "Do not be deceived, God is not mocked; for whatever a man sows, that he will also reap."

**Ephesians 4:14:** "That we should no longer be children, tossed to and fro and carried about with every wind of doctrine, by the trickery of men, in the cunning craftiness of deceitful plotting."

**Ephesians 5:6:** "Let no one deceive you with empty words, for because of these things the wrath of God comes upon the sons of disobedience."

**2 Thessalonians 2:3:** "Let no one deceive you by any means; for that Day will not come unless the falling away comes first, and the man of sin is revealed, the son of perdition."

**2 Timothy 3:13:** "But evil men and impostors will grow worse and worse, deceiving and being deceived."

CHAPTER 11:
# Overcoming Irresponsibility

**Exodus 20:16:** "You shall not bear false witness against your neighbor."

**Leviticus 19:19:** "You shall keep My statutes. You shall not let your livestock breed with another kind. You shall not sow your field with mixed seed. Nor shall a garment of mixed linen and wool come upon you."

**Deuteronomy 23:21-23:** "When you make a vow to the LORD your God, you shall not delay to pay it; for the LORD your God will surely require it of you, and it would be sin to you. But if you abstain from vowing, it shall not be sin to you. That which has gone from your lips you shall keep and perform, for you voluntarily vowed to the LORD your God what you have promised with your mouth."

**Proverbs 2:1-5:** "My son, if you receive my words, and treasure my commands within you, So that you incline your ear to wisdom, and apply your heart to understanding; Yes, if you cry out for discernment, and lift up your voice for understanding, If you seek her as silver, and search for her as for hidden treasures; Then you will understand the fear of the LORD, and find the knowledge of God."

**Proverbs 6:16-19:** "These six things the LORD hates, yes, seven are an abomination to Him: A proud look, a lying tongue, hands that shed innocent blood, a heart that devises wicked plans, feet that are swift in running to evil, a false witness who speaks lies, and one who sows discord among brethren."

**Jeremiah 17:9:** "The heart is deceitful above all things, and desperately wicked; who can know it?"

**Matthew 12:37:** "For by your words you will be justified, and by your words you will be condemned."

**Matthew 15:18-20:** "But those things which proceed out of the mouth come from the heart, and they defile a man. For out of the heart proceed evil thoughts, murders, adulteries, fornications, thefts, false witness, blasphemies. These are the things which defile a man, but to eat with unwashed hands does not defile a man."

**John 8:43-47:** "Why do you not understand My speech? Because you are not able to listen to My word. You are of your father the devil, and the desires of your father you want to do. He was a murderer from the beginning, and does not stand in the truth, because there is no truth in him. When he speaks a lie, he speaks from his own resources, for he is a liar and the father of it. But because I tell the truth, you do not believe Me. Which of you convicts Me of sin? And if I tell the truth, why do you not believe Me? He who is of God hears God's words; therefore you do not hear, because you are not of God."

**1 Corinthians 10:13:** "No temptation has overtaken you except such as is common to man; but God is faithful, who will not allow you to be tempted beyond what you are able, but with the temptation will also make the way of escape, that you may be able to bear it."

**Romans 12:2:** "And do not be conformed to this world, but be transformed by the renewing of your mind, that you may prove what is that good and acceptable and perfect will of God."

**Romans 12:17-21:** "Repay no one evil for evil. Have regard for good things in the sight of all men. If it is possible, as much as depends on you, live peaceably with all men. Beloved, do not avenge your-selves, but rather give place to wrath; for it is written, 'Vengeance is Mine, I will repay,' says the Lord. Therefore 'If your enemy is hun-gry, feed him; if he is thirsty, give him a drink; for in so doing you will heap coals of fire on his head.' Do not be overcome by evil, but overcome evil with good."

**2 Corinthians 5:17:** "Therefore, if anyone is in Christ, he is a new creation; old things have passed away; behold, all things have be-come new."

**Ephesians 4:14-16:** "That we should no longer be children, tossed to and fro and carried about with every wind of doctrine, by the trickery of men, in the cunning craftiness of deceitful plotting, but, speaking the truth in love, may grow up in all things into Him who is the head—Christ—from whom the whole body, joined and knit together by what every joint supplies, according to the effective working by which every part does its share, causes growth of the body for the edifying of itself in love."

**Ephesians 4:30-32:** "And do not grieve the Holy Spirit of God, by whom you were sealed for the day of redemption. Let all bitterness, wrath, anger, clamor, and evil speaking be put away from you, with all malice. And be kind to one another, tenderhearted, forgiving one another, just as God in Christ forgave you."

**Colossians 3:9-10:** "Do not lie to one another, since you have put off the old man with his deeds, and have put on the new man who is re-newed in knowledge according to the image of Him who created him."

**2 Timothy 2:15:** "Be diligent to present yourself approved to God, a worker who does not need to be ashamed, rightly dividing the word of truth."

**James 5:12:** "But above all, my brethren, do not swear, either by heaven or by earth or with any other oath. But let your 'Yes,' be 'Yes,' and your 'No,' 'No,' lest you fall into judgment."

**2 Peter 3:9:** "The Lord is not slack concerning His promise, as some count slackness, but is longsuffering toward us, not willing that any should perish but that all should come to repentance."

**1 John 1:9:** "If we confess our sins, He is faithful and just to forgive us our sins and to cleanse us from all unrighteousness."

**1 John 2:1-3:** "My little children, these things I write to you, so that you may not sin. And if anyone sins, we have an Advocate with the Father, Jesus Christ the righteous. And He Himself is the propitiation for our sins, and not for ours only but also for the whole world. Now by this we know that we know Him, if we keep His commandments."

**1 John 2:16:** "For all that is in the world—the lust of the flesh, the lust of the eyes, and the pride of life—is not of the Father but is of the world."

**1 John 5:16:** "If anyone sees his brother sinning a sin which does not lead to death, he will ask, and He will give him life for those who commit sin not leading to death. There is sin leading to death. I do not say that he should pray about that."

**Revelation 21:7-8:** "He who overcomes shall inherit all things, and I will be his God and he shall be My son. But the cowardly, unbelieving, abominable, murderers, sexually immoral, sorcerers, idolaters, and all liars shall have their part in the lake which burns with fire and brimstone, which is the second death."

CHAPTER 12:

# Overcoming Anger

**Leviticus 19:17:** "You shall not hate your brother in your heart. You shall surely rebuke your neighbor, and not bear sin because of him."

**Psalm 69:14:** "Deliver me out of the mire, and let me not sink; let me be delivered from those who hate me, and out of the deep waters."

**Psalm 119:104:** "Through Your precepts I get understanding; therefore I hate every false way."

**Proverbs 8:13:** "The fear of the LORD is to hate evil; pride and arrogance and the evil way and the perverse mouth I hate."

**Isaiah 1:16-18:** "Wash yourselves, make yourselves clean; put away the evil of your doings from before My eyes. Cease to do evil, learn to do good; seek justice, rebuke the oppressor; defend the fatherless, plead for the widow. 'Come now, and let us reason together,' says the LORD, 'Though your sins are like scarlet, they shall be as white as snow; though they are red like crimson, they shall be as wool.' "

**Isaiah 55:7:** "Let the wicked forsake his way, and the unrighteous man his thoughts; let him return to the LORD, and He will have mercy on him; and to our God, for He will abundantly pardon."

**Zechariah 8:17:** " 'Let none of you think evil in your heart against your neighbor; and do not love a false oath. For all these are things that I hate,' says the LORD."

**Matthew 6:14-15:** "For if you forgive men their trespasses, your heavenly Father will also forgive you. But if you do not forgive men their trespasses, neither will your Father forgive your trespasses."

**Luke 23:34:** "Then Jesus said, 'Father, forgive them, for they do not know what they do.' "

**Romans 12:14-21:** "Bless those who persecute you; bless and do not curse. Rejoice with those who rejoice, and weep with those who weep. Be of the same mind toward one another. Do not set your mind on high things, but associate with the humble. Do not be wise in your own opinion. Repay no one evil for evil. Have regard for good things in the sight of all men. If it is possible, as much as depends on you, live peaceably with all men. Beloved, do not avenge yourselves, but rather give place to wrath; for it is written, 'Vengeance is Mine, I will repay,' says the Lord. 'Therefore if your enemy is hungry, feed him; if he is thirsty, give him a drink; for in so doing you will heap coals of fire on his head.' Do not be overcome by evil, but overcome evil with good."

**Hebrews 12:14-15:** "Pursue peace with all people, and holiness, without which no one will see the Lord: looking diligently lest anyone fall short of the grace of God; lest any root of bitterness springing up cause trouble, and by this many become defiled."

**Colossians 3:8:** "But now you yourselves are to put off all these: anger, wrath, malice, blasphemy, filthy language out of your mouth."

**Titus 3:2-5:** "To speak evil of no one, to be peaceable, gentle, showing all humility to all men. For we ourselves were also once foolish, disobedient, deceived, serving various lusts and pleasures, living in malice and envy, hateful and hating one another. But when the kindness and the love of God our Savior toward man appeared, not by works of righteousness which we have done, but according to His mercy He saved us, through the washing of regeneration and renewing of the Holy Spirit."

**Ephesians 4:31-32:** "Let all bitterness, wrath, anger, clamor, and evil speaking be put away from you, with all malice. And be kind to one another, tenderhearted, forgiving one another, just as God in Christ forgave you."

**1 Peter 2:23:** "Who, when He was reviled, did not revile in return; when He suffered, He did not threaten, but committed Himself to Him who judges righteously."

1 John 4:20: "If someone says, 'I love God,' and hates his brother, he is a liar; for he who does not love his brother whom he has seen, how can he love God whom he has not seen?"

CHAPTER 13

# Overcoming Worry

Deuteronomy 33:12: "Of Benjamin he said: 'The beloved of the LORD shall dwell in safety by Him, who shelters him all the day long; and he shall dwell between His shoulders.' "

Psalm 4:8: "I will both lie down in peace, and sleep; for You alone, O LORD, make me dwell in safety."

Psalm 27:1: "The LORD is my light and my salvation; whom shall I fear? The LORD is the strength of my life; of whom shall I be afraid?"

Psalm 37:8: "Cease from anger, and forsake wrath; do not fret—it only causes harm."

Proverbs 1:33: "But whoever listens to me will dwell safely, and will be secure, without fear of evil."

Proverbs 3:25-26: "Do not be afraid of sudden terror, nor of trouble from the wicked when it comes; For the LORD will be your confidence, and will keep your foot from being caught."

Proverbs 18:10: "The name of the LORD is a strong tower; the righteous run to it and are safe."

Isaiah 26:3: "You will keep him in perfect peace, whose mind is stayed on You, because he trusts in You."

Isaiah 54:10: " 'For the mountains shall depart and the hills be removed, but My kindness shall not depart from you, nor shall My covenant of peace be removed,' says the LORD, who has mercy on you."

**Matthew 6:25-34:** "Therefore I say to you, do not worry about your life, what you will eat or what you will drink; nor about your body, what you will put on. Is not life more than food and the body more than clothing? Look at the birds of the air, for they neither sow nor reap nor gather into barns; yet your heavenly Father feeds them. Are you not of more value than they? Which of you by worrying can add one cubit to his stature?

So why do you worry about clothing? Consider the lilies of the field, how they grow: they neither toil nor spin; and yet I say to you that even Solomon in all his glory was not arrayed like one of these. Now if God so clothes the grass of the field, which today is, and tomorrow is thrown into the oven, will He not much more clothe you, O you of little faith?

Therefore do not worry, saying, 'What shall we eat?' or 'What shall we drink?' or 'What shall we wear?' For after all these things the Gentiles seek. For your heavenly Father knows that you need all these things. But seek first the kingdom of God and His righteousness, and all these things shall be added to you. Therefore do not worry about tomorrow, for tomorrow will worry about its own things. Sufficient for the day is its own trouble."

**Matthew 6:33:** "But seek first the kingdom of God and His righteousness, and all these things shall be added to you."

**Matthew 11:28-30:** "Come to Me, all you who labor and are heavy laden, and I will give you rest. Take My yoke upon you and learn from Me, for I am gentle and lowly in heart, and you will find rest for your souls. For My yoke is easy and My burden is light."

**John 16:33:** "These things I have spoken to you, that in Me you may have peace. In the world you will have tribulation; but be of good cheer, I have overcome the world."

**Romans 8:28:** "And we know that all things work together for good to those who love God, to those who are the called according to His purpose."

**Philippians 4:6-7:** "Be anxious for nothing, but in everything by prayer and supplication, with thanksgiving, let your requests be made known to God; and the peace of God, which surpasses all understanding, will guard your hearts and minds through Christ Jesus."

**Philippians 4:13:** "I can do all things through Christ who strengthens me."

**Philippians 4:19:** "And my God shall supply all your need according to His riches in glory by Christ Jesus."

**2 Timothy 1:7:** "For God has not given us a spirit of fear, but of power and of love and of a sound mind."

**1 Peter 5:6-7:** "Therefore humble yourselves under the mighty hand of God, that He may exalt you in due time, casting all your care upon Him, for He cares for you."

**1 John 4:18:** "There is no fear in love; but perfect love casts out fear, because fear involves torment. But he who fears has not been made perfect in love."

# LIGHT OF THE
# WORD

*The Teaching Ministry of Pastor Steve Mays*

Hear the Word. Experience the Light.

## LISTEN TO THE TEACHING MINISTRY OF PASTOR STEVE MAYS
## CHECK YOUR LOCAL CHRISTIAN RADIO STATION

*"...In the times we are living, it is so difficult to find pastors that are really committed to the Lord like you. You are a great blessing to me. Your preaching is so clear, so truthful and sincere and so beautiful because you always put the Lord first." S.P.*

**LIGHT OF THE WORD**
P.O. Box 300 • Torrance, California 90507 • 800-339-WISE • lightoftheword.org

# OTHER RESOURCES BY STEVE MAYS

### A Heartbeat From Hell

BKSMAYHEA    $6.00    ISBN 0-9761478-1-5

At one point in his life, Steve Mays was desperate, hopeless, and sleeping in gutters. A .38-caliber bullet had penetrated his left leg. The authorities wanted him for questioning regarding a recent shooting. Then one day something happened; Steve became a new man. His whole life changed. This booklet was birthed from the life story of a man who at one point was a heartbeat from hell but by God's grace made a choice for life. Steve Mays has learned, and continues to learn to this day, that God has a wonderful plan and purpose for all people who choose life.

### A Un Latido del Infierno

BKSMAYLATI    $6.00    ISBN 978-0-9826042-0-5

En ciertomomento de su vida Steve Mays estaba desesperado, sin esperanza alguna y durmiendo en las cunetas de las calles. Una bala calibre 38, había traspasado su pierna izquierda. Entonces un día algo pasó; Steve se transformó en un hombre nuevo. Su vida cambió completamente. Éste libreto surgió con la historia de un hombre que a un punto estaba a *Un Latido del Infierno*, pero por la gracia de Dios hizo una decisión por la vida. Steve Mays ha aprendido y continúa aprendiendo hasta hoy que Dios tiene un plan maravilloso y propósito para toda persona que hace una decisión por la vida.

### Choices

BKSMAYCHO    $7.00    ISBN 0-9761478-0-7

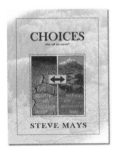

We all make CHOICES. But the choices you make today will determine the outcome of your future. Using the Old Testament book of Joshua, chapter 24 as his text, Steve Mays takes an in-depth look at the choices that knock at the door of our lives daily, and the impact those choices have in life. Steve gives practical counsel to challenge and encourage you to make good and effective decisions. You will discover that good decisions bring deeper dedication to the Lord, which will result in greater joy and peace. It's time to make good choices...start today!

### Crossing the Line

BKSMAYCRO    $8.00    ISBN 978-0-9826042-1-2

Only one step separates you from giving up your beliefs and yielding to a life of compromise. Are you willing to surrender your convictions for one moment of sin and selfishness—or will you trust God and live in obedience to His Spirit? Steve Mays presents a fresh look at how Samson's self-centered life hurt not only him, but also those around him. Samson knew the blessings of God, but chose to waste his life away, ending in apparent defeat and brokenness. But God was not done with His servant. In the end, God took a wasted life and made it a trophy of His grace.

All prices subject to change without notice.

## ALSO BY GINA HYAMS

*Country Living Decorating with White*

*Pie Contest in a Box: Everything You Need to Host a Pie Contest*

*Chili Cook-Off in a Box: Everything You Need to Host a Chili Cook-Off*

*Christmas Cookie Contest in a Box: Everything You Need to Host a Christmas Cookie Contest*

*Searching for Mary Poppins: Women Write About the Intense Relationship Between Mothers and Nannies*

*In a Mexican Garden: Courtyards, Pools, and Open-Air Living Rooms*

*The Campfire Collection: Thrilling, Chilling Tales of Alien Encounters*

*Pacific Spas: Luxury Getaways on the West Coast*

*Incense: Rituals, Mystery, Lore*

*Mexicasa: The Enchanting Inns and Haciendas of Mexico*

*Day of the Dead Box*

# The Tanglewood Picnic

The Tanglewood lawn wasn't always the manicured expanse that it is today.
Photo by BSO Archives/Howard S. Babbitt, Jr., circa 1946. Used by permission of the Babbitt family.

Opposite: Eve Dowling, age two, hitches a ride in her family's wagon. Photo by Sara Paul, 2014.

# The Tanglewood Picnic
## Music and Outdoor Feasts in the Berkshires

Gina Hyams

**MUDDY
PUPPY
MEDIA**

Housatonic
San Miguel de Allende

Grateful acknowledgment is made to the photographers and writers or their
families for permission to publish their photographs and words. Every reasonable
effort has been made to contact the copyright holders and secure permissions, as
well as to identify the people pictured and the dates of the images. Omissions can
be remedied in future editions.


Designed by Christopher Hixson

Muddy Puppy Media
tanglewoodpicnic@gmail.com
TanglewoodPicnic.com

Wholesale representative:
Janet McKean
JAM@janetlostandfound.com
(919) 949-1161
JanetLostAndFound.com

Library of Congress Cataloging-in-Publication Data is available upon request.
ISBN-10: 0692357580
ISBN-13: 978-0692357583
Manufactured in the United States of America by Worzalla.

10 9 8 7 6 5 4 3 2


Typeset in Ainslie, designed in 2013 by Jeremy Dooley.

Front cover photo by *Berkshire Eagle/*William F. Plouffe, circa 1965.
Front cover photo tinting by Christopher Hixson.
Title page photo of a Berlin Flyer "Original" wagon, courtesy Berlin Flyer Wagons.
Back cover picnic photo courtesy Arthur Provenz, 2014.
Back cover author photo by Carrie Snyder.

Opposite: Photo by
Edward Acker, 2013.

For Dave and Annalena Barrett,
and in memory of Milton Bass

Ken and Robin Koval and Diane and Arthur Provenz toast to friendship at Tanglewood, 2014. Photo courtesy Arthur Provenz.

# TABLE OF CONTENTS

# FOREWORD

I remember going to Tanglewood all the time with my grandparents when I was a kid. We'd often arrive on the late side, just as the light would scoop behind the Shed enough to set into motion the great sweep of candlelight all across the lawn. We'd weave through the blankets, simultaneously looking up for a spot and down so we wouldn't step on anyone. The smell of candles and matches would take over right then, with green grass and roast chicken and fancy perfume all together.

My grandmother had a little brown quilted blanket she was so proud of—I think she'd bought it at the Tanglewood gift shop way back, just to treat herself. It was a floral pattern, and just big enough, and it folded

up into a matching quilted tote bag with an equally matching scratchy pillow. We'd set up our little picnic, usually canned salmon and bagel slices and a salad my grandfather had dressed at home. They didn't drink, so there wasn't any wine. But I'd wander on my own through the blankets, looking for the grandest spreads. I'd hover around the wide tables with fine linens and candelabras. I felt like I was being allowed to see royalty. But then I'd always make my way back to our little brown quilted blanket. My grandparents would wrap me up, and I'd stare at the stars and fall asleep to Aaron Copland. It was heaven.

The Tanglewood lawn is truly inclusive. It's open to everyone who wants to participate, and the wonders of each blanket contribute to the experience of those blankets all around it.

Photo by BSO Archives/Minot A. Beale, circa late 1950s.

Look at any little square of grass on a packed Saturday night in August, and you'll see all the elements: a young family on an old quilt, unwrapping sandwiches and reaching into a bag of potato chips; a catered white linen-covered table surrounded by friends who make the trek up from New York every year for the all-Mozart program; a man sitting alone on a low chair with a thermos of soup and the *New York Times*. It's like a party where guests can arrive in pajamas or ball gowns, and all are celebrated for coming just in the manner that suits them.

These days, I have the great privilege of taking my own kids to Tanglewood. Our favorite time to go is for the open rehearsals on Saturday mornings, when the orchestra practices for the next day's concert. One of my favorite days I can remember started there just this past summer. I'd made a nectarine cake, which we brought in its pan, wrapped up in our old picnic basket. Our spread was simple: just the cake, some fruit, a thermos of coffee for the grownups.

My younger daughter spread out her sketchbook and pens, and there, listening to Yo-Yo Ma, she drew portraits of each tree around her. My older daughter ate her cake, and stretched out on her back with her eyes on the sky. She murmured, "This must be the most perfect place there is."

In fact, it just might be.

Alana Chernila
Great Barrington, MA

Picnickers viewed from the stage during a concert by the National Youth Orchestra of the United States at Ozawa Hall. Photo by Douglass Taft Davidoff, 2014.

# INTRODUCTION

When you ask people to describe Tanglewood picnics, more often than not, the first word they say is "magic." The experience of picnicking on the lawn clearly adds up to something that's greater than the sum of its parts.

To picnic at Tanglewood is to participate in a grand tradition. Since 1937, music lovers have flocked to the Boston Symphony Orchestra's summer home in Lenox, Massachusetts, to picnic during concerts. The 526-acre campus is a picnicker's paradise of sweeping lawns, woods, and a formal garden. Both the Koussevitzky Music Shed (a.k.a. "the Shed") and Seiji Ozawa Hall are open sided, designed so that the music pours out of the concert halls to be shared with patrons sitting in the cheap seats on the grass.

The place is imbued with a brilliant sense of artistic history and, for many, a poignant feeling of personal legacy. The tradition of picnicking at Tanglewood is passed down through generations like a beloved family heirloom. While researching this book, I met countless people who were first introduced to Tanglewood as children and who now share the experience with their own children and grandchildren.

There's a profound sense of tranquility on the Tanglewood lawn. You might battle a little traffic to get there, but once you get situated on your picnic blanket, everything seems right with the world. You slow down and connect with your companions or, as the case may be, with the *New York Times* crossword puzzle, surrounded by the bucolic Berkshire landscape and breathing in the fresh country air.

Martha Rumplik of Blue Heaven Turkey Farm, at Tanglewood, circa 1940s. Photo courtesy Nanci McConnell.

In the old days, simple picnics of sandwiches, soda, and cookies from Blue Heaven Turkey Farm, Samel's Deli, and Angelina's Subs were the norm. Alfresco dining at Tanglewood took a gourmet turn in the 1970s and '80s with the establishment of Nejaime's Wine Cellars, Crosby Catering, and Guido's Fresh Marketplace.

This book is a collective love letter to the tradition of Tanglewood picnics. It contains 150 photographs of picnickers from the 1940s through the present from the Boston Symphony Orchestra Archives and from audience members' family scrapbooks, plus a dozen classic recipes and the ultimate picnic checklist of tips compiled from expert Tanglewood picnickers. I hope it serves as both a tribute to past picnics and as inspiration for future ones.

Happy picnicking!

Opposite: Photo by Erika Stone, circa 1950.

"There is something timeless about Tanglewood picnics—the way that generations are brought together rain or shine, scattered amidst a patchwork of blankets." —Caitlin Towers

Photo by Lincoln Russell, 1978.

TANGLEWOOD PICNIC MENU INSPIRATION

Top: Photo by BSO Archives/Walter H. Scott, 1976.
Used by permission of the Scott family.
Bottom: Robin Grigg Tillotson dancing with her son,
Ian Church. Photo by Rick Tillotson, 2003.

Maureen Shambo. Photo by Al Saggese, 2014.

Top: Photo by Kathleen Drohan, 2012.
Bottom: Photo by Erika Stone, 1986.

Photo by *Berkshire Eagle*/R. Joel Librizzi, 1960.

"Thank God there are still some immutable things in this world: summer twilight with its darting swallows and softening skies; the damp grass beneath the patchwork quilt; the fragrance of Beaujolais and Blue Stilton and fresh baguettes.

The sounding of the A, the orchestra tuning, the hush of murmured conversation.

A savored repast under a canopy of just the Berkshire sky, fickle but for tonight, fair and seductive.

The Boston Symphony, elegant in white and black, pours forth its sound, signaling the start of the evening's main event?

Or maybe not; maybe this ritual, housed in wicker baskets and lit by candelabra vies for the main attraction. Picnics at Tanglewood."

—Caroline "Kim" Taylor

Country Curtains facilities assistant Chris Chamberlin and vice president of human resources Rebecca Riordan serving up whiskey sour punch at the 2014 Christmas picnic held during Tanglewood on Parade in August. Photo by Gina Hyams, 2014.

# COUNTRY CURTAINS TANGLEWOOD PICNIC WHISKEY SOUR PUNCH

Country Curtains has held its annual employee Christmas party at Tanglewood since 1968. Company founders Jane and Jack Fitzpatrick established the "Christmas at the Pops" tradition because they thought the December holiday season was so packed with parties, Christmas in the summertime would be a treat. They decorated their Tanglewood company picnics with red and green balloons, holiday napkins, and candles—a custom that continues today. Sometimes, even Santa and Mrs. Claus join the festivities.

Yields approximately 106 servings

INGREDIENTS:
2 1/2 gallons water
2 (24-ounce) packages Timmy's sweet and sour cocktail mix
3 (12-ounce) cans of Minute Maid frozen lemonade concentrate
3 (1.7-liter) bottles of Seagram's whiskey

GARNISH:
About 12 oranges, cut into half-moon shaped slices
3 (16-ounce) jars of Haddon House maraschino cherries
Ice

INSTRUCTIONS:
Pour all of the ingredients into a large insulated beverage jug and stir with a long spoon. Fill a punch bowl with ice, punch, oranges, and cherries. Add additional orange slices and cherry garnishes to each serving as needed.

Mr. and Mrs. Santa Claus (a.k.a. George and Susan Ryan) spreading good cheer at the 1999 Country Curtains Tanglewood picnic.
Photo courtesy Country Curtains.

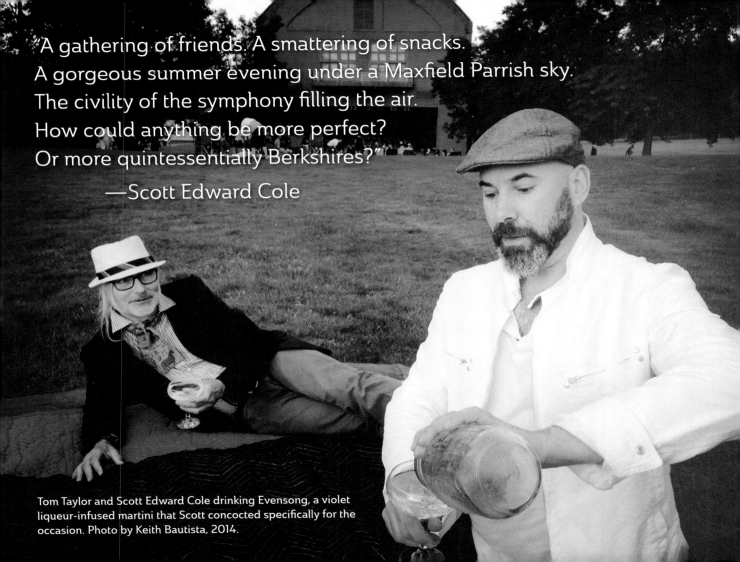

"A gathering of friends. A smattering of snacks.
A gorgeous summer evening under a Maxfield Parrish sky.
The civility of the symphony filling the air.
How could anything be more perfect?
Or more quintessentially Berkshires?"

—Scott Edward Cole

Tom Taylor and Scott Edward Cole drinking Evensong, a violet liqueur-infused martini that Scott concocted specifically for the occasion. Photo by Keith Bautista, 2014.

# EVENSONG COCKTAIL

## by Scott Edward Cole, proprietor of the Monterey General Store

Scott Edward Cole concocted this violet liqueur-infused martini to enjoy during an all-Brahms concert at Seiji Ozawa Hall. He used Berkshire Mountain Distillers limited edition Ethereal Gin, a wildly aromatic handcrafted gin with just enough juniper to hold up to its other elements, which include hibiscus, lime, and lavender.

Makes 2 generous servings

INGREDIENTS:
6 ounces Berkshire Mountain Distillers gin
1 ounce Dolin dry vermouth
1 ounce Creme Yvette violet liqueur
Twist of lemon and/or edible flower (violets, pansies, or borage) garnish

INSTRUCTIONS:
Fill a shaker with ice, and add the liquid ingredients. Shake until the shaker is so cold "it hurts." Strain into glasses and garnish with a twist of lemon and/or edible blossoms.

"We drink champagne on Sunday."

—Chris Ceranowicz

# PICNIC WINE TIPS
## from Jim Nejaime of Spirited

Wine merchant Jim Nejaime offers wine and spirits from around the world, as well as Italian, French, and Lebanese-inspired picnic fare at his Lenox shop. Some of his favorite white picnic wines are Falanghini, Gavi, and Vernaccia from Italy; Godello and Albarino from Spain; and Quincy and Sancerre from the Loire Valley in France. His picks for reds include Côtes du Rhône and Beaujolais from France; Garnacha and Tempranillo from Spain; and Sangiovese and Nero d'Avola from Italy. He also notes that dry rosés from Provence are perfect picnic wines.

Jim recommends chilling red wines, as well as whites and rosés. He says, "Reds are great to serve with a light chill on them. They are fresher and more vibrant when served cool, especially in the summer." Optimum serving conditions are to have a soft cooler bag with ice packs to keep the wines nicely chilled at about 45°F. For the reds, keeping them at about 60°F is ideal for summer picnics.

Chris Ceranowicz and her husband have attended Tanglewood together for 26 years. Photo by Larry Brandt, 2011.

Ava Crayton attends Tanglewood every summer. She says, "The BSO music under the sun, or stars, is pure bliss." Photo by Jim McCullough, 2014.

# PICNIC CHEESE TIPS

## from Bob Luhmann of Nejaime's Wine Cellars

Since 1970, Nejaime's Wine Cellars in Lenox and Stockbridge have outfitted Tanglewood picnickers with an array of fine wines, cheeses, charcuterie, and other delectable treats. Nejaime's cheesemonger Bob Luhmann dines alfresco on the Tanglewood lawn two or three times a week during the season. He says, "My favorite memories of Tanglewood picnics are a jumble of great conversation, food and drink, starry nights, sunsets, and full moon risings over the Shed."

In general, Bob advises that softer, milder, fresher cheeses are best when it's hot and more substantial, aged cheeses are good when the weather is cooler. If the cheese(s) are being served as an appetizer or dessert, plan on two or three ounces per person and double that as a main course.

He's fond of Marcona almonds and walnuts with most cheese plates and while he likes figs in most any form, quince paste, and nice fruit preserves with most cheeses, he thinks nothing beats fresh local fruit, particularly the Berkshire's exquisite berries, cherries, and melon.

"Don't get too hung up about 'correct' pairings.
Cheese, wine, and beer go together.
It's a picnic—relax and enjoy!" —Bob Luhmann

# GUIDO'S FRESH MARKETPLACE KALE SALAD
## by Guido's Kitchen

On a Tanglewood weekend, Guido's plows through 20 pounds of kale for this popular salad at its Pittsfield market. That's a lot of kale!

Makes 6 to 8 servings

INGREDIENTS:

1/2 cup sliced almonds
6 cups kale (1 large bunch, preferably locally grown lacinato kale, though any type may be used), ribs removed before chopping
2 tablespoons lemon juice
4 tablespoons olive oil
1/4 cup shallots, diced
3/4 cup Medjool dates, pitted and chopped
1 tablespoon agave nectar
Salt
Fresh ground pepper

Opposite: Guido's Fresh Marketplace founders Chris and Matt Masiero ready to picnic. Their plates are loaded with fare from their market, including grilled chicken breast, sesame noodles, Concord grapes, and kale salad. Their pick for dessert: Haven Cafe & Bakery's chocolate espresso cake. Photo by Dawn Masiero, 2014.

INSTRUCTIONS:

Toast the almonds in a dry skillet over medium low heat. Stir from time to time and watch carefully so they don't burn. Take them off the heat when they begin to turn brown and are fragrant, about 4 to 5 minutes. Transfer to a small bowl to let cool.

Toss the kale with the lemon juice, olive oil, and diced shallots. Use your hands to gently massage the leaves with the dressing for about five minutes to wilt the greens. Let the kale stand for 30 minutes. Add the toasted almonds, chopped dates, and agave nectar. Combine well, season with salt and pepper to taste, and off you go!

"Tanglewood picnics are a lot of work, but once everything is over there and arranged, it's incredibly relaxing. I love to wander around and look at other people's picnics. I'm not generally a competitive person, but when it comes to picnics at Tanglewood, my standards are high! One cardinal rule: NO Tupperware."

—Nancy Fitzpatrick

Phil Deely and Nancy Fitzpatrick pose by her artful picnic spread. Photo by Hilary Somers Deely, 2014.

# GOOD KARMA BROWN RICE SALAD
## by Nancy Fitzpatrick

Boston Symphony Orchestra Trustee Nancy Fitzpatrick has been taking this tasty salad to Tanglewood since the 1970s.

Makes 4 to 6 servings as a side dish

SALAD INGREDIENTS:

3 cups cooked medium-grain brown rice
(okay to cook a day ahead)
1/4 to 1/2 cup chopped scallions
(Nancy prefers lots of scallions)
1 cup sliced mushrooms
1/2 cup diced green pepper
1/2 cup chopped celery
1/4 cup chopped parsley

DRESSING INGREDIENTS:

1/4 cup grape seed oil
3 tablespoons apple cider vinegar
2 teaspoons Dijon mustard
2 teaspoons maple syrup
2 teaspoons Tamari soy sauce

INSTRUCTIONS:

Combine all of the salad ingredients in a medium-size serving bowl. Whisk together the dressing ingredients and dress the salad to taste (store any extra vinaigrette in the refrigerator for your next salad). Optional: Years ago, Nancy would lightly sauté the mushrooms and green peppers before mixing them into the salad. If you prefer these ingredients cooked, then you should, too.

"What I love most about Tanglewood picnics: 1. Getting together with friends and family, 2. Sharing food that is often mismatched, always too plentiful, never fussy or fancy, but tastes like summertime, and 3. Having an excuse to use my red Radio Flyer wagon." —Fran Heller

Fran Heller (right) and her sister Marlene Eichholz (left) have attended Tanglewood together since they were children. Photo by Michelle Clarkin, 2014.

# SUMMER SWEET CORN PUDDING

## by Fran Heller

Fran's favorite corn is Butter and Sugar, a yellow and white variety that she buys by the dozen at local farm stands.

Makes about 8 servings

INGREDIENTS:

6 cups cooked corn kernels cut off the cob
(6 or 7 ears of corn depending on size)
5 tablespoons butter (2 tbsp. for sautéing, 3 tbsp. melted)
1 medium yellow onion, diced (about 1 1/2 cups)
4 eggs
1 1/2 cups milk
3 tablespoons flour
1 teaspoon salt
Fresh ground pepper
2 or 3 tablespoons sugar (optional)
2 or 3 pinches cayenne pepper (optional)

INSTRUCTIONS:

Preheat oven to 400°F. Grease a 13" by 9" baking dish.

Cook the ears of corn. (Fran's preferred method is with a microwave: 2 minutes per ear, leaving the husk on to help them steam. If you don't have a microwave, use a big pot of boiling water and cook the corn about 5 minutes.) Once the corn is cool, cut the kernels off the cobs. You should have about 6 cups of kernels.

Melt 2 tablespoons butter in skillet. Add onion and sauté until translucent, let cool.

Whisk eggs and milk in large bowl. Add flour, salt, and 3 tablespoons melted butter and whisk to blend. Add sautéed onions and corn kernels and stir to combine. (If corn is not sweet, you may add a few tablespoons of sugar.)

Pour into greased baking dish.

Sprinkle with black pepper to taste and, to give it a little kick if you like, 2 or 3 pinches of cayenne pepper.

Bake for approximately 40 minutes or until set. Knife should come out clean.

# TANGLEWOOD POTATO SALAD

**by Mary F. Pisarkiewicz**

Mary adores Tanglewood, so she will cook whatever it takes to inspire an outing there. This mayonnaise-based potato salad with a twist makes her husband very happy, so she always makes it to lure him to the lawn. Mary says, "Make this potato salad with love and ideally serve it with buttermilk fried chicken!"

Makes 8 servings

INGREDIENTS:

2 pounds Yukon Gold or farm stand potatoes
1 tablespoon + 1 teaspoon kosher salt, divided
3/4 cup Hellmann's mayonnaise
1 tablespoon white wine vinegar
2 teaspoons Colman's dry mustard
1 teaspoon Hungarian sweet paprika
20 or so grinds black pepper
1 whole dill pickle, minced
3 cornichons, minced
1 pickled hot cherry pepper, seeded and minced
1/2 to 3/4 cup yellow onions, finely chopped
(Mary prefers lots of onion)
1 stalk celery, thinly sliced
1 egg, hard-cooked and chopped

INSTRUCTIONS:

Wash potatoes. Place in a large pot and cover with cold water by 1 inch. Salt the water with one tablespoon of salt and bring to a boil. Turn down heat to a simmer, partially cover and check in 20 minutes. Simmer until potatoes are tender, but not falling apart. Drain in a colander until cool enough to handle, then cut potatoes into 3/4 inch pieces, leaving skins on, and place in a mixing bowl. (It will take some time for them to cool, so be patient. You don't want to cut warm potatoes as they will fall apart and you don't want to put this dressing on warm potatoes.)

Combine mayonnaise, vinegar, mustard, paprika, black pepper, and remaining teaspoon of salt in a small bowl and whisk to make your dressing.

Add pickle, cornichons, cherry pepper, onion, celery, and egg to potatoes and stir gently to combine. Pour dressing over the salad, carefully folding it over with a spatula until evenly distributed.

Chill at least one hour before serving and take out at least 1/2 hour before your meal, so it's not so cold. Can be made a day in advance and tastes even better the next day.

*Recipe adapted from Mary's blog, LoveTheSecretIngredient.net*

# WHEATLEIGH GAZPACHO
## by Executive Chef Jeffrey Thompson

Wheatleigh Hotel is located a short walk from Tanglewood on Hawthorne Road. Built in 1893, the "summer cottage" was based on a 16th-century Florentine palazzo. Today's guests enjoy luxury picnic baskets custom-filled with gourmet treats. Executive Chef Jeffrey Thompson makes this gazpacho with locally grown heirloom tomatoes.

Makes 4 servings

INGREDIENTS:

1/2 red pepper, cored and seeded
1/2 yellow pepper, cored and seeded
1/4 English cucumber, peeled and seeded
4 medium-size red tomatoes, seeded
3 cilantro leaves
1/8 small red onion
3 ounces tomato juice
1 teaspoon olive oil
1/2 teaspoon red wine vinegar
Salt
Fresh ground pepper

INSTRUCTIONS:

In a food processor, combine the peppers, cucumber, tomatoes, cilantro, and onion and pulse until coarsely chopped (not puréed). Pour mixture into a large bowl. Stir in tomato juice, olive oil, red wine vinegar, and season with salt and pepper to taste. Cover and refrigerate until well chilled. Transport the soup to your picnic in either a plastic container or a thermos.

A towering Tanglewood sugar maple. Photo by Gina Hyams, 2014.

"I look forward to my Lesley B. sandwich from Loeb's every single year! I usually go up to a concert once a summer with my mom, and often my grandmother and great aunt. I want to always keep this tradition of Tanglewood picnics alive.

My dream is to someday have my own summer place up in the Berkshires, and be able to really pull out all the stops with my picnics! The thing I love most about them is when people add the beautiful but not 100 percent necessary details—the candles, the wine glasses, the cloth napkins, real silverware and china, the vases of flowers."

—Katherine Hughes

Former Boston University Tanglewood Institute voice student Katherine Hughes ready for an afternoon of Vivaldi in 2013. Photos courtesy Katherine Hughes.

# LOEB'S FOODTOWN LESLEY B. TURKEY SANDWICH

The Lesley B. Sandwich is named for Lesley B. Albert, who is co-owner of Loeb's with her husband, Earl. Earl and their son, Michael, invented this turkey sandwich in the late 1990s with help from the people at Boar's Head. It's the Lenox deli's most popular summer item.

Makes 1 big sandwich

INGREDIENTS:

2 tablespoons Hellmann's mayonnaise

1 teaspoon prepared or homemade pesto

Chopped fresh garlic (optional)

Fresh lemon juice to taste

French or 12-grain bread or roll, split

1 leaf crisp Romaine lettuce

2 to 4 slices tomato

1/4 cup alfalfa sprouts

1/4 pound Boar's Head Ovengold turkey, sliced

2 or 3 slices Havarti cheese

Salt and pepper

INSTRUCTIONS:

Stir mayonnaise and pesto to combine. If your pesto lacks garlic, or you'd like a little more, chop and add as much as you like. Add two good squeezes of half a lemon, and stir all to combine. Spread mayo-pesto mixture on both halves of the bread or roll (you can decide whether you want it heavily or lightly applied). Line one half with lettuce, tomato, and sprouts and then cover with turkey and cheese. Add salt and pepper to taste, and cover with the second half of bread or roll.

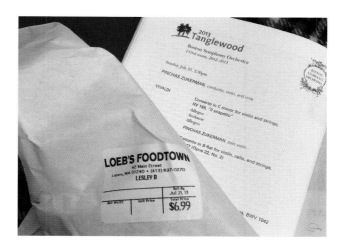

"There's a picnic one-upsmanship going on that doesn't feel competitive, but rather adds to the magic of this place. You might smile and think, 'Wow, look at that!' when you see someone with a candelabra sitting on their cooler and then do a double-take when you see a crystal chandelier strung over a tree branch hanging above a group of people enjoying a lobster dinner." —Eric Nixon

Photo by Blantyre/Sean McLaughlin, 2008.

# BLANTYRE BUCKWHEAT BLINIS WITH AMERICAN CAVIAR AND CHIVE-SOUR CREAM

## by Executive Chef Arnaud Cotar

Blantyre, an elegant resort in Lenox, is housed in a Gilded Age mansion that resembles a Scottish castle. The hotel extends its luxurious treatment of guests to Tanglewood, where they outfit their picnics with fancy quilt tablecloths, extravagant bouquets, candelabras, fine china, silver, and crystal.

Makes 12 servings

INGREDIENTS:

*Topping*

1/3 cup sour cream

2 tablespoons very thinly sliced chives, divided

2 ounces American caviar

*Blini*

1 1/8 cups whole milk

5/8 cup heavy cream

1 cup buckwheat flour

1 cup bread flour

1/2 packet dry active yeast

3 large eggs, separated into yolks and whites

4 teaspoons white sugar

1 teaspoon or more salt to taste

INSTRUCTIONS:

Stir half the chives into the sour cream. Reserve the other half for garnish, along with the caviar.

Mix the milk and cream together in a small bowl.

Stir the flours together in a good-sized bowl. Add yeast and stir to combine. Make a well in the dry ingredients. Stir in the milk mixture, egg yolks, and sugar and gently whisk to make a lump-free batter. Add 1 teaspoon salt or more to taste. Cover the batter bowl with plastic wrap and let rise for 2 hours in a warm place (at least room temperature).

Once the batter has risen, in another bowl, whip the egg whites to soft peaks, then fold them into the batter.

Working in batches, for each blini spoon 2 tablespoons batter onto a hot, lightly greased griddle or large skillet. Cook one side about 2 minutes until bubbles form on top and begin to pop. Flip and cook about 1 minute more until the bottom is golden brown.

To serve, top blinis with a small dollop of chive-sour cream mixture and some caviar, then sprinkle with remaining chives.

"What makes our picnic special is that we eat little bits of food continuously over five-plus hours while sitting on the lawn and we never actually have a meal." —Adam Kilpatrick

Cranwell guests feast on a Tanglewood picnic catered by the resort. Photo by Regina Burgio, 2014.

# CRANWELL RESORT LOBSTER SLIDERS

## by Executive Chef David Jordan

This classic Tanglewood picnic recipe is a perennial favorite of guests at Cranwell Resort, Spa, and Golf Club in Lenox.

Makes 2 servings

INGREDIENTS:

1 cup cooked lobster meat, chopped
1/4 cup mayonnaise
1/4 cup diced red onion
1 tablespoon fresh dill, finely chopped
1 tablespoon fresh chives, finely chopped
1 tablespoon fresh parsley, finely chopped
Salt
Fresh ground pepper
Brioche slider buns, halved
Mesclun greens

INSTRUCTIONS:

Mix the lobster, mayonnaise, red onion, dill, chives, and parsley together and season to taste with salt and pepper.

Place a small amount of mesclun onto the bottom half of each bun, divide the lobster salad evenly between the buns, and finish with the top half of each bun.

Photo by Kaitlyn Pierce, 2014.

# TANGLEWOOD TEMPURA PORTABELLA PINWHEELS
## by Boston Gourmet Executive Chef Joshua Ingraham

Boston Gourmet is the official caterer of Boston Symphony Orchestra and Tanglewood. Audience members can pre-order gourmet sandwiches, boxed dinners, and picnic totes from them to enjoy on the lawn.

Makes 8 to 10 servings

INGREDIENTS:

5 12-inch flour tortillas (ideally spinach or tomato flavored to add a bit of color)

1 pound portabella mushrooms, cut into thick slices, about 3/4 inch wide

20 or so sprigs of watercress

### Marinade for Portabella
3 tablespoons sherry wine vinegar

3 tablespoons soy sauce

1/2 teaspoon honey

1 teaspoon ginger root, peeled and freshly grated

1 clove garlic, crushed

### Marinated Cabbage
1 cup Chinese cabbage, shredded

2 tablespoons rice wine vinegar

1 pinch sugar

Salt and pepper to taste

### Sriracha Aioli
1/2 cup prepared mayonnaise

1 tablespoon sriracha sauce

5 sprigs cilantro, chopped

### Dipping Sauce
1 1/4 cup Kikkoman ponzu sauce

1 scallion, chopped

2 tablespoons store-bought pickled ginger, chopped

### Tempura Batter
1/2 cup egg whites (approximately 4 egg whites separated from whole eggs)

1/2 cup whole wheat flour

Water as needed

### Oil for Frying
3 1/2 cups sunflower oil

INSTRUCTIONS:

Mix the marinade ingredients; pour this mixture over the mushroom strips and leave for 3 to 4 hours. You can marinate the mushrooms at room temperature if they'll be consumed within 4 hours of prep, otherwise refrigerate until you're ready to finish the recipe.

Mix shredded cabbage with the rice wine vinegar, sugar, and salt and pepper to taste.

Prepare the sriracha aioli by mixing the mayonnaise, sriracha, and cilantro.

Prepare the dipping sauce by mixing the ponzu, chopped scallion, and chopped pickled ginger.

Prepare the tempura batter by beating together the egg whites and flour, then adding water gradually, still beating, until the batter has the consistency of heavy cream.

Heat an inch of oil in a deep skillet.

Drain the mushrooms, dip them in batter and deep fry, about 6 at a time, for 2 to 3 minutes.

Drain on paper towel and keep warm while cooking the remaining mushrooms.

Lay each tortilla flat on the table, spread a thin layer of the aioli, and then sprinkle a layer of cabbage slaw, 4 sprigs of watercress, and lastly line up the tempura portabellas in the middle. Roll the tortilla over the portabella and pull back towards you to create a tight even roll. Seal the end with a touch of aioli and wrap with plastic wrap until ready to serve.

Slice the sushi-looking tempura rolls into 1-inch pieces with the plastic on to help keep the roll intact. Once sliced, remove the plastic and arrange on a platter cut side up and serve with dipping sauce for everyone to enjoy.

Photo courtesy Boston Gourmet.

# RED LION INN BROWNIES

## adapted from *The New Red Lion Inn Cookbook*

The venerable Red Lion Inn in Stockbridge serves these brownies with vanilla ice cream and homemade hot fudge sauce. Unadorned, the brownies make for a sweet (not so sticky) treat at Tanglewood picnics.

Makes 24 brownies

INGREDIENTS:

4 ounces Callebaut semi-sweet chocolate
1/2 cup High Lawn Farm unsalted butter
4 eggs
2 cups sugar
1/4 teaspoon salt
1 tablespoon vanilla
1 cup flour
3/4 cup chopped walnuts

INSTRUCTIONS:

Preheat oven to 350°F. Line a 9" by 12" baking pan with lightly buttered parchment paper.

Melt the chocolate and butter in the top of a double boiler over simmering water, stirring frequently. Remove from heat and allow to cool.

Beat the eggs in a mixing bowl until frothy. Add the sugar and blend together well. Gently stir in the melted chocolate mixture, the salt, and vanilla. Add the flour and walnuts and stir by hand just until blended.

Spread the batter in the prepared pan and bake until crusty on top and almost firm to the touch, about 30 to 35 minutes. Allow the brownies to cool completely in the pan. Cut into squares.

"When I was 13 years old in the summer of 1947, I first attended Camp Potomac on Lake Pontoosuc outside of Pittsfield, Massachusetts. One of the activities the camp took us on was a visit to a concert at Tanglewood. In those days, there were very few people on the lawn, certainly under 1,000. Most of the audience sat in the Shed." –Richard Richter

Photo by BSO Archives/Howard S. Babbitt, Jr., circa 1947. Used by permission of the Babbitt family.

Top: Lavish picnic spread. Photo by Jane Feldman, 2014.

Bottom: Jessica Lee Close chows down at her first Tanglewood picnic. Photo by Walter Engels, 2000.

Renie Masiero feasts on a Guido's deli sandwich. Photo by Dawn Masiero, 2014.

Top: Ruth and Amy Bass with granddaughter/daughter Hannah Klupt, 2014.
Bottom: Celine Lamache's picnic of chicken salad, naan bread, cooked quail eggs, and watermelon. Photo by Paul Van Anglen, 2014.

Eric Hauser and Jen LiMarzi consider Tanglewood "the ultimate picnic spot," 2014. Photo courtesy Eric Hauser.

Photo by *Berkshire Eagle*/Joseph Contenta, 1946

# THE TANGLEWOOD LAWN EXPERIENCE

"For many people, Tanglewood is a sacred space, a touchstone. The minute you step through the gates of this Berkshire icon, you're enveloped by an all-sensory experience."  —Laura Wolf

Photo by Yi-han Cao, 2014.

# THE TANGLEWOOD LAWN EXPERIENCE

Tanglewood picnics celebrate artistry both on stage and off. The joyful spectacle of picnics scattered across the lawn is dazzling. The grounds hum with the creative energy of audience members drawing and painting, knitting, reading, and playing all sorts of games. Tanglewood picnickers have a certain *joie de vivre* about the weather, too—be it basking in sunshine or huddling together under tarps to picnic in the rain. And, well, there's a lot of sleeping. What could be more relaxing than napping outdoors while the world's greatest musicians serenade your dreams?

"I wish I could express the thrill, the swell of pride that lifts you like a ship in a fresh breeze, of walking from the Red Barn or the Chamber Music Hall through the picnics after warm-ups. You cross the lawn and 5,000 diners stop, mid-bite and mid-sentence, to watch the 'home team' heading for the Shed to await the call to go onstage. All your musical friends around you, a beautiful artistic experience ahead, and the appreciation of the most discerning audience of your life—nothing else on this side of heaven is like that moment."

—Michael Ruderman,
*former member of Tanglewood Festival Chorus*

Boston Symphony music director Serge Koussevitzky, founder of Tanglewood, cuts a piece of birthday cake while BSO concertmaster Richard Burgin and his son, Richard, and daughter, Diana, look on. Photo by Erika Stone, 1949.

Composers Arthur Honegger and Aaron Copland enjoy a working picnic at Tanglewood. Photo by Erika Stone, 1947.

Opposite: Steve Campbell, reflected in his tuba, follows conductor Roger Voisin's spirited direction of the pre-concert fanfare. Photo by *Berkshire Eagle*/Craig F. Walker, 1994.

Top left: Michael Cole holds his prized possession: a *Star Wars* score with composer John Williams's autograph. Photo by Mary Lou Cole, 2008. Top right: Photo by BSO Archives/Walter H. Scott, circa 1975. Used by permission of the Scott family. Bottom: Stefan Bauer-Mengelberg, a student of conducting under Leonard Bernstein, breaks from morning rehearsal for lunch on the Tanglewood lawn with Joanna Noble, a scholarship cellist in the student orchestra. Photo by BSO Archives, 1955.

A group of Tanglewood Music Center students gathers on the Tanglewood lawn (from left) Ernest Simms, Kermit Moore, Harry Smyles, Wayne Lazarus, James Fleetwood, Mrs. Smyles, David Abel, Adele Addison, Jay Dietzer, and Cynthia Sweeney. Photo by BSO Archives/ Howard S. Babbitt, Jr., 1948. Used by permission of the Babbitt family.

"For the last 14 years, I've been lining up at the gate at 11:45 a.m. on Sundays so I could stake out our territory under my favorite tree—a red oak close to the Shed, which affords enough shade for about 15 people. I put my tarp in the full sun, knowing that when I return with our food, drink, and newspaper for the afternoon concert at about 1:30 p.m., the tarp will be in full shade. This way, I don't need to sprint across the lawn to get my spot. We're well positioned between the speakers, and just far enough from the Shed so it doesn't obscure any part of them. We've never sat anywhere else, and as long as we and our little tree survive, we never will."

—Tom Werman

Opposite: Dr. Modestino Criscitiello, a recently returned veteran of World War II, assumes what he described in his memory book as a "special reserved seat at Tanglewood," circa 1946. Note: Due to concerns about public safety and liability, perching in trees is no longer allowed at Tanglewood. Photo courtesy Nancy and Modestino G. Criscitiello.

> "I love being on the lawn. I am not a Shed person, but a lawn person."
> —Kelley Vickery

Photo by *Berkshire Eagle*/R. Joel Librizzi, 1960.

Photo by *Berkshire Eagle*/William Tague, 195

Photo by Erika Stone, 1947.

"I love to people watch at Tanglewood—whether it be lovers on a first date,
children dancing in their diapers, or older couples holding hands

All photos by *Berkshire Eagle*/William Tague, 1956.

and tapping their feet in the green, green grass." —Carolyn Lipomi

"You don't earn your Tanglewood Badge
until you've huddled under a tarp while listening to fine music
accompanied by precipitation percussion!" —Rick Tillotson

Top: Photo by *Berkshire Eagle*, 1996.

Bottom: Ryan Brewster and Caitlin Towers, who are second-generation Tanglewood picnickers.
Photo by Gina Hyams, 2014.

Photo by BSO Archives, 1981.

"It was pouring rain for hours. We hid under two golf umbrellas tilted together over our collapsible chairs. We were wet. We were uncomfortable. We sipped our cheap Pinot Grigio and ate plain ham sandwiches, peanuts from a jar. Finally, the music started, and that was everything. The harmonies. The cello. The tones. The warmth. It was pretty darn wonderful."

—Theresa S. McMahon

Maureen White McCormick elegantly weathers the storm.
Photo by Mary Ellen Richter, 2014.

Michael Lombardi Jr.'s first Tanglewood picnic.
Photo by Marina Vandenbergh, 2014.

"A picnic at Tanglewood is like a meal at home. You sprawl, you dance, you play, you enjoy with family and friends, thankful to be in the presence of the most spectacular artists on the planet who grace our beloved Berkshires."

—John Stanmeyer

Audience members dance in the rain at a James Taylor concert. Photo by John Stanmeyer, 2014.

Nadia Szold, age 8. Photo by Honey Sharp, 1993.

Carter Marks, age 7. Photo by Scott Marks, 2014.

"The music accompanied my endless cartwheels on the lawn. I remember Tanglewood being the perfect playground—from the spooky maze, to the marble sculptures, to the people watching, to the musicians practicing in the big old houses. Little did I know I was soaking up what would grow into a lifelong love of the symphony."

—Nadia Szold

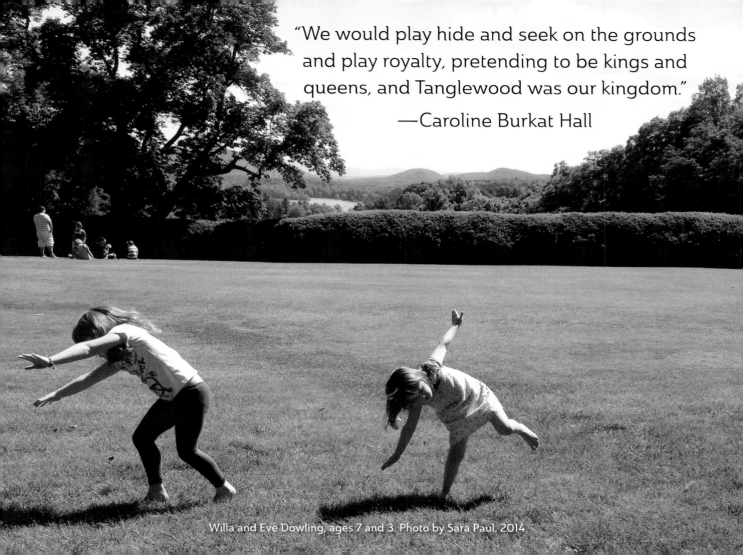

"We would play hide and seek on the grounds and play royalty, pretending to be kings and queens, and Tanglewood was our kingdom."

—Caroline Burkat Hall

Willa and Eve Dowling, ages 7 and 3. Photo by Sara Paul, 2014

"Tanglewood is a magical place. The breeze sings through the trees even when there are no musicians playing." —Katherine Hughes

Photo by BSO Archives/Hilary Scott, 2008.

Top: Jenna, Amber, and Laura Topping play 500 Rummy.
Photo by Gina Hyams, 2014.
Bottom: Photo by Erika Stone, circa 1960.

Top: Photo by Erika Stone, circa 1960.
Bottom: Photo by Susan Geller, 2013.

"Tanglewood picnics have become quite a family tradition. Each time, I double check that my mom has packed her delicious wild rice and potato salads; something isn't quite right if either is missing."

—Kevin Y. Chen

Tiger and Karis Kotschnig and Sophie and Julia Pelletier. Photo by Kathy Vera Kotschnig, 2014.

Opposite: Eighteen Israeli, Palestinian, and American delegates attended the Music In Common International Youth Summit, which has the mission to strengthen, empower, and educate communities through the universal language of music. On their visit to Tanglewood, the students listened to a rehearsal in the Shed and then romped, danced, napped, and picnicked on the lawn overlooking Stockbridge Bowl. Photo by L. Najimy/Beansprout Productions, 2014.

Allison Cole sketches during a Tanglewood picnic. Photo by Mary Lou Cole, 2012.

Artist Cynthia Wick.
Photo by Frieda Pilson, 2014.

"There is this intoxicating thing about sitting on the lawn at Tanglewood with hundreds of other humans. A cough here, a sigh there, the giggles of little children in the distance, and the deep power of Beethoven's Ninth blazing out from the Shed. It's a powerful energetic experience and in the midst of being absorbed by that bigness is the intimacy of my hand and a pen and a small notebook and being transported in the world of drawing. With all senses engaged, I draw the people sitting around me. A woman with a red hat, a pink sunburnt leg emerging from the open *New York Times*, a green glass by a blue plate of grapes. It's a never-ending supply of material."

—Cynthia Wick

Photo by
Diane M. Austin, 1997.

Jack, Kaitlin, and Andrew Vickery celebrate the 4th of July.
Photo by Kelley Vickery, 2000.

Robin Grigg Tillotson handles the picnic menu and table
décor and her husband, Rick, takes care of the packing and
schlepping logistics. Photo snapped by a friendly stranger
sitting near them on the lawn, 2011.

Tanglewood picnickers take in fireworks over the Stockbridge Bowl. Photo by Edward Acker, 2013.

Picnickers dressed up to match the "Oz with Orchestra" Boston Pops concert. Left to right: Marion Kristek (Wicked Witch), Elaine Tudryn (Scarecrow), Maureen A. Tudryn (Tin Man), Eileen Marsolais (Glinda, the Good Witch), Sharon Colburn (Dorothy), unidentified friend, Christine Lynch (Auntie Em), and Joanne Keller (Cowardly Lion). Photo by BSO Archives/Hilary Scott, 2014.

"We color-coordinated our Tanglewood outfits to match our plaid picnic tablecloth." —Paul McLaughlin

Melissa Bigarel coordinated her picnic blanket, shoes, and blueberries for the "Oz with Orchestra" Boston Pops concert to match the blue gingham dress worn by Dorothy in *The Wizard of Oz*. Photo by Melissa Bigarel, 2014.

Mary Russell, Michael Cavanaugh, and Paul McLaughlin color-coordinated their picnic outfits and illuminated their meal with festive solar lanterns. Photo by Gina Hyams, 2014.

"Beauty tip: make sure you get a pedicure before the picnic—
it's the one time your toes might be at eye level with the picnicking friends."
—Maria Nation

Opposite page: Judy Boullet (red polish), Hilary Somers Deely (coral polish), Kat Mansfield (blue polish), Sarah Eustis (black polish), and Henry Eustis (11-year-old boy toes). Photo by Hilary Somers Deely, 2014.

Left: A henna artist adorns a picnicker's ankle on the lawn. Photo by Susan Geller, 2012.

Above: Barbara Arpante offers music-themed face painting during Tanglewood on Parade and on the 4th of July. Photos by Barbara Arpante, 2012-2014.

Kathleen Drohan, Alison Thwaites, and Kelley Vickery relax on a Sunday afternoon, 2014. Photo by Eugene Carr, 2014.

Cooper Constable reads his first Tanglewood program.
Photo by Chrissie Constable, 2012.

Diane M. Austin works on the *New York Times* crossword
puzzle, 1988. Photo courtesy Diane M. Austin.

"Sometimes less is more: a tuna fish sandwich, a bottle of beer, some carrot sticks, a brownie, a blanket to sit on, maybe a chair, the symphony, and the *New York Times* on a Sunday afternoon are all you need, plus maybe a bag of chips." —Anne Simon

Photo by *Berkshire Eagle*/Arthur Palme, circa 1940s.

"When I'm packing for Tanglewood, my first priority is wine, my second is knitting. I choose projects that are pleasant and simple, so I don't need to stop and count stitches or read a chart or ignore my companions because I'm at an intricate part of the pattern. The act of knitting in public invites conversation—kindred spirits feel comfortable stopping by to inquire about the yarn or the project, and thus are new knitting friendships born." —Marie Blauvelt

Conductor Leonard Bernstein's sister, Shirley Bernstein, and his soon-to-be bride, Felicia Montealegre, knitting on the lawn, circa late 1940s. Photo courtesy Jamie Bernstein.

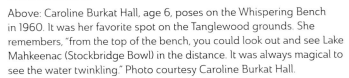

Above: Caroline Burkat Hall, age 6, poses on the Whispering Bench in 1960. It was her favorite spot on the Tanglewood grounds. She remembers, "from the top of the bench, you could look out and see Lake Mahkeenac (Stockbridge Bowl) in the distance. It was always magical to see the water twinkling." Photo courtesy Caroline Burkat Hall.

Above center: Sarah Aroeste Blaugrund and her father, Ira Silverman, in 1981. She says, "My fondest childhood memories took place on the Tanglewood grounds. My father introduced me to classical music there and I still remember humming and conducting along with him to Beethoven's Ninth Symphony." Now she's creating Tanglewood memories with husband, Jeffrey, and toddler daughter, Irit. Above right: Irit Blaugrund. Photo by Sarah Aroeste Blaugrund, 2014.

Right: Ben Baum takes his first steps ever during a Tanglewood picnic, while his grandmother, Nettie G. Baum, and great aunt, Elsie Altholz, look on. Photo by Suzi Banks Baum, 1995.

Zoe and Nathan Moskowitz in 2006 on a quilt their grandmother, Norma Strassler, created in the mid-1990s in homage to her favorite Tanglewood sugar maple tree. She brought some of the tree's leaves home and traced them to make a pattern. Now three generations use the blanket to picnic every summer. Photo courtesy Norma Strassler.

Peter C. Giftos and Judith E. Cook (Giftos) at Tanglewood in 1953, the summer before they married.
The couple happily celebrated their 60th wedding anniversary in 2014. Photos courtesy Stacia Bissell.

The Tufts at Tanglewood reunion tradition began in 2005. Tufts alumni from Massachusetts, Connecticut, Rhode Island, New Hampshire, Vermont, New York, and New Jersey are invited to attend each summer. Tufts engineers have built special carts to transport large tables from the faraway parking lots to the lawn. Photo courtesy Tufts Alumni Western MA, 2014.

Zion Lutheran Church in Pittsfield and Trinity Lutheran/Christ Episcopal Church in Sheffield hold a joint Tanglewood picnic during *A Prairie Home Companion* with Garrison Keillor. It's potluck and anything goes. Photo by Helen Kimpel, 2012.

"The summer concerts at Tanglewood evoke a feeling of almost sacred devotion in many concert-goers. It was with a mixture of pride and reluctance that some congregants would let me know that I would not see them at services during 'the season' since they would be at Tanglewood each Friday night. It got me to thinking that perhaps, we could take Hevreh to them so that everyone could enjoy the beautiful music; thus was Tanglewood Shabbat born more than a decade ago. Once each summer, we invite our congregants and their friends to share a picnic dinner on the grounds, to gather at the far end of the lawn for a brief and music-filled Kabbalat Shabbat service (a service which welcomes the Sabbath) and a sumptuous dessert reception and then, to disperse either to the Shed or the lawn to enjoy the sublime music of the BSO or the Pops. Often we are joined by others who hear familiar liturgical melodies and come to investigate what is going on. Tanglewood Shabbat has become a beloved tradition of Hevreh."

—Rabbi Deborah Zecher, Hevreh of Southern Berkshire

Clockwise from left: Unidentified nappers. Photo by Erika Stone, 1986; Charlie Cole napping in the sun before the concert. Photo by Mary Lou Cole, 2014; Wylder Vecchia snoozing on the lawn. Photo by Jessica Conzo, 2012; Hunter Runnette and Mark Vandenbosch in a reverie listening to Yo-Yo Ma and Emanuel Ax. Photo by Cynthia Wick, 2014.

Opposite: The Allied Relief Fund Benefit concert was an all-day, family-friendly event that evolved into the Tanglewood on Parade tradition. Photo by *Berkshire Eagle*/G.W. Edman, 1940.

"It doesn't matter what time of day— 10 o'clock in the morning during a rehearsal or 10 o'clock at night after a concert—people are always napping on the Tanglewood lawn."   —David Chandler Winn

# HUMANS OF TANGLEWOOD by JOSEPH MCDONOUGH

We have come here to hear Beethoven. Listening to music has become a private affair in recent years, but there is little that is private here. Blankets and lawn chairs crowd the space beneath the trees, and toddlers run freely through the grass. Teenagers trip awkwardly over reclining older couples, and their embarrassed parents abruptly fold up their seats and disappear. Grandfathers dance slowly and mysteriously across the lawn and settle quietly next to their children's children, still moving in time with the music. Picnic lunches are in progress. The Ninth Symphony calls us all to universal brotherhood.

Beethoven can make you feel that you're outside no matter where you are, or make you want to be. It's not really nature that he's thinking of, perhaps; it's some kind of ideal, but then so is this particular corner of the Berkshires. We're all looking for Elysium, some kind of rose-strewn landscape with a canopy of stars, capitalizing our nouns and wondering if this is what it feels like to be drunk with fire.

This poem originally appeared in *Dappled Things: A quarterly of ideas, art & faith.*

THE ULTIMATE TANGLEWOOD
PICNIC CHECKLIST

Rick Tillotson recommends putting your largest and heaviest items (chairs, tables, umbrellas, etc.) on the bottom of your wagon to stabilize it. Place your cooler on top of those items, along with tarps, blankets, and food. He says, "Protect fragile items and carry a couple extra bungee cords because nothing packs as tightly on the way out as it did at home." Photo by Rick Tillotson, 2014.

"What I love about a Tanglewood picnic is that the planning and anticipation are just as much fun as the picnic itself!" —Mary Ellen Richter

There is no wrong way to picnic at Tanglewood. It's perfectly acceptable to show up with nothing, rent lawn chairs and seat cushions, and pick up grab-and-go sandwiches and salads from the food vendors there. Serious Tanglewood picnickers, however, come prepared...seriously prepared! Some go fancy with lace tablecloths, candelabras, and crystal goblets and others embrace a more casual approach with paper napkins, finger food, and backyard bouquets.

Above: Jane Worthington-Roth's favorite time to enjoy an evening concert at Tanglewood is mid-August, during the Perseid meteor shower. She says, "There is nothing more magical than enjoying a delicious star-themed dinner, then lying back on a blanket and watching the shooting stars as you listen to the beautiful music!"
Photo by Jane Worthington-Roth, 2014.

Right: Laura Strickling, a Tanglewood Music Center vocal fellow, makes her own shade with an umbrella on the lawn. Photo by Vincent Festa, 2014.

# THE ULTIMATE TANGLEWOOD PICNIC CHECKLIST

Here is a compilation of tips from those who have honed their picnic strategy down to a science.

### GEAR

- ☐ PICNIC BASKET(S)
- ☐ PICNIC BLANKET(S)
- ☐ EXTRA BLANKET FOR LATE NIGHTS TO DRAPE OVER YOURSELF AND FRIENDS (*or a sleeping bag for extra coziness on cold nights*)
- ☐ BUG REPELLENT LOTION (*not spray, as spray harms the grass*)
- ☐ WARM CLOTHES
- ☐ BUNGEE CORDS (*to secure stacked baskets in the wagon*)
- ☐ PORTABLE CHAIRS (*ones with built-in awnings and beverage holders are a plus*)
- ☐ COLD PACKS OR ICE FOR COOLER
- ☐ COOLER (*preferably on wheels*)
- ☐ COOLER BAGS

- ☐ FIRST AID SUPPLIES
- ☐ FLASHLIGHT OR LANTERN
- ☐ HAT, SUNSCREEN, SUNGLASSES
- ☐ RUBBER MALLET OR HAMMER TO SECURE UMBRELLA OR CANOPY
- ☐ PORTABLE PICNIC TABLE (*ideally in a bag with a shoulder strap*)
- ☐ A PLASTIC TARP OR SHOWER CURTAIN TO PUT UNDER YOUR QUILT (*bring a tarp regardless of the weather and time of day, as the grass is always damp and nobody likes a wet blanket*)
- ☐ UMBRELLA OR SMALL OPEN-SIDED CANOPY FOR SHADE FROM THE SUN OR SHELTER FROM THE RAIN (*per Tanglewood policy, stakes must not exceed six inches in length, canopies can be no more than six feet square, and umbrellas may not exceed four feet in diameter*)

"Never, ever forget sweaters and jackets! It might be 75°F and sunny when you get there, but midway through the concert when it's dark, you'll be absolutely freezing without warm clothes!" —Alyssa Vitrano

David Chandler Winn sports a Tanglewood license plate on his picnic wagon. Photo by Gina Hyams, 2014.

☐ THERMOS

☐ A WAGON OR CART *(little red wagons are a Tanglewood tradition and wagons with sides that come off are popular, too, as that functionality is useful for carrying large items. Wagons can also double as tables during your picnic)*

### SERVING ITEMS

☐ BOTTLE, GLASS, AND CAN HOLDERS *(some are shaped to attach to your chair, others have spikes to stick into the ground near your chair)*

☐ BREAD CUTTING BOARD AND BREAD KNIFE

☐ CHAMPAGNE BOTTLE STOPPER AND/OR WINE BOTTLE STOPPER

☐ CHAMPAGNE FLUTES

☐ CHEESE BOARD AND CHEESE KNIVES

☐ CORKSCREW AND BOTTLE OPENER

☐ FORKS, SPOONS, AND KNIVES

☐ GLASSES AND CUPS

☐ ICE BUCKET

☐ NAPKINS *(cocktail and dinner sized)*

☐ PLATES AND BOWLS *(for serving and eating)*

☐ SERVING UTENSILS

☐ TOOTHPICKS

"I am quite proud of my 'table in a bag.'" —Ava Crayton

Gisela Lawton holds a farm stand sunflower given to her by her granddaughter. Photo by Francie Jarowski, 2014.

Opposite: Nathan Hanford has a collection of four vintage toolboxes that he uses as portable picnic bars. He stocks each with ingredients for one signature cocktail of the evening (in this case, a libation dubbed "The Lawn Ticket" that includes Tito's vodka, Morris Kitchen rhubarb syrup, bitters, crushed citrus, and soda water). Photo by Nancy Fitzpatrick, 2014.

## DÉCOR

- ☐ ALUMINUM FOIL OR PIE TIN *(to place under your candles, so the wax doesn't burn a spot in the lawn)*
- ☐ CANDLEHOLDERS
- ☐ CANDLES *(don't bring scented candles—with the exception of citronella bug-deterring ones—because your favorite scent may not be to your neighbor picnicker's taste)*
- ☐ DECORATIONS *(pink flamingos, balloons, solar lanterns to hang from a tree, etc.)*
- ☐ FLOWERS
- ☐ MATCHES OR LIGHTER
- ☐ TABLECLOTH
- ☐ VASE
- ☐ WATER IN A BOTTLE *(to fill your bouquet vase)*

## FOOD & DRINK

- ☐ NON-ALCOHOLIC BEVERAGES
- ☐ WINE AND/OR BEER AND/OR COCKTAIL MAKINGS
- ☐ APPETIZERS
- ☐ SIDE DISHES
- ☐ ENTRÉES
- ☐ DESSERTS
- ☐ SALT, PEPPER, AND SUGAR CUBES OR PACKETS

**Tanglewood**

To preserve and maintain
the beauty and safety of
Tanglewood property, please
observe the following restrictions:

Thank you and enjoy your visit.

Above: It typically takes five members of the Tanglewood grounds crew three hours to clean up litter after a concert. Do your part by depositing garbage into the trash and recycling bins located around the perimeter of the lawn. BSO Archives/ Walter H. Scott, 1976.

Opposite: Photo by Gina Hyams, 2014.

## FUN EXTRAS

☐ ART SUPPLIES

☐ BALLS *(per Tanglewood policy, children may play ball only behind the Visitors Center and in the Apple Tree lot of Ozawa Hall, but only if such activity does not disturb performances, rehearsals, or patrons sitting on the lawn. Ball playing is not permitted on the lawn of the Shed at any time when the grounds are open for a Shed concert)*

☐ BINOCULARS

☐ BOARD GAMES *(chess, checkers, backgammon, etc.)*

☐ DECK OF CARDS *(though wind can be challenging)*

☐ KNITTING SUPPLIES

☐ MUSICAL INSTRUMENTS

☐ READING MATERIAL

☐ SCAVENGER HUNT ITEMS *(for kids)*

## CLEAN UP

☐ GARBAGE BAG

☐ MOIST TOWELETTES

☐ PAPER TOWELS

☐ STAIN STICK

☐ ZIPLOCK BAGS, PLASTIC WRAP, ALUMINUM FOIL, OR PLASTIC CONTAINERS FOR LEFTOVER FOOD

☐ LARGE ZIPLOCK PLASTIC BAGS FOR DIRTY DISHES

"I try to get there an hour and a half or more before the concert begins. I drop off supplies and passengers just before the gate before parking." —Bob Luhmann

Photo by BSO Archives/ David Milton Jones, circa 1936.

Photo by *Berkshire Eagle/*Mark Mitchell, 1977.

Photo by Lisa Landry, 2014.

# ACKNOWLEDGMENTS

This may be a little book, but it carries within it the goodwill of a great many people. Tanglewood picnickers are an extraordinarily generous tribe and I'm so grateful to all who shared their picnic memories, wisdom, recipes, and photos. At the BSO, thanks to Sam Brewer, Bridget Carr, Bobby Lahart, Bruce Peeples, Barbara Perkel, Hilary Scott, and David Chandler Winn for graciously answering my myriad research queries. *Berkshire Eagle* librarian Jeannie Maschino excavated Tanglewood picnic treasures that were buried deep in the paper's archives and Jane Feldman opened doors to amazing photos and wrangled scanning logistics in New York City. Dawn Masiero of Guido's Fresh Marketplace, Berkshire Visitors Bureau's Laura Wolf and Lindsey Schmid, and Kelly Bevan McIlquham of Berkshire Family Focus helped spread word of my call for submissions far and wide.

Hearts and flowers to Team Muddy Puppy: copy editor Lesley Ann Beck, sales representative Janet McKean, attorney Paul Rapp, administrative assistant Annalena Barrett, research assistant Jennifer Pelzman, and designer Christopher Hixson. Chris deserves extra gold stars for his contributions to this book, which extend far beyond typefaces and kerning. He is a true partner in crime and I'm most grateful.

Savvy publishing friends Leslie Jonath, Bob

Hannah Klupt, age 7, swings from a Tanglewood sculpture. Photo by Amy Bass, 2014.

and Kaarin Lemstrom-Sheedy, Annie Brody, Michelle Quigley, Eugenie Sills, and Anastasia Stanmeyer sprinkled magic fairy dust on this book. Cheers to the recipe-testing posse: Lauren Brown Adams, Gary Bates, Lesley Ann Beck, Monica Bliss, Carolyn Gratzer Cope, Christine Deucher, Jean Flynn, Diane Clark Johnson, Beth Lee, Albert Leu, Ericka Lutz, Jennifer Yunginger Madden, Arlene Murdock, Colleen Neff, Robin Parow, Sara Paul, Carolann Patterson, Pamela Pescosolido, Barbara Schulman, David Chandler Winn, and to Betsy McNair for her eagle-eyed recipe edits.

I count my lucky stars for Dave Barrett, my husband who is always game for a picnic.

Photo by *Berkshire Eagle*/William Tague, 1956.

KODAK SAFETY FILM
KODAK PLUS X PAN FILM

→18 →19 →20 →21

KODAK PLUS X PA
KODAK SAFETY FILM

 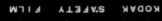  

→26 →27 →28 →29

Photos by Erika Stone, circa 1960.